Publisher: Gary Baddeley

Designer: Leen Al-Bassam

First Printing September 2002

Library of Congress Card Number: 2002107524

ISBN 0-9713942-1-0

Printed in China

Distributed in the United States and Canada by:
Consortium Book Sales and Distribution
1045 Westgate Drive, Suite 90
St Paul, MN 55114
Toll Free: +1.800.283.3572
Local: +1.651.221.9035
Fax: +1.651.221.0124
www.cbsd.com

Distributed in the United Kingdom and Eire by:
Turnaround Publisher Services Ltd.
Unit 3, Olympia Trading Estate
Coburg Road
London, N22 6TZ
Tel.: +44.(0)20.8829.3000
Fax: +44.(0)20.8881.5088
www.turnaround-uk.com

disinformation®
THE INTERVIEWS

RICHARD METZGER

For Naomi Nelson, who taught me half of everything I know.

WILLED INTENTION

Although this book is intended to stand alone, it is actually one half of a multi-media set. The interviews herein were culled from the transcripts of a *Disinformation*® television series that ran for two seasons on Britain's Channel 4 network.[1] These shows were then edited into four one-hour programs intended for the SCI FI Channel in America, but when the first show was delivered, certain decision makers at the network declined to air it, not even asking to see episodes two, three and four. Hopefully the *Disinformation*® series will eventually be broadcast on U.S. television, but at the time of this writing that is not the case. Despite this, these shows have now been seen in many countries around the world and are available on DVD. Many of the chapters in this book have their audio-visual counterparts on the DVD.

The *Disinformation*® series' object was to present the kinds of ideas you never see on television —complex, often intellectually *subversive* thoughts— in ways that are compulsively watchable, stirred within a stew of "underground culture" that included the *Jackass*-like carnage of *Uncle Goddamn*, comical exposes of "conspiracy theories" that played out a la *Spinal Tap*-style mini-*mockumentaries* and one-on-one interviews with various counterculture luminaries. I saw *Disinformation*® as a punk rock *60 Minutes* and I wanted to take the general idea of "reality TV," which is constantly being shoved down our throats, and really play with that concept to fuck with people's heads. *Reality?* Or what major multi-national corporations want you to *accept* as reality? In the programs we explored such topics as "Satanism," transsexuals, the sex life of robots, CIA mind-controlled sex slaves, outsider music, time travel and extreme pornography. The series was an audio-visual assault; if the viewer was traumatized, *then so be it!* At least they *wouldn't forget it* and they'd probably still be thinking about it several days later. If the audience wasn't constantly wavering between thinking it was real and wondering if we had actors reading lines, it didn't work. This had to happen several times in one show for it to live up to it's name: *Disinformation*®, right? But it was *all real*, sometimes frighteningly real and sometimes just hilariously real. As a friend in England told me after watching one of the shows: "Midway through it I completely disconnected from reality." Well, that was the intended reaction, certainly, and I don't foresee anyone coming along with something that'll top *Disinformation*® in the high weirdness sweepstakes any time soon. It will happen eventually, of course, after five to ten years, but not in the near term. Call me smug if you want —it happens all the time— the series, especially the condensed version we made for the SCI FI Channel, is perhaps the most uncompromising *fucked up* TV show of all time. I see this less as a boast and more as an historical fact.[2]

The interview subjects were hardly chosen at random. As the host of the show, I certainly didn't want to interview people who I didn't agree with or felt antagonistic to: I'm not a Bill O'Reilly kind of interviewer. I wanted to present and promote people whose work I admired, so in most cases, I was already friends with the people involved or else we became friends during the course of working together. This has been a source of tremendous satisfaction to me and I'm blessed with the presence of these people in my life.

When we'd finished the post-production, I started looking through the three feet high stack of transcripts I'd stuck in the closet. It seemed a pity to have to leave so many wonderful ideas and moments from the shoots on the proverbial "cutting room floor," and I began the task of assembling the present volume, giving me a chance to really mull over the radical ideas espoused by the people we'd had on the program.

One goal of this book is to reveal something about the lifestyles of these varied artists and thinkers and perhaps inspire some readers, especially the younger readers, with the potent examples of these people who in their lives and in their careers, walk roads less traveled, to put it mildly. None of these people chose the *9 to 5* option and in some cases it was probably not very easy for them to keep going financially, yet all of them eventually found a niche for themselves and a place within the culture by never losing sight of their vision and I think this is important to point out.

Not long before the interview with him that appears here was conducted, painter Joe Coleman told me about a book he was very intrigued by called *The Soul's Code: In Search of Character and Calling* by Dr. James Hillman, a post-Jungian psychologist and originator of "archetypal psychology." The central thesis of the book is the "Acorn Theory" of personality, as Hillman terms it, the idea that we are all "seeds" when we're born and our mature selves are the "trees" that we were destined (or *geneti-*

cally fated) to become. Hillman uses personalities as diametrically opposed as Winston Churchill and Adolph Hitler to illustrate his point and serial killers like Jeffrey Dahmer and Charles Manson ("Bad Seeds" obviously) make appearances contrasted with decidedly more positive role models like Eleanor Roosevelt, Yehudi Menuhin and Ella Fitzgerald. Joe was very taken with the book and his enthusiasm was contagious, so much so that I picked it up that evening on the way home. It was immediately apparent why *The Soul's Code* appealed so much to Joe and I got a lot out of it myself.

A few weeks later I was visiting Genesis P-Orridge and I told him about this interesting new book which I'd bought on Joe's recommendation. He wordlessly gestured to the bookshelf above his desk where *The Soul's Code* sat. It turns out he too was turned on by Hillman's ideas and it made lot of sense why Genesis would choose to interpret his life in this way, as well.

In the epigraphs that serve as a preface to *The Soul's Code*, Hillman quotes Jerome Brunner from his book, *In Search of Mind, Essays in Autobiography*:

> "It was Karl Marx, I think, who once proposed that evolution
> be studied in reverse, with an eye firmly fixed on the evolved
> species while glancing backwards for hints."

Examining a life by running the film backwards is a very useful one for an interviewer. I tried in many of the interviews included in this book to draw out pivotal moments and life-changing events from the subjects' lives to better explain *how* and *why* they are who they are: what happened, what turning point in their lives occurred to place them on the trajectory to *becoming themselves*? Joe Coleman tells of how he was drawing blood stained depictions of the Passion Play as an eight-year old in Catholic church with his mother. With Kembra Pfahler, her description of her childhood in Hermosa Beach contrasts her high Goth fantasy life with the reality of life in a small Southern California surfing town. Paul Laffoley had a strange dream when he was a child about *living* art that inspired his adult artistic oeuvre. Grant Morrison discusses reading his Uncle Billy's "scary" occult books and so on. Almost without fail, there was a moment of clarity or even something accidental that revealed a roadmap or a blueprint that shaped the course of their later lives.

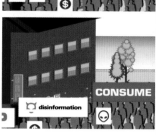

I'm often asked by people "How did you get interested in this kind of stuff?" and I think that I have a pretty straightforward answer that's relevant to this discussion. For those of us who came of age in the 1970's there really weren't a whole lot of places where you could find out about *unusual* things. Back then there were few independent magazines or outlets for culture that was outside of the mainstream. Even record stores weren't that plentiful then, maybe in the bigger cities, but not in the Mid-West, and certainly not in my hometown of Wheeling, West Virginia, which was a barren cultural wasteland, with one notable exception, but I'll get to that in a moment.

By about age 11, I'd graduated from James Bond films and comic books to "Rock," becoming obsessed with David Bowie, The Velvet Underground and Iggy Pop due to reading about them in CREEM, probably the best distributed "underground" music magazine in America at that time. CREEM has helmed by the late, great Lester Bangs. Anything that Bangs recommended, I wanted to hear immediately. I loved his writing and I loved his taste in music, even if I was forced to resort to mail order (and unpleasant chores) to get my hands on the stuff. If Lester Bangs thought it was worthwhile, it was worth checking out for that reason alone and Bangs never disappointed me or steered me wrong. His musical taste was impeccable and I, like many people my age, had my innocent young mind *fucked up beyond all recognition* by the things Bangs rhapsodized about in CREEM. Even though Bangs has been lauded *ad infinitum* over the

[1] During the first season it came on after *Ally McBeal* if you can believe that!

[2] The amazing thing is that it got funded in the first place. We were paid in full, incidentally.

years since his death, it is almost impossible to overestimate his influence on the growth of deviant culture in America during the 70's. In CREEM I was exposed for the first time to things like punk rock, John Waters films, William S. Burroughs and *Eraserhead.* It all seemed so cool, decadent and glamorous to me in Wheeling, a backwater burg where there was nothing of the sort. I'd read CREEM and see myself doing what these people were doing when I grew up and got out of this town.

It's important to remember that in the 70's (pre-MTV, of course) an appearance by someone like David Bowie on the *Cher* show or seeing The Sex Pistols for the very first time on NBC's *Weekend* was *really* wild. You didn't see things like that on American TV back then, *ever!* Like *never ever.* It was such a rare experience that witnessing such things became life-changing events for teens and pre-teens, like myself. I recall vividly seeing the Sex Pistols on *Weekend* (a show in the *Saturday Night Live* 11:30pm timeslot once a month, a late night "edgy" *60 Minutes* wannabe) and thinking to my then 11-year old self "Wow, there's got to be a lot more of this kind of stuff out there," and there certainly was. By the time the punk era was in full swing, there was a veritable flood of weirdness making its way into the culture, even to the sole crappy mall near my hometown. I was completely hooked on punk and what came in its wake. I bought records like crazy back then, the weirder, the freakier, the more mind warping, *the better.*

On a parallel track, I had to visit a clinic twice a week for allergy shots and afterwards I would wait in the local library until my parents finished work. For some wonderful and unexplained reason, the public library in this rusted-out old town was *utterly superb,* a veritable treasure trove of strange and wondrous information if you knew what you were looking for. Books by William Burroughs, Jean-Paul Sartre, Timothy Leary and Aleister Crowley — books now often incredibly rare and expensive— filled the shelves and I would check out ten at a time, pouring over them, devouring them voraciously. Robert Shea and Robert Anton Wilson's *Illuminatus! Trilogy* were favorites as were the books of Kurt Vonnegut and Albert Goldman's *Ladies and Gentlemen, Lenny Bruce* which I must've read over 100 times, memorizing each and every detail of Bruce's life. I became obsessed with Andy Warhol's *A to B and Back Again,* Yoko Ono's *Grapefruit,* Firesign Theatre records, Antonin Artaud and *everything* related to Salvador Dali.

In this unassuming little library, I stumbled across books like *Underground Film* by Parker Tyler, where I read about people like Kenneth Anger, Harry Smith and Alejandro Jodorowsky, director of *El Topo* and *The Holy Mountain.* I found to my surprise that I was able to special order 16mm films (this is about seven years before VCRs were commonplace), including David Lynch's then new *Eraserhead* and *Performance* starring Mick Jagger, from a nationwide inter-library lending system. I projected these films over and over again watching them by myself smoking pot in my parent's basement and deciding that I was going to move to New York as soon as I could, hang out with the Warhol crowd and *become an underground filmmaker!*[3] If my strictly religious Methodist parents had had even the slightest inkling of what I was up to or what I was feeding my impressionable young head with, they'd have *shit themselves!*[4]

[3] In an interesting twist of fate, in 1984 within about five hours of my arrival in NYC, I was introduced to Andy Warhol at the *Area* nightclub by future "Club Kid murderer" Michael Alig.

[4] Or had me exorcised.

My interest in Kenneth Anger's films soon led to my discovery of *The Great Beast* himself, Aleister Crowley, at approximately the age of 12. The Wheeling Public Library had both *Magick in Theory in Practice* and *The Confessions of Aleister Crowley*. For whatever reason, his ideas resonated profoundly within me and I read his autobiography over and over again, discovering a *very* kindred spirit, something which gave me the courage to say to my parents "I'm not going to church with you again, *ever*" which was a really, really big deal in their house. From a very early age, the Christian religion seemed about as valid to me as Santa Claus, the Easter Bunny or the Tooth Fairy, *obvious bullshit,* not even worth considering and I was sick of putting up with this sanctimonious nonsense. After I read Crowley, I simply *refused* to go to church and it was never discussed in my family again and "Amen" to that.

But anyway, all of this is leading up to *my* pivotal, life-altering moment; an anecdote that will shed some light on how the book you are holding in your hands came to be:

Sometime in 1982, a few of my "punk" friends and I decided we'd drop acid (something we did *a lot* back then) and drive to Pittsburgh to see "X" perform at a club there, but we found we were too young to get in. Despite John Doe and Exene Cervenka trying to OK it with the manager of the place, we were only allowed to watch their sound check, during which a heavy mirrored tile fell from the ceiling and just about beheaded the guy who would not allow us to stay for the gig. I glowered at him like I was Damian Thorne (and it seemed to really freak him out) before we headed over to the local "New Wave" record store, "Eides" (still there) where this "life changing" moment occurred.

I was kneeling down, still tripping pretty hard, looking through a wooden crate of what I guess they considered to be their most *far out* merchandise of all: books, records and magazines that seemed *so insane* that to this day I can recall many of the items in the bin. Books like *The Anarchist Cookbook* and French Situationist philosopher Guy Debord's *Society of the Spectacle* were nestled alongside various punk zines, a *Virgin Prunes* album and a weird-looking red and black publication called *RE/Search #4/5* which featured articles on William Burroughs, painter Brion Gysin and "Industrial" rock group, *Throbbing Gristle*. My attention went to this immediately and I flipped through it before my eyes landed on the following words, spoken by Genesis P-Orridge:

> "One example I used with people to try and make them update their concept of magick is—you get the old-fashioned or everybody's archetypal view of it, which is a guy in robes with a wand saying sort of Latin incantations and so on. But the *modern* magician uses a Polaroid camera and a cassette recorder, like this. Because you use what's the appropriate tool to the time you live in. So in the medieval ages that was appropriate, because it fitted the culture, with a sort of strong religious cult. But now that's not appropriate. *A computer, a cassette recorder and a Polaroid is what's appropriate; and a video camera now.* Because you're dealing with what's *powerful,* and what *works*, and what manipulates what happens. That's what it's all about. And you apply your will to what's already available to make things happen...
>
> And it's a very selfish idea in one sense, because the whole point is that you're trying to make the world how you want it, so that you get the maximum pleasure!"
> (Page 84)

As soon as I read those words, *instantly,* ALL of the various things I'd been interested in seemed to cohere in a workable artistic, philosophical —and of course, magical— worldview. It was one of those cinematic moments —almost hokey— when everything just comes sharply into focus and the moment seems frozen in time. It all made crystal clear sense to me and a sort of path appeared for me, call it instinct, fate, a "calling" or what you will, but I became very possessed of the concept of what would later become *Disinformation*® —the notion of taking these kinds of ideas, dangerous ideas, ideas that could cause social transformation and a withering away of superstition and religion— and placing them in a context that would be as intriguing for a mass audience as it was for me personally. It seemed the next logical step, especially as cable TV was just then starting to really ramp up, that an "underground" television network (I loved *Max Headroom* obviously) would eventually occur and I wanted to be the one to program it or better still, *own it.*

A few years ago, while visiting my parents, I found a notebook from that time that I'd long forgotten about where I'd written down several slogans that would later be used with *Disinformation*®, such as

"Buy Things You Don't Need," "Higher Revolutionary Mutation," "Find the Others" and "Everything You Know is Wrong." I had long lists of films that existed already and a longer list of subjects that I'd make films about one day myself. I'd even sketched out a *midnight mindfuck* style TV show with myself as the host. But the real kicker? I also found a logo that I'd designed/drawn, or rather ripped off, from a Robert Fripp album cover:

How weird is that, right?

And what does this mean?!

A Warning:

I think it's only fair that I inform you that *this book is a spell.* You had *better believe* that everything herein has been thought about, vetted and mulled over to have a maximum effect on the reader.

The idea is that you will be *different* after you've read this book. Changed permanently.

I'm telling you now: I don't fuck around.

If this *worries* you, then perhaps this book is not for you and you should ponder putting it aside and not reading it. My goal isn't to upset anyone. Consider yourself warned.

The following quote, taken from Crowley's *Magick in Theory in Practice* should help further clarify this concept:

> **Magick is the Science and Art of causing Change to occur in conformity with Will.** Illustration: It is my Will to inform the World of certain facts within my knowledge. I therefore take "magical weapons", pen, ink, and paper; I write "incantations"—these sentences—in the "magical language" i.e., that which is understood by the people I wish to instruct; I call forth "spirits", such as printers, publishers, booksellers and so forth and constrain them to convey my message to those people. The composition and distribution of this book is thus an act of Magick by which I cause Changes to take place in conformity with my Will. (Note: In one sense Magick may be defined as the name given to Science by the vulgar.)

Crowley also said that the "magical" way to open a door was to walk across the room, turn the doorknob and *pull,* if you take his point.

Therefore, according to Crowley, every *intentional* act can thus be defined as a *magical* act.

This book intends to fuck your head up, *real good!*

It's also a *manual* of magick, a new kind of magick for a new millennium. It's high time to demystify what magick is (as well as what it *isn't*), so by examining the strategies of magically inclined artists and thinkers, you can see magick, *real magick,* at work in the culture and draw your own conclusions. See what works for them and learn from that. Try to figure out for yourself how you, too, can get maximum pleasure from the universe and how these methods might be adapted to your own pursuits and desires.

Not everyone in this book, of course, consciously considers him or herself to be a practicing magician, but many of the subjects do *in fact* see magick as the overall framework that their creative work falls under or as the overarching metaphor of their life in general. It will be quite apparent how these diverse people have all found ways to work their magick in ways never imagined by the medieval sorcerer with the cup, the wand, the robes and the Latin.

Throughout this book you will see examples of how someone who views the world that way is empowered by magick and how they enrich their intellectual space. If you see the universe as an alive and vibrant space that you can influence with your own particular energies, this is a powerful —and pragmatic— metaphor to live by.

Magick enhances the possible.

For our purposes here, *this is the entire point.*

How it works is another conversation entirely…

Richard Metzger
Los Angeles, Summer, 2002

ACKNOWLEDGMENTS

By way of acknowledgments, there is a long list of people who helped bring this book to your hands:

I am deeply indebted to Nimrod Erez, who both shot and edited the entire second season (as well as doing a lot of work on the first series as well) from which many of these interviews come. To say that he worked *damned hard* is a laughable understatement (as he and I both know) and Gary and myself are ever grateful to him. There is no way, none, that the show could've been produced without his gargantuan efforts, even as his health was affected. I'm paralyzed with fear that this technological whiz kid will be too busy to work with us on future projects. Nimrod, thank you very, very much!

Gratitude is also due my co-producer and longtime friend, Bradley Novicoff, whose unerring good taste, impeccable ear and *sharp-as-a-Ginsu-knife* mass media instincts steered the ship of fools where it needed to go.

And to my dear friend Adam Peters, a true artist who produces things of rare beauty in a world that no longer cares about beauty. Adam did the amazing music heard in the television program. You can buy the soundtrack on Steven Severin's RE imprint. Look out too for Adam's *Family of God* and *Neulander* CDs.

Leen Al-Bassam, who we've worked with closely for many years, for the wonderful design of this book and Jose Caballer, who we've worked with for even longer, for the design and art direction of the TV show.

Brian Butler, who introduced me (and the world) to the charms of one "Uncle Goddamn" and who produced our classic expose of Satanism and the mega-insane Rocketboy piece. Brian's unforgettable contributions to the show ramped up the weirdness factor *considerably*.

I'd also like to thank:

Joe Comperiati, who I closely collaborated with on the first season of the show, a good friend who likes "the green" as much as I do.

Stevan Keane, formerly with Channel 4, who commissioned the series and Zizi Durrance and Darren Bender who minded this wayward child during the second season.

Steven Daly, my dear friend who suggested the show to Stevan Keane in the first place. If he's not the wittiest man alive, then he's standing in line right behind Gore Vidal and Christopher Hitchens.

Alex Burns and Russ Kick for their kind editorial input.

Peter Giblin for producing the Disinfo.Con event with us.

Mike Backes and Brian Tibbetts for their friendship and encouragement during the edit process.

Adam Parfrey for always being an inspiration.

George Bunce for doing such a meticulous job with the transcripts and really making my job *a lot* easier.

Thanks also go out to Brian Pang, Nick Hodulik, Lee Hoffman, Ron Butler, Jeff Halpin, Deb Yoon, Doug Stone, Steve Nalepa, Jodi Wille, George Petros, Marilyn Manson, Ann Magnuson, Hope Urban, Bill Brown, Irwin Chusid, Skee Goodheart, Howard Hallis, Mike Sullivan, Frank Bruno, Mark Pesce, Chica Bruce, Mark Indigaro, Laurie Leighton, Jason Boughton, Gretchen Schwartz, Joshua Levin, Paul Dougherty, Mark Posillico, Brian Pratt, Paul Romaldini, James Fideler, Sean Fernald, Charlotte Chatton, Oberon Sinclair, Jon Carin, Eric Mittleman, Susan Mainzer, Lynn Hasty, Douglas Walla, Preston Peet, John Tully, Robert Sterling, AJ Peralta, Mike Glass, Eric Schmid, Nate Cimmino, Yasuharu Konishi, Teri MacMillan, ID, Nick Mamatas, David Pescovitz, Chris Campion, RU Sirius, Vanessa Weinberg, Amy Samuelson, Dr. Dana Zappala, Craig Kanarick, Jeffrey Dachis, Michael Simon, Robin Epstein, Peter Mattei, Chris Neitzert, Allen DeBevoise, Morgan Newman, John Jeffery, Kathryn Daly, Oliver Stone, Janet Yang, Naomi Despres, John Malone and my parents for giving me such an unintentionally *long* leash.

I'd especially like to thank my business partner Gary Baddeley, who edited and published this book and who made literally thousands of suggestions, 99% of which I took him up on. When you're in business with someone it's almost like being married to them and I can think of no one that I'd rather be married to than Gary. (That didn't come out right, did it?). He's the brains behind *Disinformation*®, I'm just the mascot.

And finally, I'd like to thank my beautiful love, Naomi Nelson, the coolest, funniest, sexiest and *wisest* woman I've ever met, just for putting up with me for so long. I could spend every minute of every day of the rest of my life with you and never get bored.

And I intend to.

ROBERT ANTON WILSON

Douglas Rushkoff once told me that of all of his heroes that he'd had the chance to meet, the only one who didn't disappoint him was Robert Anton Wilson. I thought it was such a wonderful thing to say about Bob that I wanted to see it in print.

Robert Anton Wilson is one of our greatest living social philosophers, but most people think of him as a Science Fiction author because of his classic trilogies *Illuminatus!* (co-written with Robert Shea) and *Schrodinger's Cat*. A better-informed readership also knows him as the author of *Cosmic Trigger*, a classic of occult speculation (which also became a trilogy, inspiring two sequels) and numerous books of *science fact*, trenchant social commentary, and optimistic Futurism such as *Quantum Psychology* and *Prometheus Rising*.

Illuminatus! brought together elements of Swift, Thomas Pynchon, William Burroughs, *Mad* magazine, The Warren Report, the John Birchers, The Firesign Theatre, Orson Welles, James Joyce, the enigmatic joke religion of Discordianism and every far out conspiracy theory that you'd ever heard of, to expose —or so you are led to believe, dear reader— *the really big conspiracy that rules the world.* Somewhere within its three volumes were hidden occult secrets. Maybe they were right out in the open; the authors seemed to be hinting as much to the reader, winking, in fact, that right out in the open might be the best place to hide these secrets *from them*, so look carefully. As a result, many readers thought *Illuminatus!* was real, theorizing that it was a message from an underground resistance group *written in code*. Others saw it as a deliberate attempt to confuse the population and *accused its authors of being agents of the Illuminati themselves* (something neither one confirmed or denied).

To outsider teenagers in the 1970's, *Illuminatus!* became an intellectual touchstone, a way of figuring out a world they'd been born into that seemed increasingly surreal. Once you read it, you were changed forever. There was no way you could look at the world around you in the same way once you'd digested its subversive message. The *Illuminatus!* trilogy was a nifty way of imprinting a skeptical worldview on an impressionable mind. A magical initiation in book form, you might say, on sale in shopping malls across America. And our parents were never the wiser!

Cosmic Trigger was different. This time the mask came off. In this book, Wilson came clean, in the most intellectually honest way that anyone ever has, on the subject of "What happens when you start fooling around with occult things? What happens when you do psychedelic drugs and try to contact higher dimensional entities through ritual magick?" *Cosmic Trigger* is a serious mind fuck of a journey into realms of thought and behavior most people would never go near in their lives, but if you were so inclined to take a walk on the darker side of things, you'd find no better guide than the always agnostic Wilson, ever ready to shed his best explanation or his current belief system lest it impair his critical abilities to accurately report on what was really happening. And he wasn't afraid of embarrassing himself either, which was a great gift to his readers. (There was a hyper weird period in my life when *Cosmic Trigger* kept me from thinking that I'd gone insane. I won't go into it now, but my day-to-day reality turned into a psychedelic funhouse much like Wilson describes in the book. I'm glad I had RAW's help in navigating this particular hall of mirrors! It was *fucked up!*)

I've interviewed Bob several times and he was the headliner at our Disinfo.Con[5] event, something that thrilled me to no end. I'm happy to say that I've become friends with one of my biggest heroes and let me tell you, Doug was right! He's the greatest.

I hear from Bob, nearly everyday, as a member of his small group of Internet friends, shooting the shit and passing along interesting articles we find on the Net. If you'd told me when I was a teenager that one day I'd be getting little electronic notes and messages throughout the day from the enigmatic author of *Illuminatus!*, I wonder how I'd have reacted. Does this make *me* a member of the Illuminati? Or am I just a dupe of Wilson's emailed "disinformation"? Or... or what?? Most days find Bob forwarding news regarding wild scientific discoveries, medical marijuana updates, various Fortean items, Scientology stuff, dirty jokes, etc., but a lot of it seems to do with politicians and how stupid they are, so I thought that might be a great topic to get him off to a good start!

RM: Are politicians and politics irrelevant?

RAW: Well, they're irrelevant *to me*, that's for sure. I'm over 70-years old and I've been studying this

for quite a long time. I have observed we have the same number of wars under the Democrats as we have under the Republicans, and that the United States invades as many foreign countries under the Republicans as it does under the Democrats. The people who do all the invading of foreign countries to kill people, men, women and children in their homes, they're not even called the Department of War anymore. They're called the *Department of Defense!* How the hell can we be *defending* ourselves 8,000 miles away attacking people in their jungle huts? I can't understand that and it goes on no matter which party is in control.

I began to get suspicious as far back as the 1950's when I was working as an engineering aide for a very large engineering company. One of the chief engineers told me that the company had a Vice President in Washington all the time. His job was to be their lobbyist and he gave equal amounts of money to the Democrats and Republicans so that no matter who won, the company would be represented in Congress and in the White House.

And I'm sure they all do the same thing: they give approximately equal amounts to both major parties and they make damn sure no third party ever gets strong enough to pose a challenge. Voting is choosing between Tweedle-Dee and Tweedle-Dum. Which gang of Wall Street bandits does this guy represent as opposed to which gang of Wall Street bandits does this guy represent? They both represent the same gang of Wall Street bandits so there is no real choice.

RM: What's the alternative to the two party political system in this country?

RAW: As far as I can see, the only hopeful alternative is the Internet. Like, say, now you can do all your stock brokering online, I think eventually political power will devolve back to the people by way of the Internet in a similar way. The whole theory of representative government is an innovation of the last 200 years. After they discovered that the hereditary governors —the kings and their relatives— were a bunch of bandits, they said, "Well, we'll elect our own bandits and they'll represent us." But they don't represent *us*. They represent the people who pay for their elections.

The idea was we needed somebody to represent us because we couldn't all go to Washington to represent ourselves. On the Internet we can all represent ourselves and I would much rather represent myself through my computer than have [U.S. Senator from California] Dianne Feinstein sitting there claiming that *she* represents me. She represents me about as well as a hungry lion represents a running gazelle.

RM: Why is the so-called war on drugs doomed to failure?

RAW: There are two kinds of crimes. Crimes which everybody agrees are a crime, that's crimes with victims. If I get mugged or burglarized or somebody in my family gets hurt or killed I want the police to do something about it and I'm eager to cooperate with them and so is everybody else of a sound and rational mind. We don't want burglars and thieves and muggers and murderers running

5 On February 19, 2000, The Disinformation Company organized a large counterculture event in New York City's Hammerstein Ballroom that was described by The New York Times as "Cyberpalooza." The event featured several of the individuals featured in this book: in addition to Mr. Wilson, Marilyn Manson, Douglas Rushkoff, Grant Morrison, Paul Laffoley, Adam Parfrey, Kembra Pfahler, Mark Pesce, Kenneth Anger, Genesis P-Orridge and others performed. Joe Coleman blew himself up, as is his wont at such events, having the unfortunate effect of also igniting several members of the audience.

ROBERT ANTON WILSON

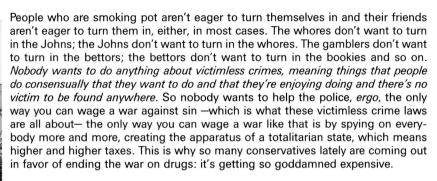

around loose. On the other hand, when you're trying to control *victimless* crime, nobody is very eager to help the police.

People who are smoking pot aren't eager to turn themselves in and their friends aren't eager to turn them in, either, in most cases. The whores don't want to turn in the Johns; the Johns don't want to turn in the whores. The gamblers don't want to turn in the bettors; the bettors don't want to turn in the bookies and so on. *Nobody wants to do anything about victimless crimes, meaning things that people do consensually that they want to do and that they're enjoying doing and there's no victim to be found anywhere.* So nobody wants to help the police, *ergo*, the only way you can wage a war against sin —which is what these victimless crime laws are all about— the only way you can wage a war like that is by spying on everybody more and more, creating the apparatus of a totalitarian state, which means higher and higher taxes. This is why so many conservatives lately are coming out in favor of ending the war on drugs: it's getting so goddamned expensive.

The only way the government has any chance at all of winning is to establish a totalitarianism wackier and more total than Orwell's 1984. We've already got the "Piss Police" which is something that Orwell didn't even dream of. *Even Franz Kafka couldn't imagine a society so crazy that you have to give urine samples before you can hold a job!* There's no way of winning without totalitarianism far beyond anything ever practiced by Hitler or Stalin or imagined by the wildest satirist. That's the only way they can win. And that costs too damned much money. The people who are running it, they're not trying to win. They know they can't win; they just want to keep the war going because it makes money for everybody.

It's a wonderful excuse to increase police power and surveillance so that they know everything that we're doing so that nobody can be plotting subversion of any sort without them knowing about it. Like the old joke goes, "When four men sit down to plot against the government, three of them are government agents and the fourth is a damned fool." Well that's getting more and more true all the time. The *war on drugs* is an excuse for more and more surveillance. They're scared stiff of us. They're more afraid of us than we are of them.

RM: You have studied the Illuminati for years. Have you come to any conclusions about their aims?

RAW: Usually when people ask me that question, I give them some kind of a put-on, but I can't think of a good and original put-on that I haven't done several times before. So I'll tell you the truth, for once. After investigating the Illuminati and their critics for the last 30 years, I think the Illuminati was a short lived society of free thinkers and democratic reformers that formed a secret society within Freemasonry, using Freemasonry as a cover so they could plot to overthrow all the kings in Europe and the Pope. I'm very happy that they succeeded in overthrowing all the kings, I just wish that they had completed the job and gotten rid of the Royal family in England too, but they did pretty well on the continent. I'm sorry they haven't finished off the Pope yet, either, but I think they're still working on the project and I wish them luck.

RM: Why do you think the central secrets of Freemasonry have, after hundreds of years, still remained secret to the public at large?

RAW: Because the public at large doesn't spend as much time browsing around second hand bookstores as I do. You could find all the secrets of Freemasonry in print. Well not always in print, but you could find them in second hand bookstores. The Encyclopedia Britannica will tell you most of it. They'll tell you who the *Widow's Son* was and what the Mason word is. The secrets are pretty well known actually.

RM: Was Beethoven a member of the Illuminati?

RAW: I can't say for sure. He was certainly very closely associated with them. His first music teacher, Neefe, was a member of the Illuminati. Then when Beethoven arrived in Vienna, that teacher gave him letters of introduction to all the noblemen who were members of Freemasonry, most of them also members of the Illuminati. The Illuminati commissioned Beethoven's first major work, the Cantata on the death of Emperor Joseph II which praised Franz Josef as a "bringer of light," an Illuminati symbol there. "A bringer of light, a foe of darkness." And I read over the life of Franz Josef trying to figure out what he did to deserve that.

The huge thing he did was to legalize Freemasonry in Austria and the second thing he did was he closed all the Catholic schools and replaced them with public schools. So yeah, I think he *was* a bringer of light and a foe of darkness and I can see why the Illuminati liked him. And I can see why Beethoven liked him too.

RM: When you wrote *Illuminatus!* with Robert Shea in the 60's, did you think you were writing a prophetic novel? So much stuff in it that seemed so far out when I was a kid, now seems to predict *exactly* what would happen 25 years down the road!

RAW: No, I thought we were writing a classic, but I didn't know it was going to be prophetic too. When I made Beethoven a member of the Illuminati —that was my idea, not Shea's— that was a parody of the Christian right claiming the Beatles were agents of Communism. Imagine my shock when I read a biography of Beethoven and found all the evidence that he may have been a member of the Illuminati. I started to wonder, do I have unconscious ESP or am I just a lucky guesser?

RM: In the *Schrodinger's Cat* trilogy, you predicted homeless people all over America and that was written at a time when the homeless problem was scarcely on the national radar.

RAW: Well, that was based on watching the rate at which rents were increasing in this country and I figured, eventually, it'll take $900 to rent a broom closet in downtown Berkeley and eventually there would be more and more people living on the streets

And of course, this *still* seems to me to be the major cause of homelessness in this country; this is the increase in rent. But you can't talk about that in the public media. My wife Arlen used to say "There's never a story about the homeless on the major networks or in the major newspapers or magazines in which the word "landlord" appears." It seems everybody working in the news business, whether it's radio, television, newspapers, news magazines, they all have a sign over their desk, "Do not use the word 'landlord' when writing about the homeless."

It's obvious to anybody who is not brainwashed by the media that the reason people are living on the streets is because *they can't afford to pay rent*. And the reason for that is it costs as much to have a one room apartment now as it did to have a penthouse in the 1940's. When I was a little kid, my parents were paying $48 a month rent for a house for both of them and my brother and me. $48 a month. Now as the rents go up and up and up and up and up to over $1000, over $2000 and so on, there are going to be more and more people living on the streets and the cause is very, very simple: *it's the greed of landlords*. But you can't say that in the major media. They've got to come up with complicated sociological problems, impersonal market forces. As if there was no first name, last name or address of the person who made that decision to raise your rent!

RM: When they changed the design of American money, a friend of mine remarked that they looked like coupons and it made me think how abstract money really is. It's no longer a certificate that you could redeem for its value in silver or in gold, it's just some kind of arbitrary "cred-

ROBERT ANTON WILSON

it" that you have in your bank account. Obviously there is a sort of a "belief" in the monetary system that keeps it afloat. What would happen if everyone just stopped believing in money?

RAW: If everybody went to the bank and took out their money, the whole damned system would collapse, because the banks are allowed by law to loan eight times as much as they have on deposit. That's considered safe because it's unlikely that everybody will go in and take their money out all at once.

Actually, according to Penny Lernoux, in a very good book on modern banking called *In Banks We Trust*, they habitually loan more than eight times than what they've got on deposit, or a hell of a lot more than eight times. When the SEC catches them they get fined and the case is not publicized, not just because the bankers own the government but because if they *did* publicize it then it might start a run on the banks and the whole system would fall down like it did in the 1930's.

It's very strange, but these pieces of paper that people have so much faith in, as you point out, if you read them very carefully, they're not promising to give you *anything* in return. They used to when I was young: every dollar bill said on it you could redeem it in silver on demand. Now it just says that it's legal tender for all debts. Which means you can't exchange it for anything but *more paper*. If people lost faith in this paper the whole system would fall apart. Money in the modern world is just pure information. It's as abstract as information in cybernetic theory. Which brings up the question: how come people get to charge interest on distributing information? (Laughs)

Ezra Pound said we're living in a "*Usuracracy*," that is a system dominated by usury, and it sure does look that way especially when you realize that we're paying interest on money that doesn't even *exist* except by some kind of social convention. At my workshops, I ask, "What's the difference between a counterfeit dollar bill and a real dollar bill?" Eventually it comes down to we've got to have faith that the Federal Reserve has a magic wand and when *they* print paper they pass the magic wand over it and it becomes money. When the Mafia prints paper in their cellar, they don't have the magic wand so it's not real money. But supposing Andy Warhol found a Mafia dollar and put a frame around it? It'd be worth more than the Federal Reserve money. How does the Federal Reserve get away with this swindle and no one ever suspects it?

RM: With something like *The X Files* or Art Bell's radio show becoming so popular in the American culture, "conspiracy theories" are being talked about everywhere and people are, you know, not trusting the government or not trusting the media or this and that... On the other hand, they seem to believe *anything*.

RAW: (Laughs) I blame that on the churches and the ignorance of the public at large. The major thing you should learn in any decent education is to how to judge and evaluate new sources of information. If I say to you "The people in the next apartment are all Zebra-striped and they fly around three feet above the ground," how are you going to judge and evaluate that? One way: does it sound plausible to you? Another way is: how honest do you think I am? And there are lots of other ways. But most people have no standards of evaluation at all to judge between something that's plausible, something that's totally impossible, something that's possible but not probable, something that's probable but not yet proven.

They don't have those distinctions because any teacher in the United States who's caught trying to teach children how to judge statements *logically*... immediately, the whole school board, all the parents and especially the local clergy come down on his or her case and he or she gets fired, thrown out on their ass, and has to find work in another field. *You can't teach children to think. It's against the law.* So of course nobody has any standards how to judge whether Martians are in the White House or if General Motors owns the President or whether there are fetuses of extraterrestrials at Fort Bragg; they have no standard by which to judge. So they judge by whomever they heard speak most recently! "Oh that must be the truth, I just heard it five minutes ago." They don't have an attention span that goes more than ten minutes and that's because they've never been taught how to use their brains. I used to advertise my seminars as "How to Use Your Brain for Fun and Profit". These days most people don't even know how to use it for fun, much less know how to use it for profit.

RM: Don't you think that many Americans are just looking for someone to blame? Might this impulse explain the interest in conspiracy theories?

RAW: Well that's a great deal of the appeal of conspiracy theories. Most people are frustrated, angry and miserable. When I was young man, I supported a wife and four children for a long time. Nobody can do that in America today. The wife has to go out and work too. Which means that she's got to earn as much as her husband or more, so they can afford somebody to look after the children. Or you appoint the older children to look after the younger ones and you end up with four juvenile delinquents on your hands. Everybody has plenty of reason to be angry, frustrated and pretty miserable and they want to know who to blame because they haven't got the mathematical sophistication to understand the concept of information flow and the way information flow leads to social chaos and transformation.

RM: What are the real conspiracies going on in the world?

RAW: At Esalen,[6] a guy in one of my workshop groups told me "I used to be the District Attorney of Santa Barbara, and I can guarantee that every time there's a major land deal there are at least 25 conspiracies fighting over who's going to get the biggest profits out of it." That's in one town. You multiply that by the size of the United States and there are thousands and thousands of conspiracies fight-

ing with each other. Which is why I can't go along with the liberal dogma there are no conspiracies. Nor can I go along with these crazy far-Left and far-Right theories about one big conspiracy that runs everything.

The most successful conspiracy that I can find real documentary proof of in recent times was the P2 conspiracy in Italy and almost everybody involved in that either died mysteriously or went to jail and I don't think it survives any longer. I think conspiracies, like Redwoods and mountains and bears and beetles and people, have a natural life span, they do not go on forever. P2 ran most of the Italian banks and most of the Italian government back in the 70's and 80's. Licio Gelli, who founded P2, was a very clever guy. During World War II he worked for both the Gestapo and the Communist underground and convinced both of them that he was really working for them and betraying the others. After World War II he worked for both the CIA and the KGB and did the same: he convinced both of them he was really working for them and betraying the other guys; meanwhile he got fabulously rich by betraying everybody in sight. When he formed P2 as a secret society within the Grand Orient Lodge or Egyptian Freemasonry, everybody had to give a full confession, not only of their sexual peccadilloes but of their financial crimes, so then he could blackmail anybody who wanted to leave P2. The more vicious the conspiracy is, the more criminal it is —like P2 was involved in gun running and laundering drug money for the CIA— the shorter lived it will be, because they all double-cross one another and get killed one way or another in fighting over the profits.

[6] The Esalen Institute, located on the Big Sur coast of California, was founded in 1962 as an alternative educational center. Esalen is known for its blend of East/West philosophies, its workshops, and its visiting philosophers, psychologists, artists, and religious thinkers.

RM: There is no word in the English language for rational fear. What is the difference between paranoia and rational fear?

RAW: That's a good question. If somebody points a gun at you and says, "Give me all your money or I'll blow off your head," I think that would be rational fear. If you get a letter that's slightly damaged and you think "Well, the FBI must have opened my mail and been clumsy in resealing it" then I think that's pretty dumb

ROBERT ANTON WILSON

because the FBI… well, I'm sure if they're opening your mail they're resealing it *very carefully*. You've got to judge each case on its own merits. Besides, paranoids have real fears as well as irrational ones.

In a very interesting paper I read about 30 years ago, a sociologist investigated a lot of conspiracy buffs and he found real evidence they were all being persecuted in some way. He couldn't attribute it all to their imaginations. And the thing was, it wasn't a matter of which conspiracy they were denouncing, they all got persecuted equally. So you figure there's some way they manage to maneuver their environment so that they get persecuted to fulfill their conspiracy theory. (Laughs)

RM: That sounds like a character in one of your novels.

RAW: Or a Philip K. Dick novel. It also sounds like a sinister variation on Jung's theories of synchronicities: *if you think black thoughts often enough, then dark things will gather around you*.

RM: That segues nicely into the next question: what is the 23 enigma?

RAW: Well, William S. Burroughs told me about the 23 enigma back around 1965. He had observed a lot of coincidences connected with the number 23 and as soon as he told me that *I* started noticing coincidences involving the number 23. I put a lot of them into the *Illuminatus!* novels and I put a bunch of them into the *Cosmic Trigger* trilogy and ever since then I've been getting letters from people who have observed odd 23s and there's no end to it.

I'll tell you a very amusing anecdote. I was in St. Louis giving a lecture and a guy came up after the lecture with his wife and said "I figured out how your 23 gimmick works." And I said "Oh? Then tell *me*." And he said, "It's a neurological grid. You make your readers very conscious of 23, more conscious than they are of the other numbers." And I said, "Congratulations, you've found the great magician who makes the grass green." That's a sign of enlightenment in Zen, which I thought was an adequate answer, and then a little while later it turned out that we went out to have a pizza together, he and his wife and me, and it was one of those places where you get a number while you wait for your pizza and of course we got number 23 and he said to me, "How do you do it?" And I said "I thought you did it that time!" and I suppose he's still wondering about that… well so am I!

It *just happens*, that's all. That's the enigma. Why does it keep happening? A neurological grid is part of it, but that's not all of it.

RM: It's also something that's popping up more and more in Hollywood films. Some movies or music videos have 23s all over them. I figure that the people behind them must be Robert Anton Wilson fans….

RAW: It pops up a lot on the *Rockford Files* too. And it was on *Max Headroom* quite a bit as well, that was Channel 23. I think I must have a lot of fans in show business; either that or the 23 thing is even more mysterious than I realize.

RM: Will it ever be possible to abolish stupidity?

RAW: Well I sure hope so. I regard that as the number one problem on this planet. I know most people think starvation is the number one problem, but I think starvation is caused by stupidity. That is to say, *starvation is caused by* —as Buckminster Fuller said— *ignorance, fear, greed, and zoning laws*. Well the fear, greed and zoning laws are caused by the ignorance and the ignorance is caused by the stupidity and the *stupidity is caused by the fact that any teacher who really tries to teach children how to think is going to get their ass fired out of the school system*. Which is the result of the fact that the people believe in traditional family values, i.e., the right to hate the same people Grandpa hated. I see more and more evidence that that is the one value on which most Christian Americans do agree.

RM: How much longer do you see Christianity lasting?

RAW: (Sighs) I wrote three historical novels in the 1980's and one of the most disillusioning things I found out was that Voltaire, that paragon of reason and skepticism and caution —who was not nearly as utopian as most of the other French intellectuals around him— Voltaire had a period in which he thought the Catholic church would be gone in 20 years. When they dissolved the Jesuits, he wrote an ecstatic letter saying, "The Catholic church is falling apart. It will be gone in 20 years." Considering how persistent the Christian virus has been, I don't see any hope of eliminating it in the near future. I just hope for more and more amelioration. Like the First Amendment over here and the similar laws in other advanced industrial nations which prevent the Christians from burning us at the stake. Which they would do again the minute they had the freedom to do it. They *would* do it, you know. As Nietzsche said, it's not their love for us that keeps them from burning us at the stake; it's the impotence of their love.

They don't have the power to burn us at the stake. If they can save our souls by burning us at the stake, don't you think our souls are worth more than our bodies? They'd burn us at the stake again as soon as they had the right to do it. So as long as we have that much protection against them, the virus will go on raging indefinitely, I suppose.

RM: You've written about the phenomenon of how information keeps leap-frogging over itself. How is this going to change society with what's coming after the Internet has been ubiquitous for a while?

RAW: Between the time of Christ and the birth of Leonardo da Vinci, information doubled in that 1,500 years. You take the next 250 years up to the invention of the steam engine, and information doubled again in that interlude. The next time information doubled it only took 150 years and by 1900 we knew four times as much as anybody living at the time of Christ did. And information has doubled in between 1900 and 1950, between 1950 and 1960, between 1960 and '67, between '67 and 1973. It's been estimated that by the end of the 1980's it was doubling every *eighteen months*. I've seen recent estimates that it's doubling every year now. Every time information doubles, society goes through a tremendous transformation.

For instance, around 1500, we had the first two successful Protestant revolutions and the end of Papal dominance over the West. At the end of the second doubling, in 1750, we had the Industrial Revolution which ended the agricultural societies that had existed all over the world up until then, replacing them more and more with industrial societies in the last 200 years. The American Revolution, the French Revolution, insurrections in Holland and Sweden and Switzerland. The first Mexican Revolution, the Bolivar Revolutions in South America. After 1900, after that doubling between then and the next doubling in 1950, we had two World Wars and the rise of Fascism and Communism. Every time information doubles, everything gets shook up and the world goes through violent upheavals. *The reason for remaining optimistic in spite of all that is the world always tends to improve in the long run with more information.* By and large, the poorest people in the worst slums in the industrial world are living better than they lived at the time of Christ. That's for damn sure. And they're living a lot better than they lived at the time of James Watt, when he invented the steam engine.

RM: So you see a hopeful future for humanity?

RAW: I see a possible hopeful future, and I've invested a lot of time, energy and emotion in promot-

ROBERT ANTON WILSON

ing a hopeful future. I feel it's possible and it's desirable and the more people can see it and think about it and envision it, the more energy will go into producing it. I agree with Nietzsche that peddling pessimism is like selling poison. Pessimism ruins people. It ruins societies. It ruins cultures. Pessimism is a great killer. My optimism is partly based on probabilities, but it's partly based on a deliberate choice. I don't want to add to the amount of pessimism in the world. Pessimists never do anything, they sit in the corner and moan and piss and groan and bitch and complain, but they never do anything. The optimists are the ones who do things. At least they're trying. I'm an optimist on principle.

RM: Looking back to the 1960's and comparing that decade's promises to the way things are now, it would seem that a lot of the countercultural values of that time are now widely held viewpoints, and that there are numerous alternative lifestyles which are totally acceptable to the general public. Do you think that the counterculture actually won?

RAW: I don't think anybody has won yet. I think the war is still going on different levels. According to one reporter from the *Atlanta Journal* we have a 70 million-person drug problem in this country. That means 70 million people use drugs the government disapproves of. Of those, 65 million are using pot. If we were to legalize pot, we'd suddenly have a five million-person drug problem. To the extent that we've got 65 million pot smokers, obviously the counterculture has won. To the extent that they're still subject to being thrown in jail even when they're using it to treat cancer and AIDS and other conditions, it hasn't won. The same bastards are still in charge.

RM: If you were elected president what's the first thing you would do?

RAW: Resign.

RM: Why is Aleister Crowley still important?

RAW: As Timothy Leary used to say, he was one of the four most intelligent men of the 20th Century. Crowley was the first writer of so-called "New Age" or mystical or occult tendency that I ever took seriously. I took him seriously because he had such a great sense of humor. I figured somebody this funny must have been saying something behind all these jokes. So I started studying him and I found he did have a lot important to say and I value him highly and the fact that he has such a low reputation doesn't bother me at all. I think Relativity is one of the most important ideas of the 20th Century. Einstein gave us physical relativity; Joyce gave us artistic relativity by telling *Ulysses* in a hundred different narrative voices instead of just the one allegedly "objective" detached observer of 19th Century fiction. Crowley did the same things for the mystical occult world, with his Law of Thelema, "Do what thou wilt shall be the whole of the law," which fills every moron in the world with terror, anxiety, paranoia and general discombobulation. It's okay to say "Do what *I* will shall be the whole of the law." Every religious teacher in history has said *that*, and everybody went, "Yes, yes, tell us what to do. Tell us what to do, yes, master. May we kiss your feet, master?" But if you say, "Do what *thou* wilt"—"What, you're giving *me* the responsibility? I can't take on that responsibility. You tell me what to do."

I've defined the "disciple" as "an asshole looking for a human being to attach itself to." The Crowley system does not have any disciples. It doesn't tell *you* what to do, it tells you to decide *for yourself* what to do. I think it's the most libertarian philosophy to ever arise out of the mystical occult mish-mosh.

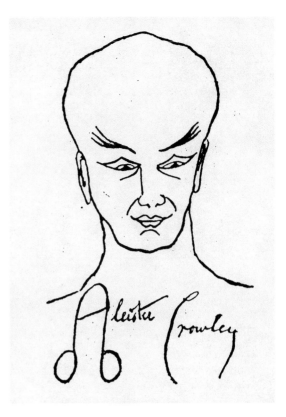

ROBERT ANTON WILSON

HOWARD BLOOM

In our first *Disinformation*® anthology, *You Are Being Lied To* (Russ Kick, editor), I wrote the following about Howard Bloom: "I have met God and he lives in Brooklyn… Howard Bloom is the next in a lineage of seminal thinkers that includes Newton, Darwin, Freud, and Buckminster Fuller." When I introduced him on television I added that I could try to convince you of that statement but that "Howard can probably do a better job of convincing you himself," which is true —his arsenal of expression is extraordinary, a marvel to behold— but why take my word for it, *or his?*

Here's what others have said about Howard Bloom:

> "Bloom's work marshals a quantity of evidence reminiscent of Darwin's *Origin of Species*."—Dorian Sagan, *Wired* magazine

> "Howard Bloom just may be the new Stephen Hawking, only he's not just interested in science, he's interested in the soul." —Aaron Hicklin, *GEAR* magazine

> "I doubt there is a stronger intellect than Bloom's on the planet" —Joseph Chilton Pierce, author of *The Crack in the Cosmic Egg*

And Leon Uris, celebrated author of *Exodus*, had this to say on Bloom's then unpublished masterpiece *The Lucifer Principle*: "An astonishing act of intellectual courage."

Obviously I'm in agreement with the above statements or else I wouldn't be quoting them here. I *do* indeed think that Howard Bloom's ideas are amongst the *very most* critically important of our time and that his books should be read by anyone seeking a better understanding of what's going on in today's turbulent world, *The Lucifer Principle* being especially handy in making sense of the mess in the Middle East and the more violent impulses of the Islamist and Zionist mindsets.

Bloom takes a broad —make that *very broad*— view of history, closely examining, in a manner never explored before him, the biological and psychological roots of mass behavior with his science of *Paleopsychology*. What Bloom gives his readers is a new and extremely compelling *revisionist history of the entirety of the history of life on this planet* —microbial, mammalian and otherwise— and nothing less. His books are absolutely essential —and riveting— reading.

Yes, it's true, missing out on Bloom *would* be like missing out on Newton, Darwin, Freud or Fuller. You'd lack a fundamental cornerstone of modern intellectual life. The public doesn't realize this yet about Bloom, but *it will.*

What great minds have done throughout history is provide an aerial view of things. A larger more encompassing view that often —but not always— subsumes the previous paradigm and then surpasses it in completeness and vividness of its metaphors. Consider how the evolving notions of a flat earth, Copernican astronomy and Einsteinian physics have sequentially changed how mankind sees its place in the cosmos, continuously updating the past explanations with something superior to what's been before. For what else do intellectuals really do but *describe nature* and how it works and the state of human affairs in relation to the whole. You can "discover" a new planet or a new species, for example, but they were already doing fine *without* you…

Great thinkers and scientists provide us with the best and the biggest, most all-encompassing worldview available at the time, but they also need to steer the trajectory of public discourse towards their ideas. Scientists, as much as anyone else, are subject to the dictates of public relations in the marketplace of ideas. To accomplish injecting their ideas into the culture, they must also be *heard*, as in the relatively recently coined Zen adage that asks, "If a tree falls in the forest and there is no one around to send out a press release, did it really happen?" For a new scientific theory to make a significant ripple, it must first find a way of making it into mass culture. There is no other way.

How fortunate then that Howard Bloom began his career as one of the dominant forces in the public relations industry, publicizing some of the biggest acts of the 80's: Prince, Michael Jackson, Kiss, Joan Jett, Billy Idol, John Mellencamp and ZZ Top were but a few of his clients. Working with such personalities allowed Bloom to abstract what makes these people tick and what makes them compelling to a wide audience. When *Gear's* Aaron Hicklin compared Howard to Stephen Hawking, what I think he was indicating is that Bloom has the potential to be a science star of the magnitude of Hawking's *uber celebrity*. I agree, Bloom has charisma and passion to spare and he is a compelling televisual presence.

There's also the matter of Bloom's physical infirmity —a bad case of Chronic Fatigue Syndrome has kept Bloom bedridden for better than a decade— which encourages the Hawking comparison, too, something Howard is certainly aware of, but being a former PR flak, he's smart enough to play along: when the media starts comparing you to the most famous scientist alive, it is a very positive thing.[7]

Photo: Naomi Nelson

Of Bloom, it can safely be said: *he knows how to make a stir*, effecting what amounts to a scientific revolution from his bedroom, whether engaged in cyber-kibitzing with fellow travelers, on the phone doing radio interviews or entertaining television crews and visitors to his bedside. The Mountain is certainly obliged to go to Mohammed as has been said about many a trip à chez Bloom but —as will be evident from the interview below— the CFS seems to have little effect on Howard's ability to talk your ear off!

So without further fanfare, I will allow the man himself to convince you, in his own way, of the validity of my initial statement. Once again here's another lively installment of the continuing conversation that I'm having with Howard Bloom. Here we discuss the central thesis to his book *Global Brain: The Evolution of Mass Mind From the Big Bang To the 21$^{\underline{st}}$ Century* (John Wiley & Sons, New York).

RM: Howard, your book, *Global Brain*, takes issue with the more McLuhanesque concept that the global brain is something that happened with telecommunications in the last 100 or so years, as Peter Russell[8] and others have argued. Let's begin at the beginning, how do you define *the global brain*?

HB: Well the global brain is not something that's electronic and it has nothing to do with the World Wide Web and it has nothing to do with the Internet; we were *World Wide Webbed* and *Internetted* 3.5 billion years ago when life first began.

Now life first began about 3.85 billion years ago. We have no idea of what went on during the first 350 million years, but we do know what was going on about 3.5 billion years ago. There were giant colonies of bacteria, megalopolises of bacteria far beyond anything we've known as humans with our empires and city-states. One colony alone, the size of your hand or less, would have more members than all the human beings that have ever been. And those members would be in constant contact. They'd be in contact via chemical means. They'd be giving each other chemical attraction and repulsion cues, chemical warnings of danger, and chemical warnings of all kinds. They'd also be exchanging information via DNA.

[7] Let's just say the *Gear* article is right up front in his press kit, okay?

[8] Peter Russell's book, *The Global Brain* predates Bloom's book of nearly the same title by about 17 years. Their respective theories are not the same, nor are they that dissimilar. Neither are they contradictory and they share many common characteristics.

HOWARD BLOOM

Now DNA is the equivalent of —a small swatch of DNA, which they could exchange quite readily among themselves— would be the equivalent of an entire encyclopedia or more. A vast instructional book.

Basically bacteria were capable of doing something that goes utterly beyond even our electronic capacities, as great as they are. A bacterium could take the equivalent of its brain, it could take a hard drive, imagine a hard drive which we've got now, it could take that hard drive, switch it over to another bacterium, that bacterium could switch it over to another bacterium, or it could put that hard drive into circulation so that it went all through the bacterial colony and every bacterium could copy it. Every bacterium then would know everything that every other bacterium knew, at least all the basics. But even more important, you could broadcast that from one colony to another. These little bacterial bits could go traveling around, and they did. As a matter of fact, once there were birds, birds were used as couriers, so bacteria already had an airline service for transferring these little hard drive's worth of information around 220 million years ago when birds first came along. Why? They worked out a simple deal with the birds, "Look, we won't bother you if you simply transport us." And since birds travel tens of thousands of miles going from one continent to another, it was the airline service of the day. Bacterial airlines. Humans wouldn't get anywhere near that for a long, long time and in many ways we're still not anywhere near that. With all of our Internetting, with all of our World Wide Webbing, with all of our URLs, we're still not anywhere near being able to swap the quantities of information that bacteria were able to swap via the bacterial airlines, which means your everyday goose flying from one continent to another.

RM: So the global brain has existed a lot longer than we've thought?

HB: The global brain has existed far, far longer than we thought and the big problem for humans is: in the same way that bacteria were always making war on each other —one bacterial colony would make war on the bacterial colony of another kind and they'd use chemical warfare, very sophisticated stuff— they also make war on us. We're their dinner platters. We're their walking canapés.

We're their walking hors d'oeuvres and we need to be able to protect ourselves against these things, but we really haven't had effective means of protecting ourselves until recently.

About 350 years ago we began to develop something called *science*. Now at that point we'd already developed books, we'd already developed language —we'd had language probably for somewhere around 200,000 years, it's hard to tell, maybe only 35,000 years— but that was the beginning of our being able to swap a zillionth of the information of what bacteria could swap. They were swapping these entire hard drives while we were only swapping bits and bytes.

In 1630 science began, and there were lots of reasons why science could begin. We had cities. We had roads. We had the mail system, this was very, very important to us. It was slow in comparison to the goose flying 10,000 miles, but at least it allowed people like Erasmus in 1500 to form an international society of people who agreed with him, of people who shared his attitudes on things.

This is another strange thing, a very valuable thing about people that plays a great part in *The Global Brain*. People —once they became metropolitan, once they developed cities, and once they developed a high degree of trade between cities— began to gather together, not on the basis of tribal loyalties, but on the basis of *mental loyalties*. People who shared a common idea or people who shared a common emotional set could find other people like them in other cities and gather together in international subcultures.

And those international subcultures would become tremendously important because subcultures, just like bacterial colonies, are constantly struggling to take over the mind of a society. In 1630 there would be a new subculture of scientists. A subculture of people who were curious about cutting up the human body and finding out what was inside or taking a lens and actually looking at sperm, which is what Anton von Leeuwenhoek did. Nobody tells us the details of how he got that sperm, we have to guess, but the fact is he was looking at it. What was he discovering? Little "animalcules" he called them, these little things that wriggled around all by themselves. He used the mails and he wrote a letter to the Royal Society in England all about these little animalcules in his sperm. And the Royal Society was absolutely aghast, but still kind of delighted that they had discovered this new thing, that there was life on a level that they had never recognized before.

One of the strange things about humans, primates, or even guppies, is that we have a very fine-tuned mechanism for finding others who are like ourselves. There's a very good example that comes from Harry Harlow who studied primates. Harry Harlow took chimpanzees and other monkeys and he gave lobectomies to the chimps or monkeys he was working with. Only two of them. This is a complex brain operation. He gave them to only two and then he let them back into the colonies of the other monkeys.

Now this means there were dozens and dozens of monkeys of the very same kind. Monkeys have different personalities, just the way we do, but they tend to gravitate toward others who are most like them. Their ability to spot those who are like them is so uncanny that the following happened: when Harlow asked his student assistants to identify the two monkeys who had the lobectomies and to keep track of their actions, they couldn't. They had to constantly refer to their notes in order to even attempt to keep track of who these monkeys were, but when it came time to mate the monkeys had no trouble whatsoever. The male monkey with the lobectomy found the female monkey with the lobectomy and that was the female, and the only female, he had any interest in. We human primates also tend to be able to feel out those who have a similar brain chemistry, a similar structural organization, a similar set of attitudes, a similar set of modes of emotions, and we hang out with them. Once we had cities and a great deal of trade going on between cites, if we couldn't find somebody at home, here in, let's say Rome, we could always find somebody in Athens we could relate to.

And ideas were beginning to float back and forth in the liquid stream of travel and of trade. This thing that we see taking place where two monkeys with similar brains manage to get together became very important in 1500 or so, when Erasmus began writing letters to people in other countries who he felt would share a common emotional sense of things. Those people were called the Humanists, and they were located all over Europe. This was sort of the first chat group and this was a chat group formed via the technology of the time, the mails.

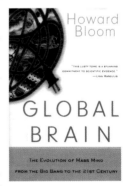

Howard
Bloom

"THIS LUSTY TOME IS A STUNNING
COMMITMENT TO SCIENTIFIC EVIDENCE."
—LYNN MARGULIS

GLOBAL
BRAIN

THE EVOLUTION OF MASS MIND
FROM THE BIG BANG TO THE 21ST CENTURY

Those mails would become extremely important in 1630 when science was founded. People who had a material approach to things and an analytic approach to things could find each other and they could stay in touch with each other. Then the Royal Society of London started up and it was able to start entirely because of the mails, because it was independent of geographic boundaries.

HOWARD BLOOM

RM: So there's a parallel society of bacteria growing apace with human society. Are we in kind of a competition?

HB: There's a very strong competition going on. A lot of bacteria have decided to become our allies. You carry around within your gut right now more bacteria than —how shall I put this— the number of human beings that have ever been is smaller than the number of bacteria living in your gut. There are 50 trillion of them inside of you at this very second. They're friendly bacteria. They're manufacturing Vitamin K, B vitamins, pantothenic acid and a lot of other things that we can't manufacture for ourselves. But there are other bacteria who aren't entirely so friendly to us... In 1348 some of those bacteria started out somewhere around China and made their way via the trade system all the way over to Iceland and in the process of making their way across *they munched humans*. They had quite a feast. The feast was so large that they managed to kill off one third of all of the population of humans on this Earth. That was called the Black Plague and we are, according to the leading experts of our time, still in a race with bacteria and we're about to lose it. We're in danger of another Black Death.

But let me go back to science for a minute, because science started out at about 1638 and again it started out as a matter of mailings, using mailings, using snail mail in order to exchange information. Now we couldn't exchange as much information as an entire hard drive the way bacteria could, but we could at least exchange letters and we could exchange books and those were a substantial improvement over what we had had before. Scientists then went on a research and development rampage which has increased in its pace tremendously over the course of the last 30 or 40 years, and we've done more science and we've come up with more scientific discoveries over the last 30 or 40 years than all of mankind has ever come up with in its past.

Theoretically this should put us ahead of bacteria, but I've got news for you: *it doesn't*. Bacteria are too swift with their research and development and too swift in transporting their information, especially now that they can use jetliners to transport their data in the bodies and on the skin of human beings. We carry the information for them, not just birds anymore.

About 1928 Alexander Fleming noticed that an awful lot of bacterial growths in petri dishes were being spoiled in the lab. People had noticed this for a long time, but Fleming had a unique point of view on it. Everybody else said, "Goddamn it, these darn petri dishes are spoiled," and they'd

throw them out and that was it. Fleming said "Hmm, spoiling bacteria? That means that some of these bacteria are being killed. That means *something* is killing them. We can certainly use something that kills bacteria. What's killing them?" Well, as I said, various microbial colonies are constantly at war and their war is very sophisticated and it is chemical warfare. What Fleming managed to do was discover that one microbial form was using chemical warfare on another and he isolated the chemical. Nothing happened with it for 20 years, but ultimately they discovered how to put this chemical stolen from bacteria into pills, and it started what's called *the antibiotic revolution*. The antibiotic revolution simply consisted of stealing one chemical weapon after another from bacteria in order to attack other bacteria and defeat them. We had a grace period of approximately 50 to 60 years in which antibiotics —the stolen weapon of bacteria— managed to protect us human beings from disease.

Well bacteria aren't dummies. They were not going to sit around and allow this to happen for very long. They worked and worked and worked at research and development. They passed information back and forth. They were using their avian carrier, that is the birds who carried them, to splash down in a new pond somewhere and use the pond water to spread to domesticated ducks and use the domesticated ducks to spread themselves to pigs. In pigs there were human bacteria because pigs are very much like us. The traveling bacteria would mix and mingle with the human bacteria and in the process swap these giant hard drives with each other. Once they'd swapped enough hard drives, bingo, they'd have the ability to both invade a human being and to use all the tricks that they'd been developing plus going through further improvements in the pig. And they hit us human beings. Every year we have a new flu virus and that's it. It's the new strain that has the new improvements in it. The real problem is this: the experts on the subject say that we're overdue for the next pandemic, that the antibiotic revolution is over, so soon we have no more means of defending ourselves against bacteria.

Many of the bacteria have learned how to overcome every antibiotic and every pill we've ever been able to come up with. So the experts say we're in for the next major pandemic. This, they say, is going to kill between two billion and three billion human beings. It's going to make the Black Death look like *nothing*. This means that the World Wide Web and the Internet that we've come up with, our ways of quick-swapping information and doing research and development, had better speed up and speed up real fast because we are running very, very hard against a World Wide Web that is much more sophisticated than ours, an Internet which is much higher in its data carrying and swapping capacity than ours and it's about to outrun us and run us into the turf.

Bacteria have learned how to overcome their own weapons in all of the forms we've been able to conceive so far and that we can put in a pill. And as a consequence, leading experts on this subject are saying a very simple thing: *it's the end of the antibiotic age*. We humans are going to have to come up with something genuinely original this time, because we're overdue for the next pandemic.

What does a pandemic mean? It means one of those incidents in which bacteria go hog wild and have a massive human feast. And the next massive human feast is due to kill off, according to these experts, between two billion and three billion human beings. The only way we'll get out of this problem is if we take the research and development system we're so proud of —which is still primitive compared to the bacterial research and development system— and bring it up to speed *very fast*. This means that a lot of the people who are anti-knowledge, anti-science, anti-Darwin, anti-stem cell research and all that kind of stuff, the *know-nothings* who seem to be taking over modern culture in America, in Europe, in Russia or wherever you turn, they have to get out of the way and leave room for the intelligent people and the scientists again, because if they don't, they're going to be dead, it's as simple as that.

RM: Is science up to this task?

HB: Science has to be up to the task. If science isn't up to the task it's the end of civilization as we know it, some time in the next 20 to 30 years. The fact is that the Internet was originally developed to allow scientists to do experiments together. A scientist in San Francisco could do an experiment with a scientist in Brussels and with a scientist in Moscow and they could all work on it as if they were in the same laboratory. Now we haven't gotten to that point yet despite the World Wide Web, but we've got to.

One of our problems are *conformity enforcers*. *Conformity enforcers* are something that I talk about in the book: we have an automatic tendency to impose conformity on other people. We look for outcasts: people with funny names, people who are wearing big glasses, and we make fun of them. We toss them out of our society and we make life so rough for them that the message becomes obvious to everybody else: *toe the company line.* Wear the kinds of clothes you're supposed to wear, use the kinds of phrases you're supposed to use, think the way everybody else does or you're in trouble.

There's another thing in the book called *diversity generators*, and we need those like crazy.

Science itself is one of the major conformity enforcing areas. There are dogmas in science that are held to as if they were religions and people who say things that are against those dogmas are cast out just as viciously as they are from any other subculture. We've got to get beyond that, we've got to get to the point where the outriders, where the eccentrics, where the people who come up with the really wacky ideas that turn out to be the ideas of the future are allowed into the establishment, and are incorporated much more quickly than they've been incorporated in the past. There's an old saying in science, "A new idea can't take off until the old guys have died," so you have to wait 20 years. Well we can't wait 20 years anymore. We have to start incorporating the ideas of the heretics, the diversity generators, within the first two or three years of the time the heretics express their ideas and we have to start testing those ideas. Science has to speed up. Why? Because bacteria go through 72 generations a day. That's the equivalent of 1,500 years in human time. That means they're infinitely speedier than we are and we have to speed things up, period.

"Throughout history organized religion has been the enemy of science; how is that still going on today?"

HB: If you stop the teaching of Darwinism in schools you lose track of that central element that allows you to understand biology, psychology, bacteriology and all of those things we need in order to get a grip and put an end to or at least topple this bacterial foe. It's two worldwide brains up against each other.

If we lobotomize ourselves via religion, if we allow religion to throttle us, we're going to be in big trouble because we tend to imagine that our enemies are human beings.

We've also got to continue allowing something that we've actually been doing for 10,000 years, which is genetic engineering. That's how we got wheat to begin with. We've been doing it for a long time and we can feed the starving people of the Earth, but there are other things that are about to occur. This is the longest period of stable climate in the history of the Earth, this last 10,000 years. Whether or not we have the greenhouse effect, we're going to have violent climatic change. That violent climatic change means that those areas of Earth that we've been accustomed to using for agricultural purposes including here in the United States, where we produce vast surpluses, they're going to not be agricultural lands anymore. The rains are simply not going to arrive and the weather patterns are going to change. With genetic engineering, we can develop plants that will grow in a dry environment. Or that will grow in a saline environment, in other words so close to the sea that the seawater has permeated the water table. If we develop these things we'll be ready for these new catastrophes. And catastrophes come all the time in nature; we've just been blessed by 10,000 years without major catastrophes.

We're overdue for the next major climatic catastrophes, but we can overcome those. We can overcome those. If we use all of our collective intelligence, complete with its diversity generators, complete with the eccentric ideas that come from left field that aren't acceptable —we have to look into them and say, "What validity do they have?"— we can't close our minds to them immediately. And stop the Luddites. Stop the people who want to stop technology and genetic engineering. All of these people have to get out of the way and get out of the way fast and leave room for those who are driven by their curiosity and who want to spend every day and all of their nights pursuing the questions of how in the world these microorganisms work that we're up against and what kind of new technologies we can develop in order to defeat them.

RM: And if mankind drops the ball on this?

HB: If we're not up to the task, then the bacterial global brain will put our global brain to shame and a third of us will die. And when two to three billion humans go it doesn't just mean that you have a good chance of death and that your neighbors will disappear, it also means that your telephone systems will disappear. It means that your governments will disappear and that your ways of getting food will disappear. Everything you've come to rely on as part of life will disappear because the structures depend on the people who are part of them; without the people the structures will break down and we'll be in *Mad Max*. Post-apocalyptic.

Another aspect of the global brain that we don't recognize is that to sustain you and to sustain me on a daily basis takes food being trucked in from hundreds or thousands of miles away, sometimes from as far as Argentina. It means the shipping lines have to operate. It means the railroads have to operate. It means that the highway system has to be maintained. It means that the retail apparatus that sells us our food, all of the super stores, have to stay in business. The corner grocery stores have to stay in business and all of this takes a tremendous amount of coordination. Wipe out a third to two-thirds of the human beings on this planet, *all of that crumbles*. All of that goes. All of the global brain that we've been developing since 10,000 years ago in the Stone Age disappears in an instant and we will be in *Mad Max* land, we will find it impossible to live. We will not find food, we will not find water and we'll be killing our neighbors for the sake of food. It could get really ugly. There's no telling what would happen.

Global Brain is the first book ever to describe the evolutionary and biological history of the global brain and to tell us how the global brain works. That can be very useful knowledge. We have tremendous possibilities ahead of us. All of the delights and dangers dreamed up by techno-lovers and by sci-fi fantasists are about to come true. We're test pilots for the cosmos. We're on the verge of redefining human capability. We're about to give evolution, nature, and biomass powers they've never had before. But we're also in a war to the death with another global brain; we have to understand how that bacterial global brain operates and this is the first book really to point that out. We also have to understand how our own global brain operates. We need that knowledge, because if we don't use that knowledge and use it very swiftly, it's the end of what we know as civilization and it's the end of most of what we know of humanity.

Photos: Naomi Nelson

HOWARD BLOOM

PAUL LAFFOLEY

Imagine the Buddha reincarnated as a mild-mannered, science fiction obsessed architect and you'll have an easier time understanding the enigma that is artist Paul Laffoley.

Laffoley's futuristic blueprints and text-covered mandalas take the viewer on a journey to the furthest reaches of metaphysical speculation, bridging consciousness and matter. Stare at one of them long enough and an entirely new cosmos is revealed.

As a child, Laffoley dreamt of a strange museum filled with alien life forms and biological machines. These surreal living statues contemplated him as much as he contemplated them. Maybe more so. Laffoley awoke from this dream with a mission, creating what some critics have called an authentic new art form.

Born in Boston in 1940, Paul Laffoley has spent a lifetime exploring a singular form of visionary art through paintings, inventions, architecture and essays. For four decades he's been the sole member and *artist in residence* of *The Boston Visionary Cell,* a one man think tank devoted to the study of alchemy, architecture, fringe science, unorthodox botany, time travel, weird areas of physics and the occult.

The Boston Visionary Cell is housed in a single room office of a respectable looking older office building located in the heart of Boston's tony financial district. More of a storage space than an office, the room is a riot of books (stacked from floor to ceiling), half finished sculptures and canvases and mutant experiments in plant grafting going on around a janitor's sink. It has a narrow path circling through it like a track. More than five people in the room at one time would be impossible.

Laffoley has worked in this room since 1968, often sleeping face down on his drafting table like Ayn Rand's ascetic, driven architect Howard Roarke in *The Fountainhead*. But Laffoley resembles Rand's uncompromising fictional architect in more ways than one: like Howard Roarke, Laffoley toiled in obscurity for years, decades even, without giving up hope that his vision would one day be recognized. And like Roarke, Laffoley also steadfastly refused to change his direction one bit, despite the art world's indifference and incomprehension.

The comparisons to Howard Roarke or the Buddha are good ones, but they don't even begin to tell the whole story. I think you'd need to mix in a heaping dollop of Merlin the Magician, Nikola Tesla and an Elizabethan alchemist like Robert Fludd to gain a fuller picture, yet this is still a woefully inadequate description of Paul Laffoley, because *he's not really like anybody else.*

Here's something that you should know about Paul Laffoley before you get to the interview: when he was a young boy, his father liked to take him to New York every year so they could look at the newest iteration of the giant Coca-Cola sign that still hangs as a capitalist constant in Times Square. What Paul discovered in that sign was a powerful lesson in the study of semiotics, or how human beings communicate in symbolic ways: *no matter what level of sophistication one would bring to the viewing of that sign, if you were a small child, a banker or a Jivaro shaman, you would know that that sign somehow represented something that was mass produced*. It might imply more things to you, such as the concept of *marketing* to a greater or lesser degree. But the one certain thing it would do is communicate the concept of *a product* in a rudimentary sense to all onlookers. *You wouldn't be able to help it.* In this sense, advertising performs an occult act, simply by using graphic design.

Remember that. It's going to help later.

Here's another thing you should know about Paul Laffoley: *he's smarter than you are*. No matter how smart you think you are, Paul Laffoley knows more things about more things than you do. It's a fact. This is an individual who possesses *singular erudition*. And it is the reason why many people in the art world are completely baffled by his work: they have no way of properly evaluating his ideas. No yardstick from the past to judge him by, either. No facile comparisons to this or that artist. As a result, he's often dismissed as a crank *due to the ignorance of others!* It's a ridiculous —and I'm sure *annoying*— position to be put in, but I've never seen Paul be anything but good-naturedly bemused by this reaction to his work.[9]

Educated in Classics and Art History at Brown, Laffoley speaks French, Latin and Ancient Greek. He was trained in architecture at the Harvard Graduate School of Design (where he was dismissed for "conceptual deviancy," whatever that is, becoming a registered architect in 1990) and apprenticed with both Andy Warhol and the visionary architect Frederick Kiesler in New York during the early 60's.

Despite the Ivy League credentials, Laffoley is mostly self-taught and therefore delightfully free of academic compartmentalization in his intellectual make-up. Laffoley is nothing if not a trans-disciplinary autodidact, so much so that the lack of ways to categorize his thought may have been to the detriment of his early career (which I'd define as the first four decades, more on this below). He speaks so far over most people's heads that he is often misunderstood to the point of tragicomedy: a television documentary called *Mysteries of Genius* used voiceover narration saying "But sometimes there is a fine line between genius and madness" –cue shot of Paul Laffoley. This illustrates just how far out of context Laffoley seems to even intelligent people, as I am assuming the people behind this program must be, for he is, for so many reasons, unlike anyone else who has ever lived.[10]

The first museum level survey of Paul Laffoley's work didn't happen until 1999, at the Austin Museum of Art in Texas. It was the first time these paintings were ever in the same room at the same time. Many of them Paul hadn't seen himself for over 20 years.

How to explain why Paul Laffoley had never had a one man retrospective before this? His large-scale paintings can take up to a year each to complete. Throughout the 60's and 70's, it was often the case that a painting would be shown as part of a group show, once, and then sold. It wasn't until the 1980's, when his association with New York City's Kent Gallery and its owner Douglas Walla began, that he started to gain major attention.

Walking into the museum's main gallery was nothing short of astonishing. Having seen several of his large scale paintings before, but never so many of them at the same time, in the same place, I can best sum up the effect in this way: if you saw just one of these paintings, you'd think "Wow, that is truly amazing." If you saw two or three of them together you'd think, "This artist is a genius." If you saw ten or so in a gallery, you'd think "This artist is a genius of the highest caliber."

But walking into the main room of the museum that day and having more than 30 of them crowding my visual field was breathtaking.

It was really something to take in. I'd never seen anything like it.
I literally swooned. The effect was that powerful.

[9] The Wright Brothers, da Vinci and Galileo were considered kooks in their day, too, so he's in good company of course.

[10] For the record, Laffoley was *quite* amused by this program.

PAUL LAFFOLEY

Imagine if Dali or Picasso hadn't been discovered as teenagers who would flower and develop in the public eye, but as senior citizens, with a fully formed body of mature work stuffed in the closet.

It's a moment of my life I will never, ever forget.

The subtitle of Laffoley's 1999 book, *Architectonic Thought-forms* is "Gedankenexperimente [thought experiments] in Zombie Aesthetics." Zombie Aesthetics? When I first read that I thought this was just Paul being willfully obscure, but I now realize just how accurate of a description that is. In a sense, you do sort of "zone out" in front of his paintings —especially the ones he calls "operating systems"— *as they work on you.*

By way of illustration, I was at a party one night when this book was being passed around. One guy remarked that he loved the "little symbols" that Laffoley used and I told him (he had never seen one in person and so was unaware of the size, 73" by 73") that, in fact, they weren't little at all, they're each (roughly) the size of street signs.

Now street signs, of course, are thought out and engineered by experts to communicate, not via language, but by symbol or a two-dimensional pantomime (such as stick figure pedestrians) of various things and concepts and you are supposed to have an emotional response to them. Simplicity is the key to this communication.

Okay, if you are still with me, if one street sign communicates something that you just simply "get" then how complicated of a message can, say, ten such primal symbols get across as a group?

In this way, I also detect the formative influence of Andy Warhol on Laffoley's thought. Consider the most iconic images of Warhol's work: James Dean, Marilyn Monroe, Elvis, Jackie Kennedy, etc., kitsch symbols, *human trademarks if you will*, of virility, beauty, animal sexuality, wealth and breeding. And tragedy. Warhol was a shrewd magician: James Dean and Marilyn Monroe have *resonances* in the pop culture *over-mind*. It's no coincidence that he chose images and icons that were the same choice of Times Square tourist trap tchotchke merchants (and vice versa), as they *evoke primal emotional responses.*

Remember that for later, too.

_SYMBOLIC EVOCATION

RM: Paul, even though I know it's an almost absurdly large question to ask of an artist, what are you trying to communicate to the human race with your artwork?

PL: I take cosmic themes and I turn them into finely detailed works for the Earth.

This is the reason why I like diagrams so much, because a diagram is a neutral system, which can allow you to diagram anything. There are no limits to it, so as an architect I always appreciated that. It's like drawing the floor plan of the building on the ground and then starting to build it.

A mandala is a type of diagram, so I think that the *diagramesqueness* of them is the core and in that sense, this is another way of defining the word symbol: it connects thinking and feeling.

[11] A term coined by Rudolf Otto (1869-1937) in a book titled *Idea of the Holy*. It is also often associated with Carl Jung. *Numinosity* connotes an intensely personal experience of spirituality, a deep connection to the beautiful, the sublime and the *sacred*. Numinosity is not merely a normal religious experience, as Kelley L. Ross, Ph.D. writes in "The Roots of Rudolf Otto's Theory of Numinosity in Immanuel Kant, Jakob Fries, and Leonard Nelson":

Otto takes the Latin word *numen*, "the might of a deity, majesty, divinity," and coins the term "numinous" to describe either religious *feelings* or the religious aspect attributed by those feelings to *experiences* and *objects*. He characterizes the feelings as involving 1) ultimacy, 2) mystery (*mysterium*), 3) awe (*tremendum*), 4) fascination (*fascinans*), and 5) satisfaction. Unassociated with any objects, the sense of the numinous is a feeling of "daemonic dread," a sense of the uncanny, frightful, eerie, weird, or supernatural. These feelings make us feel vulnerable and overpowered, what Otto calls "creature feeling."

The way Otto defines numinosity provides a compelling lens through which we can evaluate Laffoley's artwork, as something that is literally *designed* to be *awe-inspiring* —no more, no less.

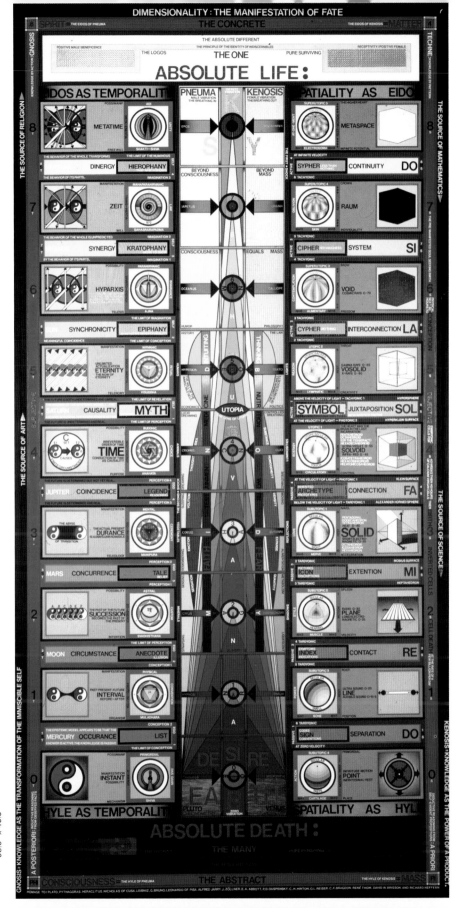

Dimensionality: The Manifestation of Fate, 1992
98.5" × 49.5"

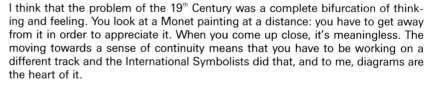

I think that the problem of the 19th Century was a complete bifurcation of thinking and feeling. You look at a Monet painting at a distance: you have to get away from it in order to appreciate it. When you come up close, it's meaningless. The moving towards a sense of continuity means that you have to be working on a different track and the International Symbolists did that, and to me, diagrams are the heart of it.

RM: The first time that I stood in front of one of your paintings, whether it was the color palette or the way the paint was applied, I felt that it pulsated. I really felt drawn in. It was somehow "electric" and *psychoactive*. Your paintings are very magical and you paint with intent... what is that intent?

PL: *The intent to remove the unmagical* (laughter). I think that in the same sense that Aldous Huxley wrote about people taking psychedelics to remove the unmagical, the goal is just simply to get at what's really there... and what's there is *Revelation*. What we call the non-revelatory aspects of nature is simply what I call the bureaucracy of biology, which other people call *evolution* (more laughter). Our brains are these valves where we only let a little bit through. I think that it's basically nature doing that. In other words it's the bureaucracy of biology that won't let us have the whole thing.

We turn our attention towards a painting called The Metatron. *Like most of Laffoley's paintings, this one is 73" by 73". Huge. The main image is what appears to be a strange creature, open-mouthed with tonsils flaring, about to eat the viewer (or at least hiss at them like a cobra), sitting atop a building that could*

be a governor's mansion, a museum or an opera house. Apocalyptic warnings from the Hopi Indians and the pictorial representations of the 'epistemic ladder' (described below) flank the central image.

RM: What about this one? Tell me what's going on this canvas. On a visceral level you're hit with symbols, and symbols have a resonance. With all of these occult symbols displayed as they are here, what are you trying to get across with *The Metatron?*

PL: *The three modalities of Revelation.* The Metatron, in Hebrew mythology, is one of the basic angels, like an angel that is part of the Seraphim. The Metatron is a real messenger and so it's providing a kind of intellectual structure for revelation, to give you clues as to when you would receive it, both from the sacramental, the prophetic and the mystical.

RM: What's the psychoactive component of this painting?

PL: There's an epistemic ladder in Symbolism, going from a sign to an index to an icon to an archetype and into a symbol. A lot of people use these words and they use them to mean each other and I think that that is actually incorrect. I think there's a technical distinction. A sign is something like a code, an arbitrary association of like A = B or A = 1 and you just start a code. An index is more like forensic medicine or like animal tracks in the snow, where you sense that something exists objectively, but apart from your direct experience of it.

When you begin on the ladder, you have what would be called the epistemic model: *the knower and that which is known are in a mutually interdependent*

Metatron, the Angel of Methodological Revelation, 1975
" x 73.5"

relationship where the knower is active and the knowledge is passive. That begins it. So as you proceed from a sign to an index to an icon, when you get to an archetype, you're moving to a point where you're recognizing that this is happening all around the world. It's more than, say, the way that Jung talked about archetypes. The concept of a collective unconscious is a diminution of the original alchemical notion of an archetype.

Finally we get to a symbol where the epistemic model has inverted so that the knowledge is active and the knower is passive.

In other words, you're going from a situation where you have a sense that you're totally in control of the information. You are this evolutionary bureaucratized creature who feels by its ego that it's completely in control of everything and if something magical comes along, it's an exception that you can *avoid*.

PAUL LAFFOLEY

Get Thee Behind Me, Satan, 1974
20" x 20"

As you get into the epistemic ladder it becomes harder and harder to avoid it, until finally, when you reach the state of a singularity and pure numinosity,[11] *the revelation has taken over you*. The content has become *the active*, *you become passive* and then you are completely one with the universe.

_TIME MACHINE GO!

RM: Paul, H.G. Wells' time machine is one of the few inventions from his science fiction work that hasn't been built yet, and you have plans to change that don't you?

PL: That's right. Most people consider that the *sine qua non* of science fiction, meaning that they feel that this will never leave the realm of science fiction. I have a pet theory that science fiction itself died in 1955 because that's when the software industry was actually starting to occur. What most people do when they write science fiction is that they're actually doing *ad hoc* research and development for some company that will exist the minute it's read, like NASA used *Star Trek:* they just took it right off line and, you know, like the communicator that Captain Kirk had is now the cell phone (laughs) and all those various things. So that sense of there being a tremendous amount of time before the science fiction comes true which was the case with Jules Verne in his day, to me that no longer exists. Given this, given the idea of a time machine, I said, "It's overdue." I thought it was overdue, probably in the 1930's. When I became interested in it, I kept thinking "I've got to be late in the game, I got to get in there quick." This is like 1975-76 when I came up with this idea right here (points to a detail in a reproduction of *Geochronmechane: The Time Machine from the Earth*, serigraph, 1990) which I call the *Levogyre* and this is the main device. The theory that I have is: *if you can control and amplify pre- and retro-cognition, pre-perception of the future and retro-perception of the past into an exaggerated form, that you will then fulfill the definition of time travel as Wells presents it in his novel.*

RM: What are you saying, that in a sense you could use this device to amplify ESP and that's how time travel will work?

HOMAGE TO: H.G. WELLS, ALFRED JARRY, J.B.L. FOUCAULT, N.A. KOZYREV, HENRI BERGSON, J.W. DUNNE, F.J. TIPLER, GEORGE VAN TASSEL, R. BUCKMINSTER FULLER

chromechane: The Time Machine from the Earth, 1990
x 32"

PAUL LAFFOLEY

PL: Well it's not just ESP, it's pre-perception of the future, and retro-perception of the past. ESP covers a lot of things, but essentially it is psychotronic and with the generic notion of the so-called Sixth Sense and so forth. What I'm talking about is specifically pre- and retro-cognition, pre-perception of the future, and retro-perception of the past, examined totally by itself and the instrumentality that would control and amplify that beyond what we normally experience.

The definition of history is an imaginative reconstruction of the past, as opposed to *retro-perception*, which is perceiving the reality of events as if you were actually there, in the same way that we can know the present, because we are in it.

RM: Is this like "remote viewing"?

Utopia: The Suspension between the Possible and the Impossible, 1974
73.5" x 73.5"

PL: "Remote viewing" could be defined that way but remote viewing involves something that only has to do with that person, and the techniques that are taught to increase it are like a yoga.

What I'm talking about is *connecting to it*, so that that you have a device that doesn't depend upon the person's natural ability or abilities that are to be developed. Because you still could only do that to a certain limit. I'm talking about having access to something that's 500 billion years into the future or 500 million years into the past, with an accuracy that you have investigating the present. Take psycho-kinesis; a person who's gifted in it can produce four pounds per square inch in a transitional motion. It takes five pounds per square inch to open the door, so you still have a toy.

My device uses an Orgone motor to control and amplify psycho-kinesis so that it becomes a viable motor that could move tons, you see, of weight. What I'm saying is I want to be able to take people who exhibit no ability in pre- and retro-cognition and hook them up to the device so that they can do it in a way that exceeds any definition of success with pre- or retro-cognition or remote viewing that has yet been presented.

RM: What's the significance of the Levogyre?

PL: The Levogyre disconnects itself from at least eight motions in the universe, of any form that's connected to it. The more gimbals that are involved in a gyroscope, the more degrees of freedom you have. Every time you spin something on its own axis you're altering the space-time around it, just slightly. But when you multiply it, you then have a time dilation —because it's a space-time dilation— which is highly exaggerated.

Alchemy: The Telenomic Process of the Universe, 1973
73.5" x 73.5"

Eternity has energy but it doesn't involve motion, whereas time has energy that involves motion, so here is a device that allows a connection between time and eternity. I'm trying to either bring meta-energy into the system or move it out. If you bring it into your mind you will create a distortion much greater than you normally could, in terms of anticipating the future. If you remove it, it will then create a remembrance of the past, more than you would normally have. What I have here is like the human soul embedded into a temporal dimensional system —with the chakras— and as a result you have a natural ability to anticipate the future or to remember the past.

_VEGETABLE HOUSE

Laffoley's plans for *Das Urpflanze Haus*, a house grown from seeds, incorporates the principles of sacred geometry with living architecture. He's like Buckminster Fuller, *with chlorophyll*.

PAUL LAFFOLEY

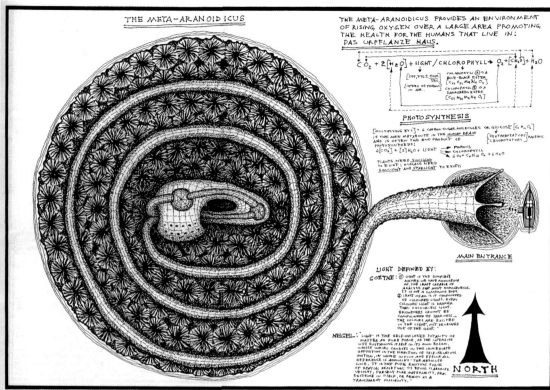

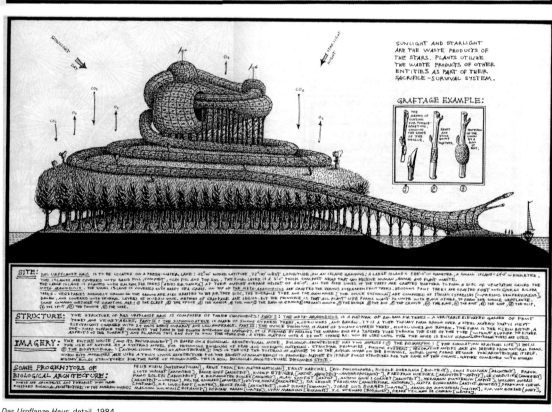

Das Urpflanze Haus, detail, 1984

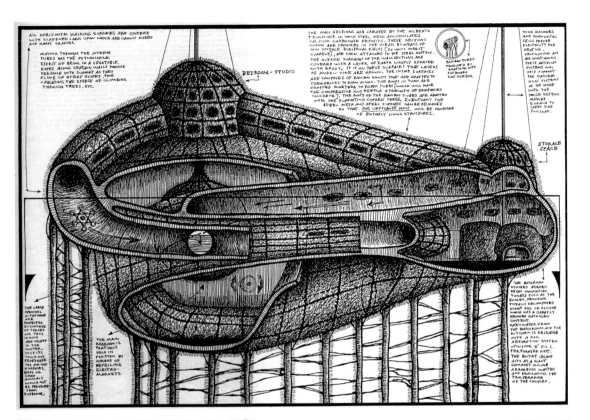

ALL HORIZONTAL WALKING SURFACES ARE COVERED WITH SCREENED FOAM UPON WHICH ARE GROWN MOSSES AND HARDY GRASSES.

MOVING THROUGH THE INTERIOR TUBES HAS THE PSYCHOLOGICAL EFFECT OF BEING IN A VEGETABLE. ROPES ALONG CERTAIN WALLS PROVIDE PERSONS WITH SUPPORT AS THEY CLIMB UP STEEP SLOPES, THUS CREATING THE EFFECT OF CLIMBING THROUGH TREES, ETC.

THE WALL SECTIONS ARE CREATED BY THE HILBERTZ TECHNIQUE IN WHICH STEEL MESH ACCUMULATES CALCIUM CARBONATE DEPOSITS. THESE SECTIONS WHICH ARE PRODUCED IN THE OCEAN BY MEANS OF LOW VOLTAGE ELECTRICAL FIELDS (24 VOLTS DIRECT CURRENT), ARE THEN ATTACHED TO THE STEEL MATRIX. THE OUTSIDE SURFACES OF THE WALL SECTIONS ARE COVERED WITH A LAYER OF EARTH LIGHTLY SPRAYED WITH EPOXY. IT IS ON THESE SURFACES THAT LAYERS OF KUDZU VINE ARE GROWN. THE INSIDE SURFACES ARE COMPOSED OF BAMBOO KNOTS THAT ARE GRAFTED TO THEMSELVES TO FORM RINGS. THE RINGS IN TURN ARE GRAFTED TOGETHER TO FORM TUBES [WHICH WILL MAKE THE COMPRESSIVE AND TENSILE STRENGTH OF REINFORCED CONCRETE]. THE ROOTS OF THE BAMBOO TUBES ARE GRAFTED ONTO THE SUPPORTING CYPRESS TREES. EVENTUALLY THE STEEL MESH AND STEEL SUPPORTS CAN BE REMOVED SO THAT ONE UNFRAMED HAUL WILL BE COMPOSED OF ENTIRELY LIVING STRUCTURES.

BAMBOO TUBES PRODUCED BY GRAFTING WITH EXTRUDED ROOT SYSTEMS.

BEDROOM — STUDIO

WIND MACHINES AND PHOTOVOLTAIC CELLS PROVIDE ELECTRICITY FOR HEATING, VENTILATING AND AIR CONDITIONING. THESE ARTIFICIAL SYSTEMS WILL HELP SUPPORT THE NATURAL HVAC SYSTEMS OF THE HOUSE UNTIL THE HOUSE SYSTEMS MATURE ENOUGH TO CARRY THE FULL LOAD.

STORAGE SPACE

THE LARGE OPENINGS IN THE HOUSE ARE PROTECTED BY CHARGES OF FOAMED AIR JETS WHICH ARE HEATED IN THE WINTER. INSECTS COULD NOT PENETRATE THE AIR JET CURTAINS, BIRDS OR SMALL ANIMALS WOULD NOT BE PREVENTED FROM ENTERING.

THE MAIN BEDROOM IS PARTIALLY HELD IN POSITION BY MEANS OF REPELLING ELECTRO-MAGNETS.

THE BATHROOM UTILIZES AEROBIC DECAY COMPOSTING TOILETS SUCH AS THE ECOLET, PROVIDING TOTALLY DECOMPOSED NIGHT SOIL OR SLUDGE WHICH HAS A GREATLY REDUCED PATHOGEN CONTENT. GREYWATER FROM THE BATHROOM AND THE KITCHEN IS RELEASED INTO A SOIL ABSORPTION SYSTEM UTILIZING 6" P.V.C. PERFORATED PIPE. THE ENTIRE ISLAND ACTS AS A PLANT COMPOST MOUND ABSORBING WASTES AND ANIMATING THE TRIM PERENNE OF THE COMPLEX.

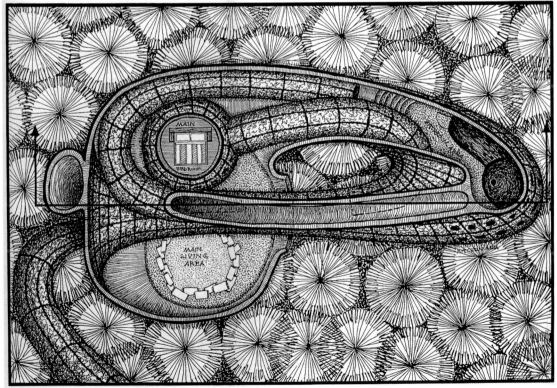

MAIN BEDROOM

MAIN LIVING AREA

PAUL LAFFOLEY

43

Cosmolux, 1980
73.5" x 73.5"

RM: Paul, tell me about your plans for the vegetable house.

PL: It's called *Das Urpflanze Haus* in homage to the poet Goethe.[12] The idea of a *primordial plant* —a plant from which all other plants come— was his idea, but biologically he never found it, so it remained an idea. So I thought perhaps you could create the idea from the other way around... that if you actually grafted together all forms of vegetation across the surface of the Earth, you would then have a single plant, and all of the different species would come to that. And people say, "Well, how are you going to do that?" I mean it's possible to graft the same species to itself, but how would you cross graft, in other words, go from one species to another?

[12] Johann Wolfgang von Goethe, 1749-1832, German poet and dramatist; greatest figure of German Romantic period; contributed to *Sturm und Drang* movement; masterpiece *Faust*.

reached a stage away from it —in other words the millions of years that have gone by and that thing still exists. It has the genes that can now make the connections. When it first was around it was simply like another plant that was there. If say a new plant forms now it would have millions of years before it could qualify to be an Urpflanze in relation to what's left. A lot of the original plants that happened during the Jurassic period are gone. Some are now extinct. This was almost extinct, but somewhere in the Eastern part of China, the Confucian monks saved this tree. They found it and they kept growing it in their gardens, and from the 19th Century until now it has proliferated around the Earth again.

(Gestures to schematic. See page 42-43) These represent individual pine trees and you graft the side branches together so what you then have is a single plant with a multiple root system.

RM: And the house sits on top of it?

PL: Well first of all you have to be able to use it as a house, and so you have to be able to see where the house is and notice that one part functions differently than another. The pine trees are the roots and they get you off the ground, see?

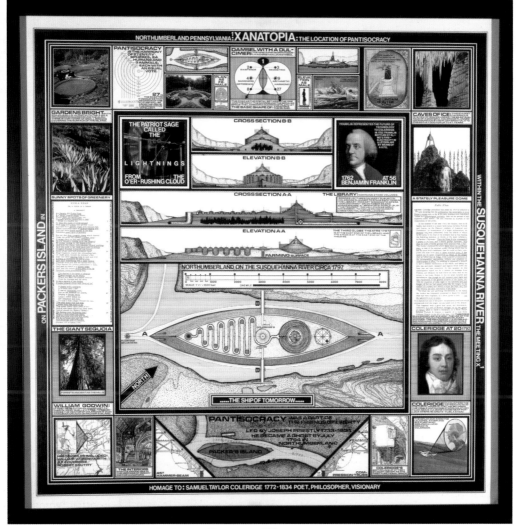

Xanatopia: Northumberland, Pennsylvania, The Location of Pantisocracy, 1995
30" x 30"

PAUL LAFFOLEY

Black White Hole, 1976
73.5" x 73.5"

with a multiple root system.

RM: And the house sits on top of it?

PL: Well first of all you have to be able to use it as a house, and so you have to be able to see where the house is and notice that one part functions differently than another. The pine trees are the roots and they get you off the ground, see? And there are fruit trees and vegetables grow here, too. As you're coming home, you can pick up the evening's dinner. This is like a farm and the lake is the water source, because obviously you're going to need water for this.

The structure itself is in the shape of a "Klein Bottle" which is a structure in geometry, which is a completely inside out shape. Its inside is its outside, you see, and vice versa. I've used this shape before in my work, and it's a very versatile form.

Let me go to a side view. First you strip the island of any existing vegetation and make a compost heap, so that this becomes like a curb around it, and then you plant the pine trees in a mature state. You see, because this is not yet a new vegetable that has reached the stage of seeds, you want to make sure that all the parts that you're using are at their mature size. For the first one. At this point I'm trying to create a new piece of vegetation which could potentially go to seed and have seeds in the same way that humans created the naval orange or the nectarine and then finally once that happened they went to a seed so that you can create more.

People often ask, "Well won't that thing just keep growing?" If you select the parts in their mature state they do not, and so that's why I start with that. These tubes are a combination of bamboo and kudzu vine, and most of the house is made of that. Bamboo is a grass, it grows very rapidly and you can do things to it. You can take it in a very young state and graft it to itself and make a ring or you can graft it to itself. You need to make sure that you do not damage the roots, because the whole point of this is that you're not taking one plant and then connecting another separate plant to it, this will all be one plant. *The entire house will be one plant.*

Aerial roots, roots that connect from one part of the vegetation to another as it comes down to the earth will be used. Mistletoe has aerial roots that grow in the notches of Elm trees or Oak trees and it stays up there and then it becomes parasitic to the tree, therefore its root system connects into the root system that goes into the ground. So when you are finished grafting, the thing is now *a single plant.* The whole point is to get the thing to go to seed and then with genetic engineering you can increase the velocity of maturation. You don't want to wait 50 years for one house if we're talking about helping to solve the housing shortage. So it's in lieu of these reforestation notions where they plant little tiny trees, but it will take a hundred years before the forest comes back. I'm talking about taking that and making it immediate.

The whole point of working with plant forms is a basic thing: without plant life we die. The population is growing and growing and growing and we're going to have 10 billion people by 2020 —that's a lot of people! If we keep cutting down the forests, we're doomed. This is almost a total cliché of the ecology movement, that we need to plant more things, so if you can grow a house, if you can give a person a bag of seeds and have an entire house grow in two months, I think you're on the track to actually solving the low cost housing problem.

We've raped the Earth from 1850 to the present, since the Industrial Revolution. Turning everything into metal or plastic… all kinds of stuff and ignoring this particular potential. And I think that as more experimenting is done with botany, biology and genetics, in a very short time it will be discovered how to make this thing work and we will create prototypes of grown buildings, let them go to seed and then find ways to speed up the growth process. Soon, it will get it to a point where it's architecturally feasible to house people in genetically engineered plant forms. This solution to the housing shortage is, I think, as radical as the increase in population.

RM: What about appliances and electrical devices?

PL: You'll be able to have all that. Let's say you could put up an antenna, like Tesla wanted to do, put up a wire and get power from the Aurora Borealis. Or maybe we'll make perpetual motion energy devices that the oil companies will hate. Solar power. Wind power. This is a big project and many, many different kinds of experts will have to be involved.

PAUL LAFFOLEY

But let's discuss the lighting. The lighting of this is also natural. There have been experiments with taking tobacco plants and gene splicing *luciferan* from lightning bugs into it. The tobacco plant will light up like a 25-watt bulb. Now that's a short distance, genetically speaking, away from a 100-watt bulb capacity. So therefore you have literally saved the entire tobacco industry. Nobody smokes anymore. You know they're the most hated guys on the planet and yet they keep growing tobacco. The tobacco doesn't care: it's a plant. And so if you can make

real Tiffany lamps out of tobacco plants whose roots are connected into this thing, you can then have it lit up with cold light.[13]

RM: I think that you ought to hit the Philip Morris Company up for a grant to build this sucker!

PL: I thought of that. It certainly would be to the advantage of the tobacco people because then you would literally have a need for all of this tobacco. There would be a specialized form of research into this and ultimately a revenue stream resulting from just the lighting system.

RM: Plumbing?

PL: The kitchen and bathroom areas are highly defined —like bushes that are really tight together so that you can have the situation where the human wastes would go into a compost heap and have a place to go immediately and be recycled into the earth.

RM: And then you can wipe with a leaf.

PL: You got it.

[13] A week after this interview was conducted, a story about scientists splicing luciferan extracted from lightning bugs into tobacco plants made the front page of *The New York Times*.

DOUGLAS RUSHKOFF

Douglas Rushkoff is one of the most widely read media critics to emerge from America in the past ten years. His thoughtful books, newspaper columns, magazine articles, television appearances and NPR[14] commentaries are intended to demystify for the man on the street the various ways we're all manipulated by the media, popular culture and especially by commerce. *New Perspectives Quarterly* called him "the heir to Marshall McLuhan" and like McLuhan Rushkoff's briefed government agencies, CEOs and heads of state. His *Coercion: Why We Listen to What "They" Say* earned him the reputation as the "go to" guy when the media needs a sharp talking head expert on matters of advertising and youth culture, and his role as correspondent for PBS's[15] highly regarded *The Merchants of Cool* documentary cemented this mark.

This reputation is justly deserved. For well over a decade now Rushkoff has sent first person dispatches from the frontlines of the future with his considered musings on advertising, rave culture, technology, designer drugs, cyberspace, Wall Street's pyramid schemes and his rejuvenated interest in his roots and the meaning of Judaism in today's society. He's the author of the "culture jamming" classic *Media Virus* and *Cyberia*, the first book to be written about the then-emerging cyber-culture centered around San Francisco's vibrant *Mondo 2000* nexus and its vivid, Technicolor gurus like Terence McKenna, Timothy Leary and RU Sirius. He's also written the novels *Ecstasy Club* and *Bull* (AKA *Exit Strategy*), his interactive, "open source" novel experiment that skewers scheming *dot.commies* with good-natured satire.

But aside from these activities and many, many others, Rushkoff is also one of the highest profile (and highest paid) corporate consultants in America today, especially on matters of communication technology and its often-unintended consequences for Fortune 500 companies. He's received a lot of flak for this in the past, especially from the bitter trolls of The WELL cyber community, who've accused him of being a turncoat, a sell-out and *worse.* I think it really hurt Doug. I know it did. But it also made him dig deeper within himself and helped him hone his arguments, so ultimately it was something that he grew from and was able to personally gain from, even if it was painful. I watched the whole thing happen and I was always very proud of the way he handled himself with these people and their short-sighted criticisms, and I am proud to be his friend.

I've seen Doug in action several times in closed door consultations as well as speeches given at large CEO gatherings, so I've witnessed first hand what he tells these companies and I can tell you here, he's not selling out the counterculture (or what's left of it) to "The Man"!

What these corporations do get when they hire Douglas is someone who is part cheerleader for change, part patient handholding explainer, and a natural teacher, notably lacking in fatuity for someone who is so often called upon to voice his opinion. He's one of those rare people who seem to genuinely want the world to be a better place and who actively work to pull their own weight in that group activity. In his guise as corporate consultant, Rushkoff takes his role seriously and in all earnestness. Part of it is an old-fashioned work ethic and Doug is a total mensch in that respect. He's obviously well paid and wants these companies to be happy with his presentations so he puts a lot of thought and a lot of time into them. He's a former theatre geek so he rehearses every speech until he gets it right and it shows. He's a marvelous public speaker: witty, funny and (seemingly) spontaneous.

And he's completely sincere about the advice he gives. It's no wonder these companies keep bringing him back again and again. As he told me one day when we were discussing the controversy over his corporate gigs, "These people are *asking* me to *help* them. What kind of asshole would I have to be to say 'No' to that? This makes me a sell-out?"

In today's culture, what the hell is a "sell-out" anyway? Is Steven Spielberg a sell-out because he makes multimillion dollar Hollywood films? Are Matt Parker and Trey Stone sell-outs because *South Park* is popular? Is Madonna a sell-out because people seem to like her music and she sells a lot of CDs? Michael Jordan because millions of people love to watch him play sports? Of course not: they're all doing what they love.

And so is Douglas Rushkoff.

Let's pick up the conversation there…

RM: Your early books, *Media Virus* and *Cyberia*, are books about counter-culture —psychedelic drugs, raves, the emerging cyber-world— written from the perspective of a young journalist who was a part of that scene. Today you give talks to corporate conventions, the United Nations and CEOs. Is there a paradox here?

DR: There's a seeming paradox in it, I guess, if you draw a clear line between what's called the *counterculture* and what's called *corporate culture*. However, if you go into almost any corporation there are tons of people working there who by night would consider themselves part of the counterculture and if you go into any rave club or bizarre event at a nightclub there will be a certain number of people who are going to work the next day in an advertising company or a major media conglomerate. So if you look at the people you're talking to as people, then ironically *they're all the same people*. This counterculture perceives itself as what could only be called *enslaved* by the corporations they work for, as if those corporations are conscious, or as if those corporations actually exercise some power over them. When I go to a corporation and talk to people I'm trying to talk to the actual human beings there and wake them up, if anything, to the reality of their situation and to the fact that they're working for, you know, a *dead thing*.

RM: *A dead thing?*

DR: Corporations aren't really *alive*. What corporations are is really very much like a computer program. They are a set of instructions for making money and that's all they are.

I'm only playing both sides of the fence *if* you think there's a fence and you think that's real. What I've been saying from the beginning, from *Cyberia* to the counterculture and with *Coercion* to the corporate culture, is that *there is no fence*. If that's true, the counterculture loses by definition. If we're in the counterculture, are we against culture? I'm not *counter* culture. Are you *counter* culture? I'm *pro* culture! Let them be counter culture, *I'm all for it*. Those people don't want to stop culture. Those people, at worst, are just miserable in jobs where they feel powerless to do anything, so if I go into a corporation and talk to those people about how they can have a better time with life and how they can make media that actually means something. I try to remind them of what it was like when they were 19-years old and decided to get into the communications industry.

And remind them that it was not about selling pantyhose to women, but about *helping people communicate with each other*. Having some real fun. I really try to empower them to make conscious changes to what they're doing. I think almost anybody brought into consciousness ends up doing some really good things, and people who are asleep or afraid or people who think they're at war end up, well

[14] The United States' noncommercial National Public Radio network.

[15] The United States' noncommercial Public Broadcasting Service television network.

DOUGLAS RUSHKOFF

they end up fighting. They end up with a very aggressive and hostile attitude towards people that really should be their friends.

So although my work has been geared towards different audiences, I see myself as saying the same thing. When I wrote *Cyberia* and *Media Virus* all I was saying is "Hey look, *we did it*. The media is alive and the media is a chaotic space. New ideas, information, political movements, spiritual movements can emerge from anywhere and catch on like wild fire. The world is in our hands now."

In *Coercion,* I'm saying to the big corporations, "Don't try to force us to do things with fear and associate your product with fear or paranoia, because that won't work." The main thing I've been trying to communicate, whether it's in terms of spirituality, in terms of media, in terms of marketing and communications, or even in terms of politics and economics, is that there's one thing going on here: people are desperately afraid to accept the fact that we are moving towards a very organismic relationship with one another: that the human being is one big thing. The problem about accepting that is if the human being is one thing, if we're all part of the same big organism, then those people starving in Africa or India are not *them,* they're *us.* So all of a sudden it's not their pain, it's *our* pain and we're *all* responsible for what's happening here. And I think the real obstacle to that kind of a sensibility is not that people want to control what's happening or that people want to be bosses, but that people are really afraid of that level of intimacy.

RM: When did there stop being an *us* and a *them*?

DR: In theory, there never was an *us* and a *them. Us and them* is an illusion that's usually perpetrated by one group of people who have an ability that

another group of people don't. You could argue that Hitler came into power because he basically had control of radio, which was a new thing, this remote, vocal presence in people's homes. And people didn't really understand radio or how it worked but all of a sudden this man, *his voice was everywhere.* Television had that effect. This was a magic box that only the BBC newscaster or Edward R. Murrow could get his face on there and no one knew how it worked. But once a kid has a Sega joystick in his hand and is actually moving pixels around on the screen, he doesn't look at that guy on television speaking the gospel truth anymore. He just sees it as a middle aged man playing with *his* joystick, if you will.

I think the latest movement towards the dissolution of *an us and them* sensibility was a direct result of young people and so-called counterculture people understanding the tools of media better than the so-called over-culture. Young people and cyberpunks and hackers understood the Internet and new media better than GE or Rupert Murdoch or any of their people.

So all of a sudden the tools that *them* uses to maintain its authority as a *them*, were in our hands. So when there is a leveling of the playing field when the technology is such that anyone can understand the magick of their time as well as the authorities can, then there are no more priests. There are no more people who seem to have this magical authority. That's why Prince Charles can't be what he might have been 100 or 200 years ago. That's why even Madonna can't be what she might have been 50 years ago.

We're all deconstructing and analyzing and remixing everything that's coming out of Hollywood and Hollywood is mining our activities for stuff for their next movie. We all have access to the same computers and digital video cameras so the fact that *The Blair Witch Project* does better than a major motion picture by a major studio means that there is no *them* anymore.

RM: That's somewhat discomforting. I like the idea of the loyal opposition. Sure we're all in this together, but I think the Leviathan needs contrarian thinkers.

DR: It's interesting. My subtitle for *Coercion* is *Why We Listen to What "They" Say*, with *they* in quotation marks. I think what's happened is we've all become sort of unwilling pawns in the market economy. It's very easy to walk into The Gap and understand that this salesgirl is using some awful technique on you; they call it GAP ACT "Greet, approach, provide add-on clothes and thank." It's this very carefully devised set of strategies to get you to buy more than you originally wanted to. To *up sell* you on more items. To get a belt or "We have new tee-shirts that go great with those jeans." So you can blame that girl and be annoyed at that girl but it's not really her fault, her managers probably made her watch those videotapes that teach her how to do that. So it's the manager's fault then. It's not the manager's fault because the manager is being judged by corporate headquarters and if they don't get more sales then the manager gets fired. So you go back to corporate headquarters: it's that marketing department's fault. Well it's not really their fault either, because they're just answering to the CEO. If they don't do a good job they'll get fired, but then is it the CEO's fault? Well no, he's answering to the Board of Directors of the company and to the shareholders. Well, okay then, it's the shareholders' fault.

Who are the shareholders? Well the shareholders are all those people with their retirement plans who have Gap stock and that's generally the same person who's walking into the store who's upset that the salesgirl was trying to up sell him with a new belt that would look *so nice*. So when you realize that you're part of that coercive cycle there, you conclude that *we're each the next guy's "they,"* so the way to end this acceleration of coercive techniques and to end the coercive arms race is to stop coercing *ourselves*. Each of us has the opportunity to end the coercion. Rather than looking at who's coercing you, look at whom you are coercing.

RM: What's a *media virus?*

DR: A media virus is really any idea that uses the momentum of the media to spread itself. A biological virus is composed of genes: it is genetic code wrapped in a protective protein shell. It spreads successfully through the body because the body mistakes it for one of its own proteins, "Oh that's me." The body has proteins running all through it. The shell of the biological virus is protein and this sticky protein shell latches onto a cell of your body and then injects its code inside. Then that code, the genes formerly inside that virus, compete with the genes in your own cells for command of that cell. And if it wins it turns that cell into a factory to make more viruses, it just says, "Make me. Make me."

As the world got more and more wired up with cable television, fax machines and the Internet, it started to take on properties of a global nervous system: biological organism. Certainly the most fun way and one of the easiest ways to spread an idea, or a strand of "thought code," through such an organismic media space was to wrap it in a shell, like a virus, protect it and serve as a container for it to spread unrecognized through the media system. But instead of it being a protein shell, as it would be in a biological virus, you'd wrap it in a media shell. All that means is creating a shell, a form of media that people haven't seen before. Something "sticky enough" to get people's attention, so that it spreads throughout the system. "Hey, check this out!" The media loves media; the news loves stories about the news. The video tape of Rodney King getting beaten by white cops in Los Angeles that spread around the world overnight: it spread not because white guys were beating on a black guy, it spread because no one had captured this on a camcorder before. The original story of the Rodney King tape was "My God, look what someone captured on their camcorder." People don't remember it that way anymore, but it's true.

Once it spread around and it was in all our homes, that's when it injected us with its code or with its ideas, which are issues like police brutality, race relations and the plight of black people in urban

DOUGLAS RUSHKOFF

America. So you can look at almost any of the media viruses that were spread over the last ten years, you know "Camillagate," the Prince Charles tapes, his little dirty phone calls with his mistress. The reason that spread was, yes, partly because it was Prince Charles but the real story of it was we had captured telephone conversations of famous people, no one had really heard telephone conversations like that broadcast on television before. So a media virus really is a way of nesting our culture, nesting our media space with new ideas by creating new and virulent forms of media.

RM: But a media virus doesn't have to take the form of *A Current Affair* type story; it can also be a popular cartoon like *The Simpsons* or *South Park*...

DR: Right. Some of the most virulent forms, the most activist forms of media are in kids' programs because they seem innocuous. Pee-wee Herman or *The Simpsons* or *South Park*, they're kiddy shows so no one expects very potent ideas to be in them, but they ended up being these hotbeds for very, very controversial memes. Very controversial ideas. Pee-wee Herman's show was really about gay camp culture. *The Simpsons* is media satire. The experience of watching *The Simpsons* is not watching to see whether Bart's going to get in trouble or if Homer is going to keep his job; the joy of that show is looking at each scene and going, "That's a satire of Alfred Hitchcock" or "That's a satire of this commercial," so the kid watching *The Simpsons*, or the adult for that matter, is really learning media semiotics. He's learning how to make connections between different forms of media, so the reward you get on *The Simpsons* is not getting to the end of the story and finding out who wins or loses, the reward on *The Simpsons* is making that connection and actually learning about media. Once you have any kind of media that seems to be about media which is about media which is about media, chances are you're dealing with a viral form of media. So on *The Simpsons* you might have the Simpsons trying to help Krusty the Klown keep his television show, so then what are we watching? We're watching a television program about kids trying to affect television. And once you have that sort of screen within a screen, or that *Beavis and Butthead* show where you have two guys watching rock videos and commenting on them, it changes the way we look at rock videos after that.

RM: Have you launched any media viruses yourself?

DR: I guess the most important media virus I launched was the *Media Virus* media virus itself. To launch the idea that ideas spread like viruses. That's what got the people who run media and those corporate conglomerates a little bit scared because they were thinking, "We're going to get infected with these *media viruses*," you know, "What is this?" So it had kind of a scary ring to it, taking those two words and putting them together.

RM: So then they invited you into their corporate boardrooms...

DR: It was weird. I didn't know whether companies were calling me in so that they could more easily dismiss what I was talking about or because they were actually afraid of what might be going on. At the very beginning, a European corporation would call me in and say, "What is this Internet? Do we need to be concerned?" An airline flew me to Europe and it was this big money thing so I'm like, "Wow, what does this airline want with me and the Internet?" They had me sign all these nondisclosures and stuff. They were all afraid, and they finally revealed the thing they were upset about was their pilots were about to go on strike and they had threatened to go online and start announcing in Usenet groups, this was before the Web even existed, they were going to announce in Usenet groups all the stories of the near misses that they had experienced over the last five years. And the company was asking, "How do we stop this from happening?" And I said "Well, you can't stop this from happening."

They didn't ask me the smart question which was "What can we do to counteract that?" and I wasn't about to volunteer it. What they could have done to counteract that was put up their own near miss stories that *weren't true* and then go on the news and pull them up and say, "Look this isn't true." Disinformation. Say "This didn't happen," and then in terms of the mainstream media it would negate everything, even the true stories posted by the real pilots.

So at first I was associated with this sort of *Mondo 2000*, rave culture, psychedelic, sub-cultural Internet thing, and it was companies wanting to know *do we need to be worried about this?* And, if so, *what are we supposed to do about it?* And I had a lot of fun. I was really, at that point, still psychedelic enough to feel like I was goofing, you know I'm just going to go in and goof on these people; imagine what Ken Kesey would have done in his Merry Prankster days.

Then I realized that really, honestly, I *like* people, even scared people, so my ambition really changed from tweaking people to trying to reduce people's level of fear. Just letting this thing happen. This Internet counterculture. This is a beautiful thing; it's going to unite people. It's going to let people talk to each other. And I really saw my next two or three books, too, were about reducing people's level of fear of change. The human species is undergoing radical change. The Internet is almost a test run for this change. I don't think the Internet, in this sense, is such a major deal at all. The Internet is a way to practice what it is that we're going to have to do for real, which is deal with privacy when we can all read each other's thoughts, deal with a global community when we're all realizing that we're part of the same thing. The Internet is like a good, dry, safe way for scared white people to experience community again, after we've

been so isolated through television. At the beginning when I went to corporations I wanted to have fun, I just was amazed that these people would even want to talk to me or that I could go to TCI[16] or Pepsi-Cola and —I mean *me*— and I'd go in my tee-shirt and my jeans and walk in and be like, "What do you want to know?" I would literally say, "You know you could read my book. $19 and you can get way more than I could possibly give you in an hour of consultation."

But they don't want to read. They don't know what reading is, or they could get an assistant to read it and give them a book report, but no, they want me in there to actually talk, because I guess there was this tradition of this idea of consultants.

One time early on, I was invited to an advertising conference and when I got there and saw posters up saying, "How to Use Viruses in Marketing" and "The New Media Viral Strategy" and I realized that they had really taken what I saw as a counterculture tool, an activist tool, and turned it into a marketing tool. So a guy like Calvin Klein can make commercials where they look a little bit like kiddy porn and they know perfectly well those are going to get pulled off the air but they're going to get more media coverage for having done those commercials than they could possibly buy with even the biggest advertising budget in the world.

Rushkoff at Disinfo.Con

So they were actually very consciously using the kinds of techniques that I laid out for activist culture, but using them instead to spread marketing campaigns. So I was actually horrified at first and it was a dilemma. People thought, "Oh Rushkoff, all you did was give the advertisers all these hacktivist tools," and I really started to think, "What side am I effectively on, anyway? Am I an unwitting double agent? Am I helping them?"

RM: Knowing you the way that I do I would argue that you are probably more like a Trojan horse smuggling subversive ideas into corporate boardrooms. When these corporations hire a consultant, they only expect that the consultant is going to tell them what they want to know. They don't know exactly what it is they want, they just know that they expect you to tell them.

[14] TeleCommunications, Inc., now AT&T Broadband.

DR: Sure. Once I relaxed, I started realizing I could play with these people. I would get my check before I'd talk to them and then I could pretty much say

DOUGLAS RUSHKOFF

whatever I wanted. So I went to the Leo Burnett advertising agency and they had me speak to 500 people in Chicago and I started the talk by saying, "The object of this talk for me is to get as many of you to quit the advertising industry as I can." And I proceeded to explain how advertising was so coercive and why it wasn't a good place for anyone who's really interested in media and how they're really sort of serfs to these corporations and I got like eight or ten emails after that talk saying, "I quit, I quit, I'm going to do something fun now." I got off on that for a while, that they had let me in and now I can sow the seeds of discontent in their companies. But then what I started to realize was rather than getting them to quit, *what if I got them to change the style of what they're doing?* So then what I started to say was "Look, corporations don't understand anything. If you're dealing with Proctor and Gamble or a cigarette company, they just want to sell their stuff. They don't understand marketing and they don't understand media. They don't understand the way ideas spread, so what if you think of these companies as sponsoring your media? You can make these little 30-second spots about whatever you want. You can make them about sex. You can make them about drugs. You can make them about media. You can make them about politics. *Just make them exciting.* Companies will love that: 'Oh, it's exciting and controversial, people are talking about it.' Think of commercials as little miniature sponsored 30-second activist movies." And then you see the eyes light up and you see these people thinking, "I bet I can get Chevrolet to do something about that," or whatever. So rather than thinking "Oh just quit, just leave this thing," I was starting to think "Well these people are in a position of power. These people are at a high leverage point and if they can start using massive corporate money to create interesting media, you know, then power to them."

RM: Well, obviously, I feel very strongly that if the large corporations will give, you should grab.

DR: Well right, *you did*, but the thing that most people don't realize is that in large corporations, *there's nobody home*. There's nobody there. There's nobody in charge. All a large corporation is is a set of commands. It's like a very simple computer program and if you look at what that program is, you can hack it to

do whatever you damn well please because there's nobody in charge. Nobody understands. I mean that's the beauty of it. Everyone's upset about these giant media conglomerates, you know, with Viacom buying MTV and buying Paramount or AOL buying Time Warner. The bigger these machines get, the smaller their little brains are in comparison with the whole thing. It's a giant media company that allows something like Beavis and Butthead or gangster rap to happen. And so I really take delight in how stupid corporations are.

Ultimately there are these two things going on in the universe: there's entropy and there's life. Entropy is trying to make everything dead and life is trying to make everything more complex and more interesting. And they've been kind of in this seeming battle, in this dance, over time. But life gets more complex, and life gets smarter over time, so life ends up winning. So you look at corporations and you look at all the means and all the things they have and yes, they seem to have power, but *they don't get smarter over time*. If we think of ourselves, not even as activists, but as the only living, breathing, thinking elements in this mess, then we're tremendously empowered to do whatever we want with it.

RM: These corporations see the profits from *South Park*, from Marilyn Manson records, from *The Matrix*, and they realize that they cannot make this kind of thing themselves and that they need to go to underground types in order to keep this cultural engine churning, so there is a real potential for mischief here.

DR: Right, so as they keep looking for coal to stoke into the fire, all you have to do is toss a few good diamonds in there and they've ended up throwing the most virulent cultural material into mainstream media and that's where you start having the fun. They're desperate for anything. Anything that twinkles. They don't realize that when they produce *The Matrix* movies, what they're doing is producing stuff that's saying, "This reality is a sham." If all a corporation wants to do is make money and make compelling media and make things that people want to go to and spend money on, then they're going to end up having to make, even by their shotgun approach, they're going to have to make media that addresses our current cultural concerns.

And what our current cultural concerns are, are things like "What is going on here? We've all been hypnotized." People desperately want to *wake up*, and *South Park* and *The Matrix* and Marilyn Manson, they wake people up to varying degrees. So the corporations, by supporting these kinds of media, end up sowing the seeds of their own demise.

RM: These days Che Guevara might as well be Captain Crunch or Ronald McDonald. That well known iconic portrait of him has now come to symbolize "rebellion" in advertising in some vague way for kids who probably have no idea who the guy was or who may mistake him for a member of Rage Against the Machine or a famous skateboarder. Tell me how that happened.

DR: Corporate America is embracing counterculture because they've found that a new way to sell us more stuff is to endorse the strident individualism of the early counterculture, and I think that the strident individualism that all this consumption promises is actually a booby prize. They want us to think of ourselves as individuals so that we buy more things; so that we don't share our toys with one another.

The better idea is to find out what do we have in common? The idea is to find out: how do I get closer to these other people? How do I transact with them on a level that's deeper than just me buying jeans from you, you know? When do we get down to the nitty gritty of actually being involved with each other?

The amazing thing about corporate America and the relationship with the counterculture is that things that used to represent a person's distance from corporations now almost represent their attachment to it. In the old days you used to be able to have a couple of tattoos and a piercing and that meant you're not part of the society; you're different; you're dangerous. The people working in the corporations have them now and it's a style statement to have a tattoo under your Prada tee-shirt or a piercing with your Donna Karan sports coat.

exit strategy douglas rushkoff

This desperate need of counterculture-type people to say, "No, we're not part of this thing," well the only way they can do it is by going into cults, basically, Heaven's Gate or Waco or something like that. They're the closest things to a counterculture we've got today because they're the ones who are, by whatever means necessary, maintaining their separateness.

RM: I agree. I think there's a good argument that cults and alternative reli-

DOUGLAS RUSHKOFF

gions are the only valid counterculture in America today.

DR: Right and they're the valid counterculture because they've found ways to insulate themselves and to isolate themselves. They formed pods that are distinct from the rest of culture and part of the premise is that it's an us versus them world we're living in. They don't ever get absorbed, but they usually die or suffer for their resistance. And their methods of separation are usually pretty damaging to their members' ability to exercise any true autonomy.

But remember that anything that the more vaguely defined counterculture does that catches on with kids is immediately scooped up by corporations and sold back to us. In some sense, I think that rather than trying to avoid that co-option, what we have to do is play with that co-option. If corporations are going to co-opt everything we do, then let's have them co-opt some really cool, dangerous, weird stuff. Let's have them co-opt homosexuality. Let's have them co-opt psychedelic drugs and designer reality. Magick. Spirituality. Let's have them co-opt environmentalism. Let's use our imaginations instead of complaining about people who sell out! Don't sell out, sell *in*.

RM: It's a bigger game than all that, I agree. With the amount of media that is being hurled at the average American today and this so-called "reality" TV programming, are we becoming an over-mediated spectator society, and is there anything even resembling "reality" —as it used to be defined— left in American life?

DR: Well there's certainly reality left, but I've always looked at media as something I call *social currency*, in other words: people don't buy records in order to have the record, just in order to have that music; people buy records in order to have an excuse for someone else to come over to their house and visit them. People watch a movie so that they can talk to their friends who have also seen that same movie. It's not the experience of the media itself as much as the way that that media can act as social currency for other interactions. Where it gets dangerous is when we're just consuming media and have no time to actually relate about it.

I look at something like people file-sharing MP3s and I think it's not really a good thing. The reason why everyone trades all these little MP3s is because the recording industry basically fucked us over when they went from regular LPs to CDs and charged 14 bucks a pop when it was actually cheaper for them to make. A revolt like what people are doing was bound to happen, but in some sense having all the music out there and all the music free, everything you want, is much less interesting than going to the record store and picking out a record. In a way it takes the joy out of it and it reduces music's value as social currency because now it's no longer like when we were kids, "Danny has the new Sex Pistols album, we're all going to go over to his house and listen to it;" now it's emailed back and forth and then what are you going to do? You listen to it while you work or you listen to it while you go on Amazon and buy something else.

I've always thought that the purpose of the media properties we create were excuses for people to have something to exchange socially. I also originally thought that the Internet was going to be this place where everyone expressed who they really are, and thought everyone's going to make their own media and all that, but frankly most people *don't* feel like making their own media. Most people are *not* artists. Most people are *not* media creators and they would rather actually create a fan site to Britney Spears where they collect all of the social currency that has to do with Britney Spears and assemble it all in one place and then they get popular and they feel good because they are purveyors of that stuff. If you look at a lot of so-called musicians today, they're really deejays and what are deejays but surrogate consumers, people who know what are the good sounds, what are the good tracks, and they play their record collection for us. So those records become social currency for that deejay to become popular in his crowd. That's the function that media often plays, but it's being devalued.

RM: It feels like we're being screamed at by idiots to me.

DR: You keep saying, "This horrible media is being shoved down our throats. Every time I turn on the TV I see this horrible thing." Well if every time you turn on the TV you see this horrible thing *then stop turning on the TV*. It's like my Tai Chi teacher used to teach us. I'd say, "When I move my knee like this it really hurts," and she would say, "Well then don't move your knee that way." *If the stuff on TV is crap then stop watching it.*

RM: Yeah, "This smells like shit. Smell this."

DR: (Laughs) Exactly, exactly, and look somewhere else for it because somewhere there are people who are doing something that's interesting and if the stuff being directed at 14-year old girls is not interesting to you, then look for something else.

RM: You were very close friends with Timothy Leary and he's now dead. Terrence McKenna's dead. William Burroughs is dead. Allen Ginsberg is dead. Do you feel in any way that you are continuing on in that sort of counterculture lineage?

DR: Well, *yes*, in the sense that the torch was passed, you know, and that Leary, who was the closest to me of all those people, he read my books and said "Wow, Doug, you really are continuing this thing." In a sense that felt great and then in a sense it was just a great big ego trap. The place I feel that the most is when I'll talk at something like at your event, like at the Disinfo.Con, to a thousand people, most of whom are ten or 15 years younger than me, and I realize that even though I don't necessarily know anything more than them and even though I don't have any more answers than they do, they are looking up at me as someone to tell them *where do we go* and *what do we do*? I think it would be flip and foolish of me to deny some sense of responsibility in that and just say, "Oh, follow your hearts and follow your bliss." At a certain point there is some responsibility that comes with the territory. When I'm trying to tell people to trust themselves, to trust their impulses and trying to wake people up to use their time on Earth wisely, the fact that I may have ten or 15 years more experience in this and that I've been gifted with the opportunity of getting to have the most outrageous experiences I could have, or of getting to sit and think about the most intense things and then share my conclusions with people, *means something*. I am paid to journey to places that most people don't go and to report my findings and to help cast some light on these areas. That's what any artist does to a certain extent, but as someone who's frequently in the media and standing at podiums and talking to people, yes, I do take it seriously and it's no longer enough for me to do what I used to do which is just say, "Hey all that stuff is crap. Don't listen to this, don't listen to that."

I think it is incumbent upon me, and others in my position, to ask, "Well then, what *do* we do?" I'm no prophet. I'm no Leary. I'm no Terence McKenna. I don't see the future and I can't tell people where it's going and what they should do, but I can give my most considered and responsible responses to their questions. I can use the fact that I have the time to consider it, the means to consider it, and I've been so privileged to get educated enough to have some of the tools I need to think about these things and I'm sure as hell going to give the best answer I can.

DOUGLAS RUSHKOFF

PETER RUSSELL

Philosopher and eco-futurist Peter Russell consults on institutional mindsets to the bluest of blue chip companies: Shell, IBM and American Express are just a few of the corporations seeking his advice. His books, which examine the ever-accelerating complexity of modern life, are hailed as classics by major thinkers, and rightly so.

Originally published in 1982, *The Global Brain*[17] is arguably Russell's most important work. All too rarely do "New Age" books offer their readers truly original insights, but *The Global Brain* is one of those rare books that allow the reader to take a major leap forward intellectually as they read it. The central thesis explores and builds on Dr. James Lovelock and Dr. Lynn Margulis's *Gaia Hypothesis*, the idea of the Earth as an integrated, self-regulated, living organism, and considers what function the human race may be playing in this system.

Its follow-up, *The White Hole in Time*,[18] speculates how our global hook-ups may be leading us toward an evolutionary breakthrough as significant as the emergence of life itself, three and a half million years ago. The essence of this leap is inner spiritual development. Moreover, Russell maintains that it is *only* through such a shift in consciousness that we will be able to manage successfully the global crises that now face mankind.

Russell is *not* a utopian, far from it, and this is what makes his message so incredibly powerful: he identifies the environmental and social crisis facing our planet at this time as being a *spiritual* crisis. We can do many amazing things with science, technology and commerce; we can master Mother Nature, but until and unless we can master ourselves, *we're racing headlong towards Doomsday.*

Period.

I found something that resonated strongly within me in these books and I do feel they changed me and the way I think as much as anything I've ever read, so it was a great pleasure to meet the wise and wonderful Peter Russell and interview him in an idyllic setting on Shelter Island, New York.

RM: Are we living in the best of times or the worst of times?

PR: We're living in the most significant, most challenging times ever, not just in human history, but in the whole history of Earth. They're the best of times —the most exciting times in terms of the potential we have with our technology— we can already change the world in almost any way we want. The way technology is going —particularly things like nanotechnology, biotechnology— ten, 20, 30 years from now we're going to do things which had been not even imaginable 50 years ago, so in terms of our ability to change the world they are certainly the most exciting and best of times *ever*.

In terms of the damage we are doing to the environment, they are definitely the worst of times. Never before in the whole of history of this planet —as far as we know— has a species arisen with the potential to actually completely destroy its own habitat, and we are doing that. It's crazy. And that's what makes these times so fascinating: *never before has there been so much potential, never before has there been so much danger*. I would say these are the most critical times in the history of the planet. We're actually living —right now— through a major species extinction. What we now know, there have probably been about five or six major species extinctions in the past. The last one was the end of the dinosaur, 65 million years ago, which was probably caused by a comet crashing into the Earth. Something like 90% of all species went extinct, more or less overnight. We are doing the same thing now; species are becoming extinct at a fantastic rate. It's suggested that three species an hour are becoming extinct in the world.

This time though it isn't a comet that's causing it. *We are doing it*. This is the first time in the history of the planet where a major species extinction is happening through our own careless actions. Maybe the good side of it is something new will emerge out of it, but it won't be human beings. In the end, if the dinosaurs hadn't become extinct human beings would probably never have arrived. We'd still be living in dinosaur times. So maybe, you know, the end of the human race is not such a bad thing. It may be we were just an evolutionary blind alley and the sooner we self-destruct the better.

RM: You know there's the old adage, "Don't shit where you eat," and yet the human race seems intent on shitting on everything. Why do we treat the planet the way we do and can we reprogram ourselves before it's too late?

PR: I hope so. I don't know what too late is. It's already too late. I don't think there is any avoiding calamity now. We are going to move into some pretty rough times, I think, over the next ten, 20 years because, as you say, we have been shitting where we eat. The way we polluted the waters, the oceans, the soil, there's no way of avoiding it. I think we're changing, but I think it's very slow. It may take a great calamity to speed things up, I really don't know. I do believe that every single one of us has the potential to change.

The sort of change I'm talking about here is the enlightenment that some of the great seekers and yogis have achieved, where they free themselves from this materialist mindset and see a whole different way of living in the world. *A way that is not one of attachment to things, not one of consumption, but a sane, wise way of living.* I don't think their brains or genetic make-up are any different from ours, which gives me a lot of hope. This means every one of us, if we had the right circumstances, training, facilitation, inspiration, whatever, could actually live that sort of life. I think the potential is there in every one of us, to be a saint.

Our culture at the moment doesn't encourage it: it almost ridicules it. It says *ignore that spiritual stuff.* It's about being successful in the world, that's what's important. *That* is what is driving our culture crazy. That's what we're going to have to learn to let go of, that whole drive to be successful in the world. *The drive should be to be wise and to be kind.* If we could drive people towards caring, if people actually just *cared for each other*, the world would be transformed.

RM: So you think that a catastrophe is inevitable before humanity will change its ways?

PR: Unfortunately, I think it probably *will* take a catastrophe. We have had the information around for ten, 20 years, more, that we are heading towards disaster. The information is *there*, staring us in the face. As each year goes by we get more and more data that says the way we are heading is just running into total disaster. We don't know what it's going to be like, we don't know when it's going to come, but there's no way we can continue doing what we're doing and not have a disaster.

And we don't want to look at it. It's like we all want to continue in our own comfortable ways. Just one example: consuming fossil fuels is bad because the CO_2 produces the greenhouse effect. What that's going to do to weather patterns, to agriculture, and many other things could be catastrophic. But do any of us stop driving cars because of it? Maybe one or two people, but we continue living the same old lifestyle. I think it's going to take a shock.

[17] Republished as *The Global Brain Awakens: Our Next Evolutionary Leap.* Element Books.

[18] Republished as *Waking Up In Time: Finding Inner Peace In Times of Accelerating Change.* Origin Press.

PETER RUSSELL

The same thing happens with individuals: if you tell somebody, "If you continue drinking like this, smoking like this, doing something else that's not good for your life, then you're going to end up with a major illness," people's typical response is "It hasn't hit me yet" or "I'll worry about that when it happens." And then when it does happen, we change. It happened to a friend of mine recently. He had a minor heart attack. Fortunately it was minor, but it was sufficient to change his life. So I think we do need disasters to bring us to our senses. My hope is it's a disaster that we can recover from rather than a disaster that totally destroys humanity.

RM: These droughts and the changing weather patterns are not encouraging. What are some of the scenarios that could happen, if the food chain starts to collapse?

PR: Then you get some pretty ugly scenarios. Obviously, food is really important, but the water supply could collapse as well. We already have a shortage of water, pesticides in the water, pollution, that sort of thing, a change in weather patterns could be catastrophic. Water is something very basic, and when people don't get the basic things coming through as they expect, they start fighting for them.

RM: Well, the whole house of cards falls if plants can't reproduce.

PR: The biggest danger —and it's a very real danger— is if we destroy the ozone layer. There's not a lot we can do about it because the ozone layer now is being destroyed by CFCs that have been released in the last 50 years. Even if we stopped releasing CFCs now —which we're not, we're still producing them and releasing them, not so much, but we're still doing it— those old CFCs are going to cause damage over the next 20, 30 years still.

If we seriously damage the ozone layer, we'll kill off all life on land. The only reason life exists on land is because of the ozone layer. For nine tenths of the Earth's history, all life existed under the sea. That was because water in the ocean filters out ultraviolet light. There was no ozone layer to block the ultraviolet light so the safe space was in the water. It was only after the ozone layer formed that it was safe for life to come out of the sea onto the land.

So the whole colonization of the land has happened in the last 10% of the Earth's history. If we destroy the ozone layer, the growing tips of plants get destroyed. Plants can't reproduce themselves, insects go blind and they won't be able to pollinate plants. In fact, everything dies. The whole of the land will be reduced to desert for maybe another billion years till the ozone layer is built up again. That's the real danger, we don't just affect ourselves, we affect the whole of life, and that is still a very, very real possibility. I'm not going to say it's *going* to happen, the possibility may be 10%, but 10% is a huge, huge risk. We take out insurance on our houses because there's a one in a thousand chance they might catch fire. When it comes to the environment there's a much, much greater chance we're going to completely screw it all up.

We continue in the hope that it may not happen. It's basically insane. We call ourselves the most intelligent species on the planet, yet is it intelligent to realize where you're going, to know what's going to happen if you continue this way and then continue doing it, anyway? That to me, is just stupid. It's a bit like we're in a car, driving around a bend in thick fog. We don't know what is coming. We know it's dangerous and we're accelerating into it. Now if you were a driver accelerating into thick fog, you'd have your license taken away. It's insane. You're just heading into disaster. That's what we're doing, we know there's danger straight ahead and we can't see what it is and we can't see where the future is going and we're just going faster and faster and faster.

I think one of the crazy things about our culture is that we do not have a mission statement about where we're going. Any corporation today has worked out this mission statement like "We are going to be the producers of the best washing machines on the planet" or whatever it is. They've got their mission statement of what they're going for. Our culture doesn't have one, we're just going blindly ahead. Why are we developing the Internet, making it go faster and faster? Why are we looking to make our computers more efficient? Why are we doing most of the things we're doing? It's just because they're there to be done, we're not saying this is really helpful for us in the long term. I've spent a lot of time living on the edge of Silicon Valley and I see all the progress that's happening there, but no one's thinking about what this is leading to in the long term. There is, in Silicon Valley today, almost zero awareness of the environment. There was much more awareness ten years ago. We've got so wrapped up in the potentials of the cyber world, we've ignored the real physical natural world and if that falls apart then the Internet economy isn't going to help us much.

RM: Everybody knows —or we should know— that the rainforest is being cut down at the rate of 50 to 100 football fields worth a day and the question must be asked, "By who's right?" Doesn't this sort of activity test the definition of private property?

PR: I think it's everybody covering their own ass and looking after their own interests. The people who are cutting it down are doing it because it's in their short term interest to do so, whether it's villagers living in the rainforest or whether it's huge corporations just cutting it down to sell the wood. A large part of the Southeast Asian rainforests have been cut down and turned into plywood to make shuttering for new buildings being built in Japan. They won't use their own wood for this; they use wood from other countries. They put the plywood up for concrete shuttering, the building's built and then what happens to the plywood? It's burnt, because that's the cheapest option for them.

A lot of it comes back to money and the money thing comes back to this belief that the more money we have, the better we're going to control the world and ultimately the happier we'll be. You've got people running corporations who are as sucked into this belief system as anybody. So I think it's all, in the end, a reflection of our consciousness. The consciousness of the people who are doing it, the consciousness of the consumer, people who go out and buy nice mahogany furniture or a mahogany toilet seat. They can be very proud of their mahogany toilet seat, but does it actually make them function any better? The result is another tree has gone down in the rainforest somewhere. We don't want to think about the consequences, we just want to get on with our little private lives and be comfortable. I think that that's the major part of the problem: we're not willing to put ourselves out. A few people may be, a few will change their lifestyles, or protest, and that's valuable, but they're still very few and far between. Most of us just don't want to have the status quo disturbed. We don't want to hear about it, even, because if we did, if we really let in what we're doing to the planet it would be too painful for most people.

RM: Well people would realize what they're leaving for their kids to deal with!

PR: Yes. It's species suicide. Planetary suicide.

RM: Peter, if one buys into the Gaia hypothesis —the idea that Earth is a living, self-regulating organism— then what is mankind, scabies?

PR: That's a very interesting question. I wouldn't say scabies. We're more like cancer. If you look at cancer, cancers tend to grow very fast. Humanity's grown very fast. They're also very selfish systems. Humanity seems to be a very selfish system. It doesn't care much about the rest of nature. Cancer's also stupid. If a cancer is successful it usually will take over the whole body and kill the host, which isn't very sensible because the cancer then dies. We're doing exactly the same thing. We're equally

PETER RUSSELL

stupid, because if we continue on our present track, we're going to foul up the planet to such an extent that we probably won't continue to exist.

However, cancers can spontaneously heal themselves. In many cases, usually because a person has a change in attitude, or falls in love, or has some mystical experience, the cancer goes into spontaneous remission and often goes away completely. So although we're behaving in a very malignant way towards the planet at the moment, it doesn't have to go on that way. That is the good news about cancer: it is healable.

On the other hand we need to ask what is humanity's role for the planet. The planet's existed very well for billions of years without humanity. The Gaia hypothesis suggests that different systems have different functions, like the rainforest would be like the lungs of the planet and the oceans are like the circulatory system. What is it that humanity is good at on this planet that no other creature does?

It is *information processing*. We are the creatures that can learn. We have language, with which we can share our experiences with each other. We are the creatures who developed a collective body of knowledge. We are the information processors of the planet, which means we are like nerve cells on the planet. Long before the Internet existed I became fascinated by the way human society seems to be growing together in very much the same way as the cells in a brain grow together. There is the same order of magnitude of cells in our own brains as there are people on the planet. We are like a young evolving nervous system.

And there's another parallel here. As the nervous system grows in the human embryo, there is first of all an explosion of nerve cells, then those nerve cells start linking up. Maybe that's what we're going through now. We've had this population explosion, and now we're linking up through telecommunications, the Internet, and other media. So I believe we are heading towards becoming a single global information processing system: what I called a *global brain*.

I think the truth is probably we are both an embryonic global brain and a cancer, a nervous system that has turned malignant, so the challenge is: can we heal ourselves of our malignancy and reap the full potential of becoming that global brain, that single integrated information process of a planet? Can we heal ourselves of the malignancy in time? I think that's the real challenge. And it comes back to each and every one of us. The misguided thinking is something that we all carry around inside us. When I say, "People are self-centered, they must change" or "This person's materialistic" or whatever, it's all in me, too. I have all those same faults and traits. It's in all of us. But the only person I really have total responsibility for is myself.

In the end it comes back to the question: *can we inspire other people so everybody can go through this process of transformation.* This change is valuable in its own right. The more we can free ourselves from these old outdated, fearful modes of thinking, the happier we're going to feel. That I think is something that people often forget. We need to do the inner work, not just to heal humanity or to heal the planet; we need to do it to heal ourselves because our lives will get a lot better if we do. We'll find the fulfillment we've been seeking all along.

RM: Right now in America we are enjoying the highest standard of living ever in history of any culture at any time, higher even than during the 1950's, after World War II. The Eisenhower era is always held up as the highest standard of living, but we've surpassed that many times over at this point. How much more can the economy possibly expand?

PR: I don't know, I'm not enough of an economist. The question though, is, do we *need* it to go any further? The standard of living is measured in material terms, what we really need to look at is the quality of life, and that actually hasn't changed much. Back in 1957, pollsters asked how many people were happy with their lot in life. About 30% of the people said they were happy with what they had. They did the same study in 1992 asking exactly the same question. Now over that time the size of housing had increased, the number of cars per family had increased, the number of TV stations had increased, the availability of foods from around the world all the year round in your supermarket, that had blossomed. But the number of people who were happy with what they had in life was exactly the same, 30%. To me this shows two things: first, what you have doesn't determine whether or not you're happy. All this increase in the external quality of life —or *quantity of life* we should say— hasn't changed our internal quality at all. And second, over those 35 years we have done absolutely nothing to educate people in the real basics of what's important in life. We are still stuck in the same old model.

RM: Well, as the philosopher king himself, Mister David Lee Roth once said, "Money can't buy you happiness, but it can buy you a yacht so you can pull up alongside of happiness." With all of the neat stuff you can go out and buy, why *aren't* we happier?

PR: This, I think, is the fundamental malaise of our culture, perhaps of any culture. We get seduced from the moment we're born into a belief system that says: *whether or not you're at peace depends upon what you have or do in the world around you*. It's almost hypnotized into us.

Now if the reason that you're not at peace is because you're hungry or you're sick or you're freezing cold, then that's true, you need to eat something or deal with the sickness, whatever. But most of us in the contemporary world have enough food, most of us have adequate shelter. The reason we're not at peace is not because there's something amiss with our external world but because there's something missing inside. It's some hunger for meaning, love, acceptance, or security. It's something *inside* that's missing and yet what our culture tells us to do the whole time is look *outside* for it. Take yourself to a movie. Go out and have a good meal. Buy yourself a new jacket.

What happens is we become addicts to *things*. And it's just like any other addiction, we take the substance, in this case the substance is a new car, a new meal, a new movie, and we feel a bit better for a while. But because it doesn't satisfy that deeper inner hunger, the effect wears off and we start looking again. The reason is we don't recognize that what we really are looking for is to feel good inside.

The Dalai Lama said it perfectly: "In the final analysis, the hope of every person is simply peace of mind." That's our basic motivation. Whatever we do, we're doing it because we want to avoid pain and suffering and feel better. Even when I go to the dentist, it isn't a pleasant experience, but I do it because I think I will feel better in the long term for it. It's an investment in future happiness.

So whatever we do, we're looking for a better internal estate. That's our basic motivation: to change our state of consciousness, to improve the quality of our state of consciousness. In our culture we're taught the whole time you improve the state of your consciousness by doing the right thing, having the right thing. That's why we love money so much. It's not money itself that's important but money gives us the ability to buy the things or the experiences or the friends… whatever it is we think is going to make us feel happier.

Yet what all the great spiritual traditions say is *it doesn't work*. In the end whether or not you feel at peace and happy has nothing to do with what you *have*, it's how you look upon it. It's your *interpretation* of it. Many of the people I know who are some of the happiest people are far from wealthy; they're just people who are just living a life which satisfies them. Not a very rich material life, perhaps, but they are living something that is in accord with their own values and needs. On the other hand, some of the unhappiest people I've seen are those who are continually chasing after the tangible signs of happiness, and never satisfied with what they have in the present moment.

PETER RUSSELL

I think this is the basic sickness in our culture and I think it arises in all cultures. We fall into this trap of thinking that if only I had and did enough of the right things, I'd be happy.

RM: Why does organized religion feel so meaningless in modern times?

PR: I think it *is* meaningless in modern times. I believe religions originally sprang from spiritual insights and truths that were very meaningful when they were laid down. They were laid down in a completely different culture, with completely different value systems.

We then take these texts and retranslate them and try to put them in the current culture, and they just don't fit. We need today a completely different restatement of those truths. It's not that the basic truths are wrong. I love to go back and look at the Greek version of the Gospels, which was not even the original, of course. In the Greek version of the Gospels, I find truths which I think are absolutely right on. You find the same in Hindu teachings, the same in Buddhism. These are eternal truths and what happens is they get shaped by that culture and then reabsorbed by other cultures. Much gets lost over time as they're translated. So we end up with something which is a very poor resemblance of the original wisdom, *whatever it was.* Most of the spark and life has gone out of it. We then try to take that distorted understanding and incorporate it into a modern framework. No wonder then that they're meaningless. They are literally *without meaning* in our culture!

What we need to do is rediscover that wisdom for ourselves in 21st Century language terms. That to me is the exciting thing that's happening today. All over the world, particularly in the developed world, which I think is where the need is the strongest, people are beginning to look within themselves to rediscover that essential wisdom.

Earlier I mentioned that we get sucked into a belief system that the material world is the real world and if we have enough control over the real world then we'll be happy. All the religions have talked about this. It's the distinction between God and Mammon. But we don't have to talk about in the language of God and Mammon, or talk about it in Buddhist terms as being sucked into Samsara. This is all foreign language for us. But we can talk about it in psychological terms, about our attachment to things. Then it all begins to make whole new sense. Maybe in 500 years time our current language will be seen as spooky religion talk by somebody, but what we have to do is rediscover that wisdom and shape it in contemporary terms.

RM: Peter, in your book *The White Hole in Time* you predict that the next stage in humanity's growth will be a new spiritual age. How do you see this happening and what forms do you think it will take?

PR: I don't think it's going to be a spiritual age as we think of spirituality today because so much of our thinking of spirituality is conditioned by old traditional religion. What I mean by *spiritual* is a deep recognition of the real potentials of the human psyche and part of that is stepping outside our mindsets and the framework in which we normally look at the world, rediscovering who we really are. That's the essence of many spiritual pursuits, discovering the real nature of the self, the real nature of consciousness behind all the roles we play and the things we think. I think *I'm Peter Russell*, this male person, etcetera, but that's just a role I have taken on. But what is the essence of that? What is the essence of *I-ness* that we all feel? That is key to our spiritual quest, along with letting go of our attachments to the material world, thinking the material world is the thing we should focus on.

What we're all looking for really is *freedom*; everybody is looking for a sense of inner freedom, but we focus on external freedom. I think real spirituality is about freeing ourselves from misguided fears, from judgments, from all the crap that runs us. We are so conditioned in our minds to think in certain ways, behave in certain ways. Spirituality for me is about becoming free of all that stuff and I think that is the revolution we are going through today. That's going to come about, not through some new messiah. Messiahs were valuable in the past, but we're living through a revolution today where there's no messiah. Instead there are millions of people beginning to value their own internal wealth and share it with other people. Whether it's through books, conversation, on the Internet, we are all learning from each other. I think that's how this spiritual evolution is going to take place. It's going to take place through a grassroots raising of consciousness. Everybody learning from each other.

When you have that sort of process happening you get an accelerating phenomenon. You get positive feedback and that's going to spiral faster and faster and faster, and that's what I was showing in *The White Hole in Time*. The idea of the white hole in time actually comes from a black hole in space. A black hole in space is the endpoint of life of a large star. As a star evolves it does so faster and faster and faster. It takes billions of years to burn hydrogen and then millions of years to burn helium and each stage happens faster than the one before. Then in the last 15 minutes it collapses into a black hole.

I think the same is happening with life: it evolves faster and faster and faster and the final stages are actually the real awakening to consciousness itself, and a lot of the great past masters, teachers and saints, they are the heralds of what is about to happen. They are people who discovered the wisdom, the richness and the wealth that there is inside our own consciousness. They've just been like little lighthouses in history.

What is happening now is we are doing this together, and I think we are potentially on the edge of an explosion of awakening of consciousness much like what a star goes through in a supernova. *We're on the edge of an explosion of inner light*. We're not there yet, but we are working our way up to that. If you look at the accelerating curves, they all seem to go vertical, sometime in the next ten, 20, 30, 40 years. This suggests this super nova of consciousness —whatever it is— is going to happen potentially within our own lifetime.

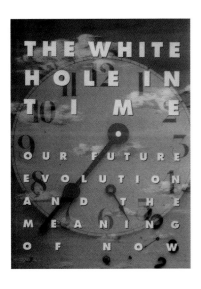

THE WHITE
HOLE IN
TIME

OUR FUTURE
EVOLUTION
AND THE
MEANING
OF NOW

_Usuracracy

RM: Peter, do you think that charging interest on loans is morally wrong?

PR: Yup. I think it always has been. It's called *usury* in many of the old religions. It's been banned by just about every religion. And it's seen be to wrong for two reasons. First it makes the rich richer and the poor poorer. The people who lend the money are the rich people, the people who borrow the money and pay the interest are the poor, and the people who gather it are the rich. Secondly, it's the idea of getting something for nothing. You lend the money, you do nothing but you get wealthier from it, so those who have money get wealthier by doing nothing. There's no useful work done by lending money.

There are many references in the Old Testament to the banning of charging interest. Jesus threw the moneylenders out of the temples. The Catholic Church banned it, until recently. When Henry VIII broke from the Vatican he did two things: he legalized divorce, and he legalized the charging of interest. Usury is still banned by many fundamentalist Islamic countries. There you can't lend money at interest. You have to lend money on an equity basis rather than just taking interest.

Yet it is so much a part of our culture we never even question it. I think that's one of the main things that's making our culture totally unsustainable. Something like 90% of the money in circulation today is borrowed money, and the interest has to be paid back on that. Say it's at 10%, that means each year 10% more wealth needs to be created to cover the interest. There's two ways of doing that. You either have inflation, but that is not good for the economy, or you have to keep increasing the real wealth of a country. That is why we are *saddled* with this idea of growth. We have to keep growing, and it's growth that is killing the environment. The more we grow, the more we consume, the more we pollute. All of the people who really look at the global situation seriously say we have to move towards a *zero growth economy*, and yet you cannot have zero growth so long as you are charging interest. Ultimately we have to go to an economic system which doesn't charge interest. How we do that I have no idea because we are so immersed in the idea of charging interest. But, I think, ultimately it has to go.

PETER RUSSELL

KEMBRA PFAHLER

Kembra Pfahler is a rock star, wrestler, fetish film star, Calvin Klein model and mastermind behind the legendary freak show known as *The Voluptuous Horror of Karen Black.* By the time I arrived in New York City at the end of 1984, she was already quite well known in East Village hipster circles. Famous even. Part of the landscape you might say. Her strange, often bewildering, and always notorious performances were staged at clubs like 8BC, ABC No Rio and The Pyramid Club, which was across the street from where I then lived, on Seventh Street and Avenue A, so I often saw her shows. Articles appeared about her in underground magazines where she discussed her artistic manifestos of "Availabism" and "Anti-Naturalism" or mentioned that she had not a single fork, knife, spoon, plate or even cup in her apartment.[19] The local artsy video emporium, Kim's Video, rented the unusual art films she'd directed and ones that she'd been in, such as Nick Zedd's *War is Menstrual Envy* and various shorts done with Richard Kern, including the infamous *Sewing Circle*, the one where she has her vagina sewn shut. A few years later, that same store started stocking dozens of almost surrealistic fetish films she seemed to be cranking out weekly. All in all, it was confusing. Observers and admirers of her work were kept guessing. I certainly was. Even though I've long been fascinated with her work, I confess I often left her performances wondering, "Why would someone do that?" Looking back on it, I suppose that was the point!

It's difficult to get across these days just how *odd* Kembra looked back then. No one looked like she did and I mean <u>no one</u>. She really stood out walking down the street. Certainly she was foxy but she was homicidal looking, too! I used to think of her as a Black Widow spider because of the fearsome way she presented herself: like the hourglass figure on the back of a Black Widow, if her looks weren't a warning to *stay the fuck away*, I don't know what was! I saw it also in how she went about her performances, calculating every movement, building a web, bit by bit, performance by performance, of an overall experience and visual language. Perhaps she sees herself in this way, too, as she certainly uses a lot of spider imagery.

Despite the fact that we lived in the same neighborhood and have many of the same friends, I'd actually never met Kembra. It wasn't until after Ann Magnuson and I watched her *Wall of Vagina* performance at Anthology Film Archives (an event fêting artist Hermann Nitsch) in open-mouthed astonishment and I was starting to plan the Disinfo.Con that we finally did meet up and we've been great friends ever since.

Kembra's Disinfo.Con performance —a reprise of *The Wall of Vagina* piece— floored everyone present. On a day that is legendary for its weirdness, Kembra took top honors. Watching it from the side of the stage, a highly amused Robert Anton Wilson turned to me and asked "You want me to follow THAT?" and he referred to the piece several times during his speech.

Don't tell anyone, but Kembra's a real sweetheart. She's not at all the homicidal maniac I'd made her out to be. She's actually really nice. Really, *really* nice… which is not to say she couldn't turn homicidal in a heartbeat if a situation warranted it!

When I did the following interview, I went in armed with questions that I hoped would coax out of her the story of how a strange little girl from a Los Angeles beach suburb found happiness and voluptuous horror in the big city.

RM: Was there a significant event or turning point in your childhood?

KP: I grew up in a small surfing town in Southern California and I guess my household was a little *unusual*. My grandmother was kind of the town… *wild woman* and she used to come into my room at night when I was asleep and tell me stories like "Your mother and your aunt went swimming off the Hermosa Beach pier and they were eaten by sharks." They were fantastic and she provided me with the fodder for what was later to become my interest in horror.

All the other kids were swimming and tanning and I used to like to watch horror films, like the Universal horror films. And I always admired the great black-haired ladies of horror like Barbara Steele and Karen Black. Karen Black made some incredible films in the 1970's that I was very inspired by. I felt like when I watched her in her films, I couldn't take my eyes off the screen. She was very strange looking, beautiful and horrifying at the same time. And one movie in particular, *Trilogy of Terror,* was very inspiring to me. I used to spend my days bicycling down to the movie theater where they'd show films and it was

a great escape and it was something that formed the artistic vocabulary that I'm still using today.

My mother was very artistic and very fashionable, and she used to make costumes for me, some of the costumes that I use to this day, like the big flower heads that I use in my band in Karen Black, my mother had actually designed that for me when I was a child... I guess I was very lucky to have a lot of artistic encouragement. My mother would also tell me that I was very special and that I was going to grow up to be a great person.

Later, I found out that in the nursery school that I attended, the Virginia McMartin School, there was a big scandal about child molestation and allegedly the teachers belonged to a satanic cult. It was all over the press for a few years in the United States. I was kind of excited. I thought does this have something to do with my obsession with horror and my darker thoughts, but unfortunately I truly believe that this was just a kind of witch-hunt that was created by the neighbors in the South Bay, but I did attend this nursery school where I was nurtured by alleged child molesters and Satan worshipers! (Laughs).

RM: So *unfortunately* as a child you were never involved in any satanic abuse?

KP: Yeah. *Unfortunately*.

RM: How did the other kids in Hermosa Beach react to you? My visual image of you as a little girl is of a Wednesday Addams-type character running around in the midst of beach culture. Did people think that you were a freak in your hometown?

KP: No, not really, they didn't, because my father was a very well known surfer and back in those days the surfers were revered as gods almost. My father made a famous surfing film with Bruce Brown called *Slippery When Wet* so every place that I went as a child it was like the red carpet was rolled out which I think might have overblown my ego a little bit because I really did feel like I was a surf aristocrat somehow. I got to go to special places and I got to travel up and down the coast of California with my father surfing, but no, I wasn't really viewed as a freak. I had a few behavioral disorders, only because I was extremely bored as a child.

Young Kembra, top right, with Virginia McMartin.

(Preceding page) Photo: Scott Ewalt

But growing up on the beach with this kind of one singular archetype available to me —the sun bathing beauty queen— I just didn't feel like that internally and I didn't resemble anything like a surfer on the outside.

RM: At what point did what would later become your performance art start to germinate in your mind?

[19] This is true to this day. Her apartment is also painted brick red: all of it! Every single surface in the place is brick red. The sink, the floor, the countertops, everything!

KP: I had been hospitalized from a gymnastics accident and I had basically mutilated my elbow so that I couldn't move for months and months on end. I just remember spending a lot of time very isolated and I started having strange thoughts, sort of thoughts of mythological proportion. I thought of ways to manifest these thoughts as well. I started thinking about making movies and doing performances.

I was pretty much left on my own and I suppose my mind just exploded, thankfully, and I got the itch to move to New York City and reinvent myself. So it happened when I was a teen-ager, like 15 or 16-years old. I was going to a lot of punk rock shows in Los Angeles, seeing bands like The Screamers and The Cramps and more of the theatrical rock bands who were playing in Hollywood. Me and my friends would hitchhike to Hollywood to see these bands and that whole scene was very encouraging of people to express themselves very individualistically. It was one of the first times that I felt like my appearance and my behavior was applauded rather than spat on. I was really nurtured by those people, by those older punk rockers in Los Angeles.

But from an early age, I always strayed from doing what I saw other people doing, like I didn't want to grow up to be in a punk rock band like those that I was seeing. I wanted to reach for something else and that's why I came to New York. I stayed away from music and bands just because I thought that paradigm was so complete and it was so well done by so many others.

RM: Aside from the punk rock, what other kind of influences went into informing your rather singular aesthetic?

KP: I was really deprived of any kind of access to European history when I was growing up so I had this desire to go to Europe, Germany specifically. I stayed in Munich, Bavaria for a while and I also visited Vienna, Austria where I saw for the first time pictures from the Vienna Action Group. They were Rudolph Schwarzkogler pictures; Otto Muehl and Hermann Nitsch, and those were some of the most intense pictures that I'd ever seen in my life. The Vienna Action Group was a group of extreme artists doing strange body mutilations, paintings and performances, in and around Vienna after World War II. Vienna was a very strange city, you know. It was so different, obviously, to what I was exposed to in Los Angeles.

Stills from *The Blue Banshee*.
Director, Mike Kuchar

I really identified with Schwarzkogler's body mutilations. They were very well composed and they were extremely violent. They were also very beautiful. The use of the body was very beautiful, I thought.

I really liked their work, I think, because of all of the history that I'd had with the body growing up in Southern California and always having to be so body conscious and always hating that so much. You know like "Oh, when you grow up you know you're going to be so pretty" and "If you just lose five more pounds and dye your hair blond." People were always inflicting their opinions on me as a young girl saying things like "Oh, you're going to be so pretty *if you just do this...*"

I grew up being extremely, um, *body dismorphic*, I guess you'd say, with these people and their opinions on me about my body and about my appearance. I always hated that so much. I'd get this running commentary in Los Angeles: "Lose five more pounds, you might get to be on TV." I never asked for that kind of input at all, it was just something that was thrown on me and it was so great to see those Schwarzkogler pictures with him wrapped in bandages and just like

KEMBRA PFAHLER

doing insane things to his body, turning this kind of pain into a beautiful picture.

I spent about a year in Germany and when I came back I moved to New York and I started some of the first performances then.

RM: When you moved to New York what was it like then?

KP: In 1979, New York City was, of course, *a little bit different* than it is now. The Lower East Side was very rundown. There were a lot of burnt out buildings and it was a very undesirable place to live. I guess that film *Sid & Nancy* had a lot of scenes of people lining up to buy drugs and so forth outside of abandoned buildings. It looked quite different then, than it does now.

There was a community of performers and places to do performances like the Pyramid Club. It was the kind of place that you could go and ask for a booking because you had an outlandish idea and you could do it the following week and show it to your friends.

(Opposite) Photo: Richard Kern

(This page) Stills from *Chopsley: Rabid Bikini Model*

That kind of place really doesn't exist so much anymore. The city's been extremely renovated and I think a lot of the youth culture just can't afford to come here and live anymore. But back then there were a lot of young people and we were doing shows and running the clubs.

There were also a lot of incredible legends around town too. Jack Smith lived on First Avenue, the great filmmaker, and Quentin Crisp was in the neighborhood. Allen Ginsberg, too. There were a lot of people from like the 60's who still lived here, so it was a really good time to be in New York. I got an apartment for a couple of hundred dollars and that enabled me to be able to do a lot of artwork and shows.

RM: Describe some of your earliest performance art pieces.

KP: I guess the first performance art piece that I did was the egg piece where I stood on my head and had the egg cracked on my vulva. That was one of the first pieces that I ever did. It was at a club called Armageddon, which was on Jane Street on the West Side. There was a raucous, violent crowd there and they were throwing bottles and screaming and yelling. It was really terrifying to be naked in front of this gawking crowd of drunk, artistic types of people. I also started doing a piece where I walk on top of bowling balls. I strap bowling balls to my feet and walk on them. That had come from this drawing that I'd seen in Austria by Hans Bellmer, a drawing of a witch that had been persecuted. They used to torture these people by affixing balls to their feet. I found bowling balls one afternoon walking home and I taped them to my feet in my performance.

I started doing the costume, *Abra Cadaver,* which is the one where I tie the strings to my labia and sort of quack like a duck... that's a good one... I feel like I look sort of like a moth with my arms outstretched attached to my labia like this. (Gestures) That was a real hit and that was a costume that I also brought into Karen Black in the later years.

I also did nude car modeling. I liked to dress up in my monster costume and lie on the hoods of cars. In a strange way, that had the same kind of symmetry that standing on my head with my legs open cracking an egg on my vulva. It made a lot of sense to me, somehow, as far as that being a letter in the alphabet of my artwork and the vocabulary that I was building. The composition is very important to me. Shapes. The lines from different poses that I strike in my performances. All of the things that I took into my band, I was developing in the 80's, in my apartment here, using "Availabism," the movement that I made up which is *making the best use of what is available*.

I was basically doing like one performance a month and we also went to Europe

KEMBRA PFAHLER

The Egg Piece

Kembra and Samoa
Photo: Michael Lavine

(Opposite page) Karen Black poster by Scott Ewalt

around 1985 with a group called the Oroboro Ensemble. That was with Samoa, my partner and collaborator at the time and a violinist. We were in our early 20's and we convinced all these great music halls to hire us and let us come in and do our performance art. We had a great time. We were in London. We went to Spain. I was doing the egg piece at that time, but it was a very raw version of it, a very undressed, unglamorous version of the egg piece that you know…

RM: A *raw* egg piece?

KP: That's right. (Laughs).

RM: It's funny hearing you describe things that I saw you do back then. I remember thinking "Where is she pulling this from? What dark crevice of her mind would inspire her to crack an egg on her vagina?" And now I know it was because it *was there*. I think I understand you a lot better now…

KP: (Laughs) Well, I'm a staunch minimalist, but also it's really trying to find some kind of beauty and transformation with everyday objects that are just around as well. Yes, the reason I did that piece was because I was employing Availabism — making the best use of what's available— and I was staying in some rotten apartment on the Lower East Side and someone invited me to do a performance piece and I had three minutes to do it. There was an egg in the refrigerator and you know it just seemed like the perfect thing to do to stand on my head and have someone crack an egg on my vulva. *There was really nothing else to do with an egg.* I wanted to make an incredible picture and so that's what I did.

RM: Tell me about meeting Samoa. I take it that the two of you must've really spurred each other on.

KP: To say the least! Samoa originally came from Hiroshima, Japan and he had a background in theater. He was on television as a young boy. He taught me about Noh plays and about Kabuki. I learned about Japanese literature from him and all of these incredible things. We had such a strange parallel existence going on: he was at home in Hiroshima listening to Grand Funk Railroad and I

was home in Southern California painting Kabuki eye make-up, trying to commit Hara-Kiri and doing strange things. I wasn't even aware of why I was coming up with these things. It was a tremendous affirmation to meet Samoa and we started working together when we were in our early 20's doing films and performances on the Lower East Side of New York.

RM: In the 80's there was a very vibrant underground film scene in New York and you were a big part of that. What were the projects that you were working on in film at that time?

KP: We were getting so frustrated that everyone else was always documenting our performances and we never had any footage of our very own artwork, so we wanted to film our own performances and that's how we started making films, just filming the performances that we did. There were people like Bradley Eros and Nick Zedd and Richard Kern on the scene then and I offered my acting skills to other directors during that time. I had people be in my films so I felt

KEMBRA PFAHLER

like it was just part of the exchange to offer my services as an actor in their films. I think that I'm a terrible actress and my school of acting I decided to call "Anti-Naturalism," which is the opposite of method acting. With method acting, you're drawing from real experiences and exuding honest emotion. *Anti-Naturalism* was more like having a cartoon character emerge and being essentially totally fake.

RM: It's kind of like drag queen acting?

KP: Dolly Parton is an Anti-Naturalist. Marlon Brando is an Anti-Naturalist, too. I read in his book that he would read lines off of the person in front of him when he was making films. He felt very strongly that you didn't need to be a method actor and that spontaneity and *unnaturalness* was just as provocative and interesting on film if you had the magic. Anyways, film being something so totally artificial, it seemed totally natural to be anti-natural...

RM: What sort of day jobs have you held when you were pursuing your career goals?

KP: For a long time I was very unemployable. I refused to change my appearance and I refused to work a regular job. Mostly I couldn't *get* a regular job because of my appearance. It was not fashionable yet to look like you poured a bottle of black ink on your head with your make-up melting off of your face, it wasn't high fashion yet to do that and I couldn't get a job. But I did procure some extra work from a porno kingpin out in Queens, New York. First I started doing the sets for his porno films in this film studio. They stopped making porno films with film — using regular film— and they started shooting them on video, so they were doing them one after the other. I somehow found myself working in this studio doing the sets and because of my appearance and my make-up and my demeanor they thought that I might be good playing a dominatrix in some fetish films.

And because they did these films so rapidly, there was never a script, but I was quite good at coming up with improvisational skits, so I got hired to be a fetish film star. I had as much interest in doing those films as I as I probably would have had doing another kind of day job. I made up skits like "The Sadistic Hair Salon" where I was a sadistic hairdresser and I'd have to beat up all the guys. I didn't have a problem beating people up. I thought it was very humorous actually. It was more fun than a regular job, that's for sure.

I made like 50 fetish films and got to go to the porno awards ceremony that they have in Las Vegas. Suddenly I found myself in the midst of all these famous porno stars. I was like the 105lb, emaciated wreck from New York who had, by accident, landed herself a table signing autographs at the adult film convention.

The Wall of Vagina at Disinfo.Con

(Opposite page) Photo: Bruce LaBruce

And from making those connections with those fetish film people, I was able to make some of my own films. I started to write and direct my own art films, I suppose you could call them, but they were made under the auspices of pornography. The content would be "The Voluptuous Horror of Karen Black" or images that were in my performance art but on the box covers they would be described as "hot thrilling girl-on-girl action," things like that, totally unrelated to the actual descriptions of my films. I made *Punk Ladies of Wrestling* or P.L.O.W., which is my wrestling federation. My specialty as a dominatrix in the fetish films was always wrestling and my tactic was the surprise element. I would just take a running jump and throw myself on these poor unsuspecting people!

I was a terrible fetish film star in that I made a lot of boo-boos. I made errors, breaking the rules of Sado-Masochism, which is a very conventional paradigm: the red, the black, a type of heel, the whole vocabulary of S/M, I strayed from.

The film work enabled me to continue with "The Voluptuous Horror of Karen Black"

because essentially we were unsupported by the music industry the entire length of our career. Doing the fetish films sponsored ten tours across the United States.

RM: Take me through the history of "The Voluptuous Horror of Karen Black."

KP: "Karen Black" started around 1990 and basically what we wanted to do was score our own performances and our own films, so we decided that we were going to play rock and roll music. We got a band together and started rehearsing every day. Samoa played guitar. I was writing the lyrics and I began singing, which was something I had never done in my films and performances. I was always afraid of the microphone. I was afraid to sing. But around 1990, I had a near death accident where I was savagely beaten up on the Lower East Side. I was taken to this abandoned building down by the FDR Drive. I woke up from this and I found myself recuperating in bed, in this very apartment. I was like a zombie lying in bed and *Trilogy of Terror* came on, the movie with Karen Black in three different stories, and it got me into such a great mood for some reason. I had been so scared to death during this attack that when I recovered from it somehow I had like… you know you've heard people say they've "found their voice" or something? It sounds very cheesy but it's true.

So we decided to combine all of the things that we'd been working on visually with our performance art history and with the costumes that I'd been wearing all of my life since a child and everything sort of merged. We felt like we'd spent

ten years doing these strange performances to a very esoteric group of people and we really wanted to make an act that we could take on the road and tour around with.

I went to a classical Chinese opera vocal coach but other than that I didn't really have any vocal training. Being scared to death by this brutal mugging was enough vocal training and I also liked the way my natural voice —or I should say my "anti-natural" voice— sounded. So we started to write songs and each song had a little prop and it had a costume and it had a storyline in it, not unlike the performances that we'd done in the 80's. Everything had a very specific intention. The

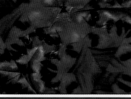

colors were thought out. The props that we used signified something that we were talking about. Even though I'm an Availabist —I make the best use of what's available— there wasn't any randomness, like in a successful magick spell you have specific ingredients that you use to make your point and to make something beautiful.

I always resented that with theatrical rock, everyone would say, "Oh, well what are you going to do? Are you going to swing a dead chicken around? Are you going to swing a rubber chicken?" or "Is there going to be blood," or whatever. There was such a large vocabulary of theatrical rock things that you could do; in "Karen Black" I wanted to stay away from that completely. We wanted to do what we had not seen before.

That was my primary motivation. I wanted to do something that I hadn't seen.

Ferrum 5000. Director, Steve Doughton

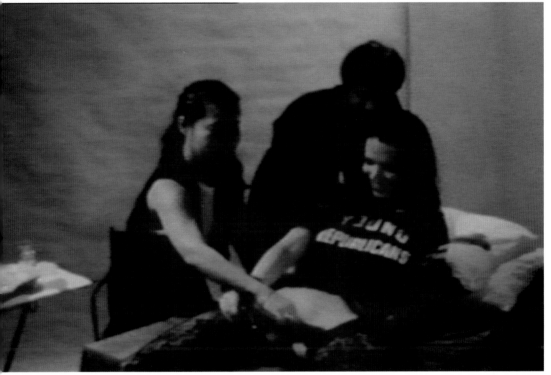

wing Circle. Director, Richard Kern

EWING CIRCLE

: I made the movie called *Sewing Circle* at a time when I was experiencing a lot of body shame and I s experiencing in my growth as a human being a lot of controversy with other people's feelings about, e, owning my very own body. Like sometimes in love, or something like this, people think that that they 'n you, that they own your body if they love you. At the time I started doing a lot of extreme body stuff d it was ruining a lot of my personal relationships because everyone was getting so angry with me for e appearing topless in "Karen Black" or exhibiting myself in an extreme fashion and I was so angry about e unacceptance of the loved ones around me that I decided to reclaim my very own body and I sewed ' vagina shut.

the other side of that coin I simply thought that it would look good, which is also basically the sole otivation for why I do things in general. I always thought that to be naked covered in body paint was mething that looked very nice.

' mother got very angry with me and she asked me why I sewed my vagina shut and I was trying to agine what it was like for a mother to have a daughter who does such extreme things to themselves, d I just told my mother that I was very *upset*.

KEMBRA PFAHLER

_CALVIN KLEIN

KP: I was in the Calvin Klein campaign that was called "Heroin Chic" in the press and I thought that was quite funny because basically none of us who were in it were on drugs at all. Well, most of us weren't. (Thinks) *Well I wasn't anyways.* I just happened to be an emaciated wreck.

I got to be on the side of a bus in New York City which I thought was very was ironic because I was always the person for years who people threw rocks at in the neighborhood, who no one would want to get near and all of a sudden I was a high fashion model.

RM: Is it true that the dope dealers on your block named a brand of heroin after you?

KP: Mmm hmm. Yes. Yes, that's true, but it was before that. They named a brand of heroin "Kembra." They did. They did actually, yeah. In the early 80's they named a brand of heroin "Kembra" which I thought was very funny because I used to hear outside of my window, "Kembra's open! Kembra's open!" and that would signify that they were ready to sell the drug, so that was kind of nice.

RM: Quite a compliment!

For information on obtaining the artwork of Kembra Pfahler, contact American Fine Arts Company/Colin De Land Fine Art, 530 West 22nd Street, New York, NY 10011. Phone: +1 212 727 7366

For more information about "The Voluptuous Horror of Karen Black," see www.karenblack.com

JOE COLEMAN

When we were putting together the portrait of Joe Coleman for the *Disinformation* television series, we were trying to figure out what we were going to do when producer Brad Novicoff hit on the winning formula: "Introduce the audience to Joe, the themes of his paintings, how intense his technique is, the serial killer fascination, his collection of weird stuff —it's all very macabre— *and then* once the audience thinks they know him as this "dark" character, we introduce Whitney, show the flip side of him and his happy home life and marriage."

It was a great idea and I think it worked in the show because it both taps into the "real" Joe Coleman and illustrates his fixation on duality in nature as well. You might *think* he's one thing, but he's really not. I'll let Joe explain duality in the interview, but here are a few observations I have on the man and his public persona.

Perception: Joe Coleman is a "dark" person.

Reality: *Joe Coleman is anything but a "dark" person*.

Would you consider Gomez Addams to be "dark"? Of course not, *that's just the way he is*. BINGO, that's Joe. He may share his domicile with two-headed monkeys, wax figures of serial killers and a baby in jar, but he is not, I repeat, *not* a "dark" guy, contrary to all expectations. He is fascinated with dark things and he may project the image of a Celine-esque[20] misanthrope glowering in his evil chambers as he paints his masterpieces, and I also think Joe would like for nothing more than to have a hunchbacked manservant named "Igor" answering the door when those foolish enough to knock do so. I think that would amuse him to no end, but Joe's not "dark;" again with the Gomez Addams comparison, it's just the way he is.[21]

He's also hilariously funny, warm, witty, well read, thoughtful, a true friend, knowledgeable on a wide, wide, variety of arcane subjects, as friendly as friendly can be, a raconteur's raconteur and when Joe takes someone on a tour of *The Odditorium*, his mind-boggling collection of *really weird shit*, they get a performance in the classic "Step right up, hurry, hurry! Gen-you-wine Fiji Mermaids!" style from a *master* showman who as a kid grew up inundated by P.T. Barnum lore and all manner of freak show and carny life near Barnum's hometown of Bridgeport, Connecticut.

He knows *very well* how to create myth and encourage public fascination with his exploits. Look at the historical figures he paints: John Dillinger, Nero, John Brown, Manson —all people who had their own particular impact on society— he's studied the best. Few people have stories funnier than Joe's, and his stories are in such demand ("Tell that story about…") that Coleman has honed them into "routines" that Henny Youngman would envy.

And of course, he is one of our very finest painters, internationally feted and recognized by the best museums and most discriminating collectors as a modern master in the tradition of Bosch and Breughel, whose work Joe's own paintings have been exhibited with. His paintings contain the same minute level of detail (Joe often paints the smallest details with a single horsehair brush!) and the comparison is absolutely warranted. He's *that* good.

Joe Coleman is quite a character, *but he's not "dark."*

The Odditorium has to be the best collection of its type in the world. Everything from serial killer art (several John Wayne Gacy paintings —including a portrait of Joe and a creepily phallic rendition of the Seven Dwarves— and an "Audubon Society" looking bird oil (quite good!) from nurse killer Richard Speck) to a bejeweled reliquary that is supposed to contain a piece of Christ's bone marrow to mummified saints exist side by side in Joe's cramped Brooklyn apartment. As Joe says, "It's almost as if these things want to be here. It's like they heard, "There's a party at Joe's" and they want to be here because they know they'll be respected."[22]

Every Gomez must have his Morticia and Coleman's found his in *va-va-voomish* photographer Whitney Ward. Recall how perfectly suited for each other Gomez and Morticia are, how romantic they are: "Cara Mia!" *THAT's* Joe and Whitney. Like Dali and Gala, they are total counterparts of each other.

Absolutely complementary beings. Their union is nothing short of *alchemical* and it is a wonder to behold them together. Never have you seen two people having this much fun with each other! Whitney and Joe exist on such a specif-ic mutual frequency that it's impossible for anyone who knows them to think of them as anything other than as a single unit. They're one of the all time great couples. Think Ozzie and Harriett meet Ozzy and Sharon and you'll get the pic-ture: they give the notion of *American Gothic* a new twist, these lovey dovey sweethearts cooing at each other like Ronnie and Nancy *from Hell*.

Their wedding, held at the American Visionary Arts Museum (AVAM) in Baltimore, Maryland on 11/11/00, was the wedding of the century. Joe was delivered in a hearse and popped out of a casket. Trapeze artists swung from the ceiling and midgets carried the bridal train. Whitney looked like Jayne Mansfield wearing an emerald wedding dress embroidered with real human hair. The service was per-formed by a ventriloquist dummy worked by an ordained priest from the Church of Satan. Women dressed as mermaids, tattooed biker types and I all wept tears of joy.

Consider for a moment how cool it is that such things can happen in this world.[23]

Who would have thought that Joe Coleman, the guy who used to bite the heads off mice and blow himself up at *other people's* high school reunions with hun-dred of dollars of Class "C" fireworks strapped to his chest and who is fascinat-ed by murders, disease, freaks and all things morbid, would turn out to be one of the most *romantic* guys on the planet?

But that's just Joe. He's a walking contradiction.

You see he was born that way…

RM: Joe, tell me about your childhood.

JC: Where do you start with childhood? I was born on November 22, 1955, so that's 11/22/55: it's all double num-bers. I grew up in a house that was across the street from the cemetery that was at number 99 Ward Street and Whitney's last name is "Ward." So all of those things have significance to me, because I think your destiny is already preordained when you're born. You're born into a *calling*. So it was already set for me, and just the fact that I was put across the street from a cemetery was mean-ingful. The date 11/22/55 was

meaningful and inspired anything from my obsession with two-headed animals to my obsession with the duality of nature and the fact that everything has two sides. These are recurrent themes. I was born into this; this is not something that I would *choose* intellectually to be interested in. I was born into it.

RM: Were you a frightened child with monsters under the bed?

JC: Yeah, I was the kid who was scared of everything, and that's actually what is the inspiration for my work, *fear* and *the conquering of fear*. I was obsessed

[20] Louis Ferdinand Céline, (1894 – 1961), French writer and doctor, wrote *Journey to the End of the Night* and *Death on the Installment Plan*.

[21] This was not always true, but as long as I've known him, and I met Joe and Whitney at the same time, he's been the happiest guy alive. Still, for some reason people are terrified of him.

[22] There is no damned comfortable place to sit at their apartment. There might be, but a wax replica of O.J. Simpson refuses to give up his seat…

[23] And consider the example of Harry Harlow's monkeys that Howard Bloom discussed in Chapter Two!

JOE COLEMAN

with the cemetery. I couldn't get it out of mind. If a fear sets in, it's like the needle on a record getting stuck and repeating and I started to become obsessed with the cemetery. First, I climbed over the stone wall. I put my foot on the other side and that was a big deal. The next day I put the other foot over; eventually I put my whole body over. As you attempt to deal with fear, as it progresses, you start to get pleasure out of it because when you're in that heightened sense of dread, some kind of primordial *scariness* causes your heart to pound faster or you start sweating and it's an intense, visceral sensation, so you kind of get to like it.

RM: It's that adrenalin rush.

JC: The first time you drink, sometimes you don't really like it, but after you keep doing it for a while, you start to develop a taste for it. The same thing happens with fear, you start to develop a taste for fear so then you need a little stronger kick to get off on the fear, and it progresses from there. It doesn't start from someone who's well adjusted and doesn't fear anything. Someone like that would never get obsessed with the kind of things that I get obsessed with.

RM: So you're saying you were *not* a very well adjusted child?

JC: No, but I think the thing that defines what your humanity is, is your *pathology*. What I mean by that is, it's what makes you unique. It's what gives you your fingerprint, your mark in the world. Even if you associate it with music or art, and say somebody's a fairly good draftsman, but for some reason this particular person has difficulty with hands, whenever this person attempts to draw hands they just don't quite look right, but they are otherwise a very good draftsman. In their weakness, they make hands uniquely to them that are the way that they draw hands, that are unlike anyone else's hands. That's what creates style, so style

Richard, Joe and the remains of St. Agnes.

is born from pathology, from a defect and that's also what creates the individual and what makes somebody unique. Even the so-called average person is really defined by their defects, because if you look at an anatomy chart and the teacher says, "Here's a normal human body," they're lying to you, because a normal human body would have some sort of defect. It could be minor, but there would be some little things in that body that would be slightly off and that would make it normal. What they're showing you is an abnormal body, and they're telling you it's normal.

RM: You would not exactly have to be Sigmund Freud to look at your paintings and figure that you have an Oedipus complex. What was your relationship like with your mother?

JC: Well my mother and I had a very complex relationship. I'd consider it very loving. My mother and I had a sexual relationship that did not culminate in fucking, but we did sexual things and it was because of certain things that my mother wasn't getting at home and that she needed for her own pathology.

Of union with the mother. That's this incredible taboo being violated.

RM: Well then! What was your relationship like with your father?

JC: The sole and only positive sides of my father were that he was *really scary* and he fought in Iwo Jima and Guadalcanal.

He had this stash, it was a hole in the wall, essentially, with a little door on it and a lock. It was his stash and I always wanted to break in there. I was fascinated by this door and had to open that door. I got the serial number on the lock and brought it to a locksmith and tried to get a key, but then the key wouldn't fit in, so then I figured I'd unscrew the whole thing, took it all apart and laid all the pieces down so that I could put it all back together, when I'm through. Then I opened the door and there's like *Climax* magazine and this is, you know, the early 60's and it was unusual to see pussy and so this was really shocking. I'm going through all this stuff in there and I'm lifting up a bunch of these amazing porno magazines and underneath them were these pictures of my father holding decapitated Japanese heads taken either in Iwo Jima or Guadalcanal and I was like, "Holy shit!" That was both frightening and exhilarating at the same time and just really a strange, strange experience.

RM: It's odd that he would keep his photographs of himself with his *hunting trophies* with this stash of porn magazines...

JC: Yeah, somehow that was this kind of taboo threshold as well.

RM: Did he ever figure out that you had gotten into that stash?

JC: Yeah, he figured it out because I broke the key that I had made in the lock, but what was stranger was the fact that he didn't say anything. If he had confronted me about it then he would have had to deal with the fact that I saw it. So instead it was even weirder, the lock was changed and nothing was said.

RM: Why did you start painting?

JC: I don't know exactly why but I always felt driven to reorder the universe and kind of put it under my control. The first time that I remember ever doing any kind of artwork was in Saint Mary's church that my mother brought me to all the time, even though she had been excommunicated, which I thought was weird. They wouldn't let her take Holy Communion because she had remarried and my father had been excommunicated and all this crazy Catholic stuff, but I would sit in the church listening to the mass being spoken in Latin, so it's all very mysterious and fascinating to me. Everybody's talking in this strange language, they're in strange robes and there's this figure of a guy nailed to a cross, bleeding, that's at the center of the room. And there were these relief sculptures around the church of the Stations of the Cross, which is Christ being brought before Pilot and Pilot doesn't want to judge him and he lets the Pharisees decide his fate, and he gets whipped, crowned with thorns, and nailed to a cross and then comes back from the dead. That's fascinating stuff.

I copied the images with a pencil and then colored the blood in with a red crayon and that was some of the first art that I ever did.

RM: It's wild that your subject matter was starting to manifest itself even at eight years of age.

JC: I consider myself very much a Catholic. I don't believe in God, but I'm a Catholic and that's not going to make sense, but the ritual and the drama and the theater of Catholicism and its iconography are so much a part of my work that I can't escape from it. I can't not be a Catholic. It's easy to not believe in God, but it's not easy to not be a Catholic. Its images are the most powerful for me and they're so rich and I can see them everywhere. I see a sideshow presenting the mummified body of John Wilkes Booth as really no different than Saint Agnes the martyred saint's body being in a church in Venice. To me they're interchangeable and it's also not that much different than a pathology museum housing a 200lb colon, like the one that's in the Mutter Museum, and the reason why is because religion has nothing to do with morality. Religion is a house of awe and mystery about life. To me, a strip club with naked girls giving guys lap dances, that's a house of religion. Those are the real churches, because that's where the real awe and mystery of life is. That's where it exists. That's true religion. True religion is not telling you how to live your life. True religion is not about saying there are a certain amount of commandments and you have to live by these commandments. That's about so-called civilization but that's not religion.

RM: You've always been fascinated with serial killers. Why are these avatars of nihilism in your personal pantheon?

JC: Well, serial killers are very much saints for our culture and this starts because we reject dark gods

JOE COLEMAN

and there's still a need for them to manifest themselves. I'm creating my pantheon in the same way that in Tibetan culture they'll have Kali or Shiva or Hari Hara and there's room for all these different gods that inhabit parts of what it means to be human, but that are rejected by the mainstream religions.

And that's a real psychopathic society. Ed Gein or Karl Panzram or Charlie Manson only represent the culture that they're in, I mean they define it. The culture gets the criminals that it deserves, so they are really *your* mirror. In a society where everything is turned upside down then of course the psychopath is a god.

RM: Well, they set the outward boundaries. Do you see nature demanding serial killers?

JC: Well yeah, they're demanded by nature, but serial killers are more like a Greek chorus because they don't tend to have a grand effect on the planet. A serial killer is not going to cull the herd to any degree that's going to matter. They're more like the Greek chorus, giving a way for the rest of the world to channel their fears into these beings...

RM: Boogey men?

JC: Yes, but real evil comes from a guy that's sitting behind a desk and clipping his nails in some corporation, or a political figure who never gets his hands dirty but he signs papers and millions of people are in misery and the environment is compromised constantly. That's real evil. The real evil is not a serial killer; a serial killer is more like the shaman who is doing these little acts so that everyone can put all their fears on him and live through it through them because it's in everybody.

There needs to be a spokesman of the dark side because the dark side has a value. Psychiatry tries to tell you that the dark side is something that has to be healed, but what if the dark side is *not* something that has to be healed? What if the dark side is something that has a function? What if the dark side is part of the balance of nature? Are you going to try to heal a tornado, are you going to try to heal a flood? It's not like there was anything wrong with those things, but we as so-called civilization think that we're better than nature and that we have to do these things in order to protect us, you know, and think we're so strong that we're above nature.

But nature is always going to figure out a way to still stay on top. One day you've discovered antibiotics and you've discovered this great thing, but all of a sudden all these people that should have been dead are still alive and then you're causing this thing that you had destroyed to become stronger because it starts to develop a tolerance to your antibiotics and becomes even more powerful than when you started because nature is going to keep upping it.

RM: I recall you telling me that you tried to put some trace elements of carcinogenic substances in your body on a daily basis.

JC: Yeah, I was doing that because I thought that the structure of the future had to do largely with carcinogens and that the only way to survive in the future was to expose your body to a certain amount of carcinogens so that you would develop a tolerance to it, because that's really the way to survive. You don't do it in an extreme way that you're going to shock your body; you do it in low levels.

There's an old fairy tale about a king who as a child was told by some fortune teller that he was going to die from his subjects poisoning him, so he would take a little bit of poison every day in order to develop a tolerance. When they actually did attempt to poison him, it didn't hurt him because he had slowly developed a tolerance for it, and it's the same thing with this environment. If you're on a macrobiotic diet or even a vegetarian, to me, I think you're in *more danger* of dying. You have to make friends with the enemy. You have to digest a certain amount of the dark side in order to survive.

_A Roadmap of the Life of John Dillinger

At this point we moved into Joe's studio to see his stunning portrait of legendary gangster, John Dillinger. It's dazzling, truly one of his best.

JC: This is my folk ballad of John Dillinger. I collect folk ballads of famous criminals like Carl Younger

JOE COLEMAN

and the Hatfields and the McCoys and different anti-hero outlaws from the turn of the 19th Century. And Dillinger, he's pretty much the embodiment of that type, and the last from that period of history who connects to Jeffrey Dahmer and Charles Manson.

The reason why Dillinger connects to them is because Dillinger, unlike somebody like Al Capone... If you talk about gangsters, they always bring up Dillinger or they bring up Capone, but Al Capone was essentially *a businessman*, and he wanted to be part of society. That was his desire and he reflected the same business policies that politicians are involved in. But Dillinger was more of a prankster. He was more of a *Trickster God*. He was more into creating chaos wherever he went and that's why he was important to me.

And Dillinger connected to Jesse James... Jim Younger... Bonnie Parker... Bill Doolin and Ned Kelly, they're on the frame here because they were these anti-heroes in the 1800's that pretty much embodied something that the lower classes desired to do, which was to take what they felt they were entitled to, because like the rich, you know, the privileged class, they got everything. They got the best cars, the best houses, the best women, the best drugs, the best booze and the best food. Why shouldn't they have it, too?

The only difference is *the will*. Maybe *the will to power* is actually the thing that's going to get you what you want. Somebody like Jesse James, under William Clark Quantrill's tutelage, learned that you can take what wasn't given to you and that you can *force people* to give you what you feel that you deserve. Dillinger was the last of those kinds of bandits and Dillinger had an incredible history. He almost lived like a great Greek tragedy life, like Ulysses. He did these amazing

Dillinger's gun gets a blowjob.

things throughout his career. One of his most famous exploits was when he broke out of Crown Point prison. He carved a gun out of a bucket. It was a phony gun, it wasn't a real gun, but he carved the wood of a bucket to look like a gun and then he painted it with shoe polish and broke out of Crown Point prison with this phony gun. He grabbed two machine guns and made his getaway in the sheriff's car.

So the grandiosity of it, the mythic quality of it, makes it even more important and if you look really closely there's already the feint of death because "He that liveth by the sword, shall die by the sword," and if you put on the goggles, his end has already been written, and also his desires. If you look closely at his gun you'll see his fake wooden gun is getting a blowjob. And if you look over here he's being dragged down into Hell.

Joe puts the jeweler's goggles he paints with on my head and yanks my nose mere inches away from an area of the canvas measuring about 2" x 3", where you see a finely detailed painting within the painting showing Dillinger mid-jailbreak. But what you don't see, indeed what you cannot see, sans goggles, is the gun getting the blowjob, as it is a detail that is, well, bigger than a speck but not much more so. There, in the texture of the jail cell wall, a ghostly woman sucks off the gun. Faintly there nearby, Dillinger's soul gets dragged to eternal damnation. I've been following Joe's work since the mid-80's, but when it finally dawned on me the maniacal level of attention to detail that he'd devoted to every square inch of this canvas, bursting as it is with details of a complicated biography, a psychedelic snowflake of pure information, I was truly and utterly flabbergasted. Every detail's detail in turn had its own details. And so on, until it got really tiny!

RM: Wow! How do you hold your hand that still? My God!

Public Enemy Number One, 1999
36" x 30"

JOE COLEMAN

Coal Man, 1998
22" x 28"

JC: It happens slowly, it doesn't happen overnight.

RM: (Still looking) Joe, there is no way that someone looking at this painting reproduced in a book is ever going to see this level of detail. Does that bother you?

JC: No. They're not going to see it, but that's not important to me because I'm doing it for *me*. I'm not doing it for them. I've had collectors that have had paintings for years and all of a sudden one day I'll get a call and they'll say, "Joe, I just discovered this thing I never saw in the painting. I've been looking at it every day and blah, blah, blah" and that's kind of like fun for me, to hear it, because it's all there if you're willing to look. I'm only giving you hints on how to look.

You start from the outside and you keep going in. We start from a folk song that was written about Dillinger a year after he was killed in front of the Biograph Theater. You can actually play this music. These are the actual, you know, notes…

RM: You found the sheet music for this?

JC: Yeah, it's out here on the borders and all the lyrics are there. Then as you get closer, you start to get the story of his life, but it's not in chronological order. It's not like you go from the left or the right. You can start anywhere, at the end of his life or the beginning or the middle. The more that you put into it the more that you're going to get out of it, the same way that I do when I'm making the painting.

Because as I'm working, painting and doing the research, I just keep getting more and more information and as it's being filtered through me, it blasts out into the painting, and then it reveals these weird things. Like I had no idea that the composition was going to be this kind of light on the top of a police car, where you already have the mug shot idea that I'd been working on that was revealed to me towards the end of the painting because I worked from the outside in. But then I realized that it's just like the top of a police car that has those red and blue lights that are spinning around. These spotlights are shooting out and lighting all the events that were important to his life.

When I'm finished with a painting, after I've put all these details together, there's a whole and that whole creates a pattern and the pattern was always there. That pattern I'm just uncovering like an archeological dig. I've just shown you where it was but it's always been there. The pattern was always there.

RM: How do you do your research?

JC: I research them in many different ways, anything from going to arcane libraries, bookstores, going to the New York Public Library and digging up old newspapers to find accounts of the events of that particular day. Obscure books on the subject. Often I have a certain amount of the books when I start the painting and then I'll look for more stuff once I begin the intense research.
But then when I'm painting actual characters, even if it's not the main character, I'm playing the parts of all the characters like an actor on a set, whether it's male or female, young or old, I'm playing all the characters. When I'm painting some figure my face turns into their face and I'm them as I'm painting them and they're living through me and being recreated.

The best composition comes from the faith that it's all going to work. And so the only thing that I have to deal with is the detail. I concern myself with nothing else, then I add detail upon detail upon detail upon detail upon detail upon detail upon detail upon detail until the whole image, the whole surface of the wood is covered. Then I paint the frame. It tells me, "This is the composition." I don't tell it what the composition is, it tells me. The only thing that I'm con-

JOE COLEMAN

cerned about is the detail. Because the detail leads me to the soul.

RM: The surface of this painting is almost like glass.

JC: It's like a jewel. That's the way that I look at it, because it's like carving a jewel, the surface of a jewel with his life. The anecdotes, things that he said, things that were said about him are what make up a life.

RM: Here's one of the more famous details, of course, *his schlong*.

JC: (Laughs) Well, yeah, that's his dick. That was the legend of Dillinger's dick. And I know the person that actually owns his dick.

RM: I thought it was in the Smithsonian Institute?

JC: Right. Well there's been a whole mythology that's built up around his dick, which is one of the inspirations for the painting in the first place. Most Americans assume that Dillinger's dick is on display at the Smithsonian Institute, which is not true, but most people believe that to this day.

RM: Where is it?

JC: It's in a private collection and this is actually what it looks like. How it became a part of a private collection was because a midget show promoter paid Dillinger's father, who became famous for doing lectures about his famous outlaw son, who sold the entire body to this midget show promoter, to do like a traveling sideshow of the mummified body of John Dillinger. Kind of like the John Wilkes Booth body. But at the last minute the old man reneged on the deal, and the guy said, "Well look, I paid you all this money, you gotta give me *something*." So he got *his dick*. (Both burst out laughing).

RM: *The father castrated the son? Yikes!*

JC: Yeah that's right. Oedipal in reverse. And that's exactly what it looks like, but I can't reveal the source that has that penis, but that is based on what it actually looks like.

RM: Oh, so this is not a fanciful representation of the penis...

JC: Nope, that's what it actually looks like. And he had such great lines like, "I'm not like some bank robbers, I didn't get elected president of the bank first!"

RM: First I was going to call him the John Holmes of bank robbers, but perhaps Milton Berle is a better comparison.

JC: Well, yeah that could be, but also there was the whole media obsession with Dillinger at the time. It was kind of like what we had with O.J. Simpson or other recent crimes. Everyone was obsessed with what Dillinger was going to do next, but he was actually a hero. They were rooting for him, because he represented the desires of the general public at that particular time. He stole from the banks that were foreclosing on people's houses and took their farms. That no longer works for our period because in our time he's kind of like a Robin Hood and he looks quaint and folksy, but the Mansons and the Dahmers represent like a new kind of anti-hero, which he kind of gave birth to.

He's the father of Charles Manson, so I wanted to bring it back to the father of who I had painted before, because I had painted Manson. Manson embodies a new mythology that can work for our culture, because our culture no longer cares about the Robin Hood because the lower class or the people that supposedly have nothing can eat meat three times a day. They can pull up to a fucking McDonald's, you know, and they have TV sets, they have stereos, they have CD players, they have computers, even the poor among us have all these privileges, but they still have all this resentment and anger inside of themselves and what do they resent? *Dillinger just represented the resentment*. Just the resentment itself, so if you bring it into Manson or Dahmer you see that the resentment really has to do with the fact that that they resent being born. And they want revenge, *just for being born*.

an Venus, 1997
22"

Lovesong, 1998
28" x 30"

_Addams Family Values

RM: How did how did the two of you meet?

Whitney Ward: We met at *Joe's Psychedelic Solution* show. This good friend of ours who's a medical examiner introduced us at the opening.

JC: Then I invited her to this birthday party...

WW: *Yeah, right*. You asked, "Would you like to come see the documentary that was made about me?"[24] (Laughs).

JC: The way that I finally got her was that I said, "I got a new jar of tumors that I thought you might like to see."

WW: Yeah, "Would you like to come over to The Odditorium and see my new jar of tumors?" (Laughs).

RM: Is that's your version of "Would you like to come upstairs to see my bullfight posters"?

JC: No, that's *their* version of "Come upstairs and see my jar of tumors"!

WW: The fine art of wooing.

RM: Tell me about *Love Song*.

JC: It's called *Love Song* because that's what it is. It's a love song in paint. It's kind of like a ballad, so it has a whole narrative. It has our first date, in this bar, and we were sucking on each other's fingers. That was one of the first images that appeared in the painting. It has her favorite cameras and people she knows. It has the people who *brought her to me*, like her father's the dentist in the painting. He's working on this woman's mouth and teeth are flying all over and blood is splattering all over the place, and around the image of her father it says, "The nut never falls very far from the tree does it, Dad?"

WW: And when my dad first met you and he said, "Oh my God, I didn't know there were *two of you* in the world."

JC: Yeah! There are many elements that make up *Love*, you know, and some of them are words, some of them are images and some of them are *objects*.

WW: We'd just gone to Venice and he was inspired by all the beautiful religious reliquaries and he bought these watch crystals and inside them he would mix... maybe his fingernails and my hair with some blood and spit and then put in pieces of our clothing and whatnot and made these really precious little reliquaries that are in each corner of the frame.

RM: So there's a magical element to it?

WW: Uh huh, so we were the only people who could logically own the painting, which is why we now have it and not a collector. That was my final argument: *nobody else can have this painting because it has our blood on it*.

RM: Whitney, is there a disconnect between the public persona of the legendary misanthrope Joe Coleman and the man at home?

WW: The Joe Coleman who blows himself up at high school reunions and things like that? Yeah... (thinks) I mean I don't let him explode in the house, but that's the only difference.

[24]*Rest in Pieces*, Robert Pejo, director, 1997

JOE COLEMAN

Joe, Whitney and Junior

_A Nuclear Family

JC: Junior is my adopted son, and the experience of getting Junior was...

WW: The proudest day of your life...

JC: It was a very proud day. I was in Coney Island and I was walking past a sideshow. All of a sudden I heard somewhere in the background, (shouts) "Hey Joe!" And I just figured, well there's probably 5,000 people named Joe in Coney Island so I just kept walking. Then I hear, "Hey Joe Coleman!" "What?" So I turn around and I see this character by one of the banners going, "Hey Joe, you wanna buy a pickled punk?" I was like, "What?" So I walk over to the guy. I knew what a pickled punk was because that's old carny slang for a baby in a jar. Usually deformed. It sounded really interesting. So he brings me behind the canvas banner and brings me to this little trailer. He goes behind a curtain and pulls out this little darlin'. And immediately, I fell in love with him and I just gave him what he asked for and took little Junior home on the subway.

RM: You really are like the Addams Family!

JC: And baby makes three!

Leonardo DiCaprio and Junior

Book of Revelations, 2000
28" x 30"

JOE COLEMAN

97

GRANT MORRISON

When Grant Morrison took the stage at the Disinfo.Con event, even though it was only 4:30 in the afternoon when the lights went down, it could've been midnight inside the Hammerstein Ballroom.

Grant's drunken but enthralling speech began with a scream, a slosh of his beer as he climbed the podium and an admission that he'd just taken drugs and would be flying high by the half hour mark —"So watch for it!" It was pure punk rock theatrics filled with sublime moments —such as Morrison explaining how to work magick spells to all assembled!— and it was certainly one of the event's highlights. The guy was on fire and he looked spectacularly cool up there in his black leather jacket, Donna Karan suit and his shiny, bald pate, just like a white "Shaft." From what I gather, many of the audience didn't know who Morrison was when they arrived, but after that bravura performance, they sure as hell knew who he was when they walked out![25]

God, where do you start when you're trying to describe *a character* like Grant Morrison? The most obvious place to start is that Morrison is Scottish. Make that *thickly* Scottish; born and bred in Glasgow with an accent so strong you'd think he was *French!*

He's also in a select group of contemporary writers who'd be on a Mount Rushmore of comics if such a thing were to exist, alongside Neil Gaiman, Frank Miller and Alan Moore, writers comics fans still *read* rather than just store in plastic bags.

His resume is pretty impressive. Here're just a few of his credits, taken from his website:[26]

> Grant Morrison has been highly regarded as one of the most original and inventive writers in the comics medium. His revisionist Batman 'graphic novel' *Arkham Asylum* was the highest-grossing hardback comic book ever, selling over 200,000 copies in its first three months of release and winning most of the industry's major awards. *St. Swithin's Day* —a story about a young man from the North attempting to assassinate Margaret Thatcher— had questions raised in the House of Commons, as did *The Invisibles*, Morrison's highly influential six-year long series about a group of anarchist terrorists. Credits also include the 'controversial' *The New Adventures Of Hitler*, *Big Dave*, *Doom Patrol*, *Animal Man* and *Kill Your Boyfriend*. He has helmed both Marvel's *X-Men* and D.C.'s *Justice League of America*, which he took from 20,000 sales to 125,000, making it D.C. Comics' biggest selling monthly title. He was the first comics writer to be included as one of *Entertainment Weekly's* top 100 creative people in America.

And he's the possessor of one of the finest imaginations on the planet, poised to take over Hollywood *any day now*.

I don't want to forget that bit.

I'm not really a comics reader and I haven't been since I was a kid. Although I did read *Arkham Asylum* when it came out because a roommate of mine had it and I did know who Grant Morrison was and I'd even liked the book, I was none too eager to start reading *The Invisibles*, a comics series that I knew would be serialized for six years, despite my old friend Jim Ferguson, a musician based in New York, pushing it on me *every* time I'd see him, usually adding *"I'm telling you, it's everything that you're obsessed with…"*

But six years? Come on, that's quite a commitment! He didn't give up though, and for that I am truly grateful. One afternoon Jim showed up with every issue of Volume I and the first two issues of Volume II. That evening I rolled a huge joint and read every single issue then available of *The Invisibles* in one sitting. The next day I did the same thing as soon as I woke up. He was right, it *did* contain most everything that I was obsessed by and I was immediately hooked. After that, for the next few years, I usually visited the comics store the day the new one came out. I'd rip it out of the bag and read it standing right on the street. When issues were late I suffered through withdrawal cramps and night sweats.

One of the fun things for me with *The Invisibles* was finding all of the obscure references within its pages. It was pretty obvious right off the bat that Grant and I must have extremely similar book and record collections, a point brought home when I read what he was listening to when he'd write the comic, as he'd often mention this in his letters column. When a story arc took *The Invisibles* back to the 1920's, the songs of Noel Coward would be playing in the background. This amused me due to the fact that I, too, had been listening to Noel Coward a lot at that time. On another occasion Grant wrote that he'd composed one issue whilst listening to Japan's top pop combo, Pizzicato Five, who are old friends of mine. I've directed a music video for them and my voice is even on one of their tracks, so in fact at one point or another my favorite comics writer was writing my favorite comic with my voice in the background. I thought that was pretty cool, too.[27]

[26] Worth mentioning is how many of my female friends (all of whom should have taken one look at him and known better) approached me that day with some variation on the theme of "Introduce me to that sexy Grant Morrison." I've seen this kind of thing at work in the animal kingdom in nature documentaries, with the females displaying themselves before the alpha male, but never in a human population. At least not like this!

[26] www.grantmorrison.com

That said, it seemed inevitable that Grant and my paths would eventually cross and that'd we'd probably get on quite well when they did. Of course this *is* what happened and we've become great friends over the years. I always look forward to meeting up with Grant and his better half, Kristan Anderson, when they're in New York or Los Angeles and I always have a great time with them, usually discussing frontal assaults on the entertainment industry over ethnic foods and copious amounts of marijuana. The following interview was conducted at the trendy Standard Hotel on LA's Sunset Strip over the course of two evenings.

RM: First off, what brings you to Los Angeles? What are you doing here?

GM: Well, basically the idea is to try and make some money (smiles evilly). This is the place where bullshit turns into money and that's an area of magick that's always interested me. The idea of just turning pure thought into pure cash, and this is the place where light becomes money. It's an interesting place, but LA's a virtual space. None of it connects. You know that, you're living here as well,

but it just doesn't add up. But it's interesting that way because it's odd and everything's fake. So I kind of like that and I want to get involved in it and see if I can profit from it (Laughs).

RM: What do you see as your relationship to what's being produced by the Hollywood culture machine?

GM: I think what's happening, in my terms anyway, is that the ideas that were once marginal and that once only I liked to play with, ten or 15 years ago in the comic books, have become the mainstream of culture and the life blood of the movies and the TV and the records and *everything that we watch and are listening to*. There's *Buffy* on the TV. We've got *The Matrix* in the cinema. Gnostic ideas are turning up everywhere. Ideas about the supernatural, the occult, the power of magick, the disintegration of reality are all coming from this place. They have all become mainstream and are fed back into our lives as "the spectacle" and it's the best spectacle we've ever had.

[27] I am the un-credited English speaking interviewer questioning Pizzicato Five lead singer Maki Nomia about her favorite perfume, make up and fashion designer on "This Year's Girl #5" a song on their *5x5* EP (Matador).

RM: Why do you think these marginal ideas have become mainstreamed?

GM: I think it has to happen, even in the sense that we've all grown up to a point where we can make it mainstream. And, that's exactly what we seem to be doing. We're selling weirdness back into the culture. The culture demands it.

GRANT MORRISON

The culture has come to us looking for ideas that have once been hidden under a mossy stone and ignored. Suddenly, things got boring. They ran out of heroic muscle men. They ran out of Rambos. They ran out of the entire Reagan/Thatcherite-driven philosophy that we were all going on.

And suddenly they've turned to the freaks and the weirdoes and the outcasts and the geeks and the Beatniks and the hippies and whoever's left to provide some infusion of interest into a flagging culture. And it seems to be working and the interesting thing is that it's bending *their* culture towards *our* culture to the point where the two things have become interchangeable and there's no difference between them.

RM: So you see a changing of the guard thing going on in the cultural machinery? There's obviously a certain pop culture dialectic that continually refreshes itself and when you note that it's people our age who are the new "commissar class," I guess that's what you mean... (laughs). Do you think it's a case of "Meet the new boss, same as the old boss" or are things different this time?

GM: I honestly believe that there's a lot more of a hierarchical caste system going on in this culture than we like to think. Like why are there always policemen? Why is there never a century where no policemen are born? (Laughs). We're always streaming people into these roles. Suddenly we're filling the roles that once Timothy Leary or William Burroughs filled. We get born and suddenly we're replacing those guys and we're looking over our shoulders at what the kids right behind us would do. So all we can ever hope to be is some cutting edge of oddball ideas that refresh the culture behind us, because we're always a little bit ahead of what's popular and what's fashionable.

And that's why it seems cool, because a little bit ahead is a little bit hard to understand. But ultimately it gets swept up. You know, *The Matrix* is mainstream. So those ideas, which to me were very unusual and abstruse back in 1984, are now part of the vocabulary of every kid that can afford to go and see a movie. But these things are multi-perspective. From our point of view, yeah, this is great: *we've taken over.* But if I were 15-years old, I'd turn on everything to do with the occult and the weird and the quirky and the individual. I'd piss on it, basically.

RM: Why do you think a 15-year old kid would look at what you and I are doing and see it as crap (Laughs)?

GM: Just because *that's what they're made for!* You know, I can elect to write for those kids because even though I'm hundreds of years older than them, I can remember that feeling of just being so angry with the way things were and having a better idea of how it should be. I want to hear how they trash me because I know I'll absorb it and reflect it back at them. I'm interested in that kind of reaction. I want to see what they'll do. That is the dialectic, they'll clash against whatever culture we're trying to sell them and create some new fabulous mutation which then we can steal from again and feed it back. And the whole thing is enriched. It's a process that we should encourage.

RM: If you were 15 today, what would you think is cool?

GM: If I was 15 today, I would just take a look, in the same way that the punks did. It's quite easy to be an adolescent rebel. You look at everything that your big brother or your mum and dad like and go in the complete opposite direction. I'm interested to see the complete opposite of what's going on now emerging and then trying to play with that. It's also what Aleister Crowley called *The Age of Horus.* What we're seeing is "kid" energy getting infused into our culture again. And it's wild and it's destructive and a lot of the old stuff's getting swept away. Which is great.

RM: I'm not so sure that I agree with you. I think that right now, especially in this country, we're being offered the blandest culture, at least in my lifetime, that has ever been foisted onto the public. Right now, we have all these damned teen pop acts and these interchangeable pretty people actors. Is it possible to come up with another iteration of these kinds of acts? To me, it's just one big, horrible, boring McDonald's blur.

And if you live in New York or London or if you live in Los Angeles, you know, the entertainment capitals, if there was something really good —if there were some really good band or something— you'd hear about it. And there's been precious little coming out of any of these cities for a *very long time* that I feel merits intelligent consideration.

GM: Well, it depends what you look for. I'd have to agree with you, as someone who grew up to punk rock, these acts are terrible. I mean, some of the worst shit that I've ever heard, but I think these things happen all the time. It's no different from the Pat Boones and the Bobby Vintons at the end of the 50's and the start of the 60's.

RM: *But there's no Elvis!* That's a significant thing to say, there's *no Elvis* today. Nobody who originates anything new or who is in any way a prime mover. Who's the new David Bowie? Where's the next Picasso or Warhol, for that matter? There are none in sight!

GM: Again, it depends on your perspective. McDonald's is as interesting to me now as Aleister Crowley once was because I've been reading their corporate manuals. The way they talk to the staff, the way they use NLP[28] and magical techniques and hypnotic techniques. That's where the interesting stuff is going on. All we need to find is a way to turn that shit into gold because there's no way we're ever getting the old stuff back. It's not going to happen ever again.

You know, I don't even want the Sex Pistols back because they're all old men. So we have to find a way to make black helicopters and Big Brother and all this horrible stuff *cool*. That's what creativity's about, it's turning shit into gold. Making it say something. So I think it's worth looking into those awful areas of corporate manuals and fast food drive-ins and bank tellers' lifestyles, to find some clue as to something new we can do; some new thing that we can make cool.

RM: Let's talk about *The Invisibles*. When you started writing the comic, you obviously had in mind a beginning, middle and end. Did the plot line that you originally envisioned change a lot over the years or did the comic end the way you thought it was going to end when you started it?

GM: Yeah. The actual last page, I always knew how it was going to end even though I didn't know what the sentence would be. But I knew what the last page was going to be. With *The Invisibles*, Volumes I and III were almost exactly as I had imagined them, but Volume II took on this bizarre life of its own. And also strangely enough that was the one that I think most people got involved in the series with, because the characters kind of came to life. In the story, there are moments where you see me as the author trying to wrest control back from the characters. In the end, I just had to let it go.

It became this dynamic thing. A lot of new ideas just kept coming in. For instance, I met a girl in New York who fancied herself as *Ragged Robin*. You know a lot of girls who read the book really identified with the female characters. She sent a picture of herself with the makeup and she'd written me and some of *The Invisibles* characters. So that kind of fed back into *The Invisibles* as the notion that *Ragged Robin* in the future could be writing the comic books. So some of the things in it were actually dynamically being written by the fans of the comic as it was being written by me. And I thought that was the most interesting part. The most occult part of the whole process was that second volume.

[28] From an NLP website: "The name Neuro-Linguistic Programming comes from the disciplines which influenced the early development of the field. It began as an exploration of the relationship between neurology, linguistics, and observable patterns ("programs") of behavior. NLP, as most people use the term today, is a set of models of how communication impacts and is impacted by subjective experience. It's more a collection of tools than any overarching theory. NLP is heavily pragmatic: if a tool works, it's included in the model, even if there's no theory to back it up. None of the current NLP developers have done research to "prove" their models correct. The party line is "pretend it works, try it, and notice the results you get. If you don't get the result you want, try something else."

RM: How did the concept for *The Invisibles* come about?

GM: Well, it probably had two starts. The first one all I wanted to do was a kind of William Burroughs version of Jack Kirby's *The Boy Commandos*, because I thought it was such a cool name and D.C. Comics owned the characters. *The Boy Commandos*. That sounds just like a Burroughs novel. It started out as this basic notion of psychic Boys Scouts and Baden-Powell[29] was even in it at one point. But I completely changed it and I decided well, this was so far from the original that why should D.C. own the title when I could just make something up? I went through *Brewer's Dictionary of Phrase and Fable* and found *The Invisibles*.

RM: Like the Rosicrucians?

GM: Pretty much any secret society in the 17th Century was known as "The Invisibles" so it was perfect. And it sounded like a 60's television spy show, which was perfect for the kind of idea that I was doing as well.

So, that was it, the first four issues I knew was going to be a boy's initiation through this occult secret society. Then when I was doing issue two, I went to Kathmandu and had basically an alien abduction experience. And that changed the entire series because what I then wanted to do was to make something that was *alive* rather than just tell a story. I wanted to do something that was an actual *spell* so that people who read it would be changed by it or would be led into situations whereby they might be changed. And also to simulate the experience that I had in Kathmandu, which I don't have any explanation for, ultimately.

When I was writing *The Invisibles* I went through every possible thing —I read Robert Anton Wilson, I read Philip K. Dick and everyone else who reported this type of unusual experience— and the parameters are all the same. All the nervous systems reported slightly differently and used their own sci-fi language or

[29] Sir Robert Baden-Powell, founder of the World Scout Movement, Chief Scout of the World.

[30] Grimoire: Medieval spell book.

Morrison at Disinfo.Con

theological language or mythological language depending on who they were, but ultimately these things are *the same*. It's like the classic shamanic process whereby you appear to be taken out of reality into a higher dimension. Your body is stripped and destroyed and then you're put back with extra knowledge, which then leads to weird synchronicities and unusual experiences that in my case began to proliferate as *The Invisibles* was being written.

I was living that comic as a diary as it was being written. The occult stuff in it and the martial arts, that's all *real* stuff that, as it was happening, it was going into the comic. So it's probably about 60% biography in there.

RM: What happened to you in Kathmandu?

GM: The short version is, simply, that I was sitting up on the roof garden in the Vajra Hotel and *this thing happened*, and it's hard to describe. We're getting into areas that are unusual. All I can remember is getting back downstairs and I lay in the bed and weird and unusual things happened and then it seemed that there were entities in the room. It was like those silver morphing blobs you see in rave videos. And it was like computer-generated things and they claimed to be cross sections of Fifth Dimensional entities as expressed through Fourth Dimensional space-time. And they claimed that I was one of them and that I had to come back and see what the old homestead was like.

And they took me out of my body and into what seemed to be the Fifth Dimension because I could see the entirety of space and time as an object. As a dynamic, living object, in which Shakespeare was over here, and I was over here and the dinosaurs were here, but were on the same object, and time was a *thing*. So, I appeared to be in a Fifth Dimensional fluid, an information space that I could say was maybe kind of bluish and extending out infinitely. These things swam through it and interacted with it. And they told me that what our universe was, was a larval form of what they are, which is Fifth Dimensional entities. And the only way to grow a Fifth Dimensional entity is to plant it in time, *hence, our universe.*

RM: Planted in time?

GM: Yeah, like we are a larva, a fetus. And they —this is shit that's pouring into my mind here, you have to remember— whether it's true or not is a matter of conjecture (laughs).

RM: Were you loaded when this happened?

GM: I was loaded for the entire week! (Laughs) But I'm familiar with drugs and I've had the full effects, and this was not that. This was like magick and I've done magick, and it's got nothing to do with drugs or anything like that, as you know. I've taken a lot of marijuana or whatever, and people assume that every experience that is mystical is some drug-addled hallucination, but as you know, most of the time when you're on drugs you *don't hallucinate*.

RM: It's hard to do, I agree. It almost never happens.

GM: Yeah, you are where you are. And this was not a hallucination. It was like no other drug effect. When I do magick without the use of drugs and I get these effects, you know, things appear as they're supposed to appear in the grimoires[30] or in Aleister Crowley's books. This experience had that same feeling and whether it was deluded or not, I could never get it back. If that experience exists then it can be repeated. So something happened personally and subjectively that was so powerful and so profane that the entire universe shook and I've been trying to understand it ever since.

It's hard to talk about. My current belief is that it's actually just a simple on/off in a structure in the brain, in the same way that when you're five-years old you can't see perspective but when you're seven-years old you can. And, I think this is something like that, but it expresses itself through what appears to be alien contact, contact with the fairies or contact with the devil or contact with something that is utterly alien. But it's not alien; it's just our own future potential.

RM: Well this is something people have looked to do for a very long time. It's the classic initiation experience.

GRANT MORRISON

GM: Yeah. I had the classic shamanic initiation experience. I *went* to Kathmandu with the hope that I might have a real shamanic experience and I got one exactly as I'd hoped. Something happened. Too many people have reported the exact same type of phenomenon, so something's going on. It feels like a download of information that I could easily turn into a cult religion if I felt like it because it's that interesting and the cosmology is quite convincing, you know.

RM: You could be the new L. Ron Hubbard if you wanted to be!

GM: (Laughs) It's all too easily done. I felt it was better to put it in the fictional form of a comic and dissect it that way. All I'm left with is an experience that I can say, "This happened." And I'm sure if you do shamanic techniques you will get a similar experience. Or if, you know, you try conjuring the devil or whatever, you will get a similar experience.

RM: Explain to me what happened. I want you to be a bit more specific. Describe it from start to finish if you will.

GM: It's a long story. It began with basically the appearance of these apparent *entities.* And I was in such a weird state that I thought, "Something's going on here." There was no control of what was happening. And, the first thing they were trying to say to me is "You must remember that you're like us. You're only here because you're playing inside this reality." Which, you know, is what *The Invisibles* became about.

RM: In other words, you had the right mental attitude for them to talk to you?

GM: I don't even know if it was that. I mean it happened to me, but ultimately everyone's involved in this. That's what they were telling me. Now the first thing they said —I kind of had an out of body experience— and they said, "Where do you want to go?" and I said, "Alpha Centauri" because that's the first thing that came into my head (laughs). And suddenly you've got all these Stargate special effects and yeah, it looked like a very convincing Alpha Centauri. And I'm like "Fine, okay" and I said, "Thanks" and "What's the deal?"

RM: I've had similar experiences when I've smoked DMT.[31] Let me guess, the next part is "Now we'll show you the *real* thing"!

GM: Yeah, "Now we're going to show you the **real** thing. Are you ready for this?" And that's when I felt that I'd been peeled off the surface of space and put into a Fifth Dimensional fluid that enclosed our entire universe from The Big Bang to The Big Crunch. And this fluid, they said to me, contained space-time but was beyond space-time. Space-time is included in it, but they weren't bound by space-time. Space-time is a constraint that they could create within a higher dimensional universe.

As I say, it was a Fifth Dimensional environment. And the creatures in it seemed to be holographic. They were blobs but it's hard to describe this because you're crunching back down into Third Dimensional language. I'd equate it with something like the Aboriginal "dreamtime." Those people are very sophisticated, a 40,000 year old culture. They talk about a dreamtime, which is a space where stories continually happen. And it seemed to be that experience. And like I said, the universe behind me was one single object where time was a *thing* that was *like a landscape* rather than what we think it is. You see, we move through time. You know you lived in 1970, so where the hell is 1970? Why can't we point to 1970? From the Fifth Dimensional perspective we *can* point to 1970 and that's the difference.

A human being has been processed through time. We come out of our mothers' wombs as babies. You were a baby, I was a baby, we were all babies, and we were all 12 at one point. All of us that got to an age beyond 12, that is. And yet where is it? Those things are behind us and the medium that is space and time stretches out like a centipede body going all the way back to the womb. And joining in with your mother and your father and then intertwined with what I saw was an entire life energy going back that floats in space-time. And it was like a huge sea anemone. And everyone is a branch of this.

And when you can get that perspective, all you're getting is a section through time. This is the way that we experience it because we can't move backward. We're forced to move forward all the time. So we can't even turn back over our shoulders and see this billion-legged, billion-eyed monster that stretches behind us. But, you know, deny it if you can, a human being unfolded through time would look like that. If you could see from beyond the time perspective, this is what it would look like.

RM: Did they explain to you what happens after death? Beyond this time suit?

GM: No. There is no death. They said, "If you look at the object all at once, everything on it dies simultaneously because it's a single object." We've only experienced it as a death that is happening serially through time because of the way we move through time. *From outside time everyone is born and dies at exactly the same time.* And what they tried to tell me was that what we experience as death is simply the unfolding into the adult form of this larva, which is growing in space and time. And whether, you know, it's mad cosmology, but I had no fear of the stuff because I'm utterly convinced it was like a religious vision in that sense where, you know, I can become evangelical about it if I don't get a grip on the madness of it. It was like a religious vision or it was like, you know, like meeting the fairies or whatever, it's got that kind of impact on how you feel. I was utterly convinced when I was there and the feeling was as, you know, I've read these accounts by everyone who's had similar things happen to them. The feeling that you belong here forever. This is where you belong.

They said they were trying to describe how they make universes and they do it by detaching parts of their substance and plugging them into the surrounding fluid, the Fifth Dimensional informational fluid that we're swimming through. And when you did that, when you plugged a fractal component of yourself into the universe, it would grow around you and become another one of these universes. And the idea was that those of us who knew, who'd had this experience, were supposedly midwives for this larva because we'd remember, then you'd go back and you'd be constantly trying to encourage the larva format because it has to grow.

²¹ DMT (N,N-dimethyltryptamine) a fast acting, smoke-able hallucinogen that often (but not always) transports the person ingesting it to a weird space inhabited by what the late psychedelic explorer Terence McKenna called "self morphing machine elves," entities which chatter at you, show you strange and wonderful things and prove, by their mere existence, that the universe is a much stranger place than you'd ever imagined before that moment. The whole experience lasts three minutes tops, but you'll be thinking about it a lot longer than that! For more information on DMT see *The Archaic Revival* by Terence McKenna (Harper Collins).

I mean it could die, it could just as easily die, but this seemed to work. You know, I'm feeling that *this one* works and I came out of it quite optimistic. I'm using science fiction language to try and conceptualize what actually went on, which I can't; I don't know how I can describe it.

RM: Did these beings represent themselves to you as gods?

GM: No, they didn't. They represented themselves to me as, as mates, you know, as friends. When I passed through one of them, I felt myself in their form as passed through another one of these creatures. And there was just this inter-

action where I felt everyone that I'd ever known was present in this thing. Again, I don't know how to describe it. It was like a movement through everyone.

RM: Did you get a glimpse of an even higher dimension beyond that one?

GM: I assumed there had to be, there was a Sixth, Seventh, Eighth, Ninth… I don't know. But yeah, there was something else going on. They were obviously something that was just a life form that exists in a different dimensional frame.

RM: Did you have any indication of what was above them?

GRANT MORRISON

GM: I don't know! I had to assume, they seemed to have their own role. It was like, they were just beings, I mean, they weren't like "gods." To us they'd seem like that, maybe, because they have complete control over space and time, but I'm sure above them there's some other unfolding of space and time. I don't know where they go when they die.

RM: So it wasn't scary?

GM: No, not at all. It was monumental. It was soul shaking but it wasn't scary.

RM: What was the next day like?

GM: The next day? What do you think it was like? I was buzzin'. I wrote like 200 pages in a notebook, just to try and get it down. And then I tried to explicate it for the next six years. And now I can just forget about it. (Laughs).

RM: Well, now you can turn it into a big Hollywood film and make a million dollars.

GM: Well, hopefully, yeah!

RM: Let's get back to *The Invisibles*. For people who haven't read the series, how would you describe the plot?

GM: Well, the plotline is fairly labyrinthine and baroque. But basically what we have is the James Bonds of the counterculture and these are five super cool terrorists, anarchists, occultists who operate in a cell as part of a vast organization,

which may or may not exist, called the Invisibles, which has existed since the dawn of time to fight against tyranny and oppression and slavery and everything that's supposed to be bad in the world. So, initially we set up this kind of conflict, the classic good and evil of freedom versus slavery conflict, where the Invisibles are on the side of love, laughs and libido, basically, and the bad guys are on the side of everyone who tries to run our lives and tell us what to do.

And the Invisibles cell attempts to recruit this young kid from Liverpool, who's a real violent punk. He wouldn't even call himself a "punk." He's just a kid off the streets of Liverpool who takes Ecstasy and steals cars and does that sort of thing. But he happens to be, or he's believed to be, the Buddha for the future, the technological Buddha of the 21st Century. And they have to recruit him before the other side recruits him and uses him to hasten the Apocalypse.

[37] Loa: Voodoo recognizes one God, Bondye or Gran Met. However, there are a host of spirits or deities called loa which act as intermediaries between humans and God. The loa, unlike Christian angels or devils, have significant powers relatively independent of God, and embody both positive and negative forces within the same loa.

There's a time travel thing that goes on. The whole thing loops through time as an object that connects all the characters through time. We have previous Invisibles groups in 1924 who do things which connect and vibrate through the ether, and turn out to be important in the present day or things that go backwards through time. So the whole thing kind of exists in its own little continuum and it has its beginning and end. But it's also meant to intersect with the real world and there are parts, you know, things that happen in the real world go instantly into the comic, like the death of Diana or the surveillance cameras going up all over Britain, and everything tied in so beautifully to the dynamic of it.

But ultimately what happens is that the plotline of that setup is subjected to such rigorous destruction that something else emerges by the end, which I don't want to say too much to people who haven't read it yet, but I've taken the classic good and evil conflict or anarchy versus repression conflict and tried to resolve it into something useful at the end. The setup is pretty high concept but I think the philosophy, in the end, is more important than the plot in the book.

RM: Who or what inspired the characters?

GM: Well, I guess when the Dane McGowan character started out, I was going to do this typical kind of character that I always write: the neurotic boy outsider with high cheekbones. (Laughs). You know, he's 17 and *no one understands him*. Dane McGowan started life as kind of a typical smart, teenage rebel, the type that I'd written dozens of in previous comics. It didn't seem right and I started looking around at the people who were actually rebellious in society. Five minutes in any direction from my house in Glasgow you'll find people who will happily cut your throat. (Laughs). So, I thought, well, one of *them* should be the Buddha because those guys don't care about any of that stuff. Dane's pretty smart; he's not completely stupid. So, there is something to work on and he's obviously got a kind of agenda, which a lot of these kids don't have. But I did want to go there and kind of give a voice to that Ecstasy-taking teenage hoodlum who was rising in Britain in the 90's.

And I kind of broke up parts of my own personality and put them into characters. King Mob became the main character, mainly because I'd just shaved my head. I was traveling around the world and I shaved my head and I thought, well, the only way to get girls to like me is turn the character into this bald guy and try and turn bald guys into the cool guys!

RM: *You* don't seem to have any problems meeting women!

GM: Well, exactly! (Laughs). So it kind of worked in that way, but the character was also the type that was beginning to appear and it was the "fetish man" of the 90's, the guy who was hanging around those fetish clubs and who had the piercings and wore that type of clothes. So he became a sort of 90's figure and so was Lord Fanny, the transvestite shaman. I thought there were a lot of interesting correlations between the shamans who would wear women's clothing to do their work and the kind of glammed out trannies that were starting to appear in the club scene in the 90's, so there was another little link there that made this connection between the occult stuff that I was interested in and the pop fashion stuff that I was interested in, too. And to try to rehabilitate and turn around this weird stuff that had previously been the province of shambling wrecks. You know, anarchists are seen as kind of shabby, hooded figures. I wanted to turn them into really sexy, glossy, James Bond-like kind of figures.

Obviously King Mob looks like me. I gave him a lot of my history. He's born on the same day as me, you know, he's obviously grown up through the same times and he was in a band at the same time as me. He went to India at the same time as me.

So there are differences, you know, he's a lot fitter and healthier than me. But it was deliberate, too, and like I said, *things happened because it was deliberate*. Things that I did to the character happened to me so he was kind of like a voodoo icon who was in the comic operating as me. He was what I called later in the series a *fiction suit* that I could enter and go in and move around in this reality and play with characters. And they didn't know who I was even though I'm the author in there pretending to be a lead character, but that's what was going on. And that became interesting to me as well that you could enter fiction and be characters.

So I began to see that kind of thing. I also fed into the whole idea of being able to enter the continuum that was *The Invisibles* and enter in a form which was this little icon who was King Mob, who himself had a character. It was enough like mine that I could ride him like a loa[32] and experience things in the story via him. So, yeah there was, for the six years of that book, a strange connection between that character and me.

But following on from the whole idea of writing something into existence, I started to think, "Okay this

GRANT MORRISON

thing could work. What if I put something in and see what happens to the character?" And I wasn't even thinking I'd made the character like myself!

King Mob was the bald guy and he wore my clothes. And even though he was an assassin and was quite different from me, it was there. He was my projection into that reality. So quite unwittingly I put him through a torture experience and it was designed to take him through a shamanic initiation experience, but in an updated way. I used the idea of the CIA torture manual technique for *The Tibetan Book of the Dead*. King Mob is put through this experience where he thinks he's in a chair being tortured. He's actually been given a drug, which makes him believe everything he's told. And he thinks his face has been eaten away by a bug. Within three months *my face* was being eaten away by a bug.

Unwittingly I have the alien beings or the Gnostic beings who are supposedly threatening Earth in *The Invisibles* story emerging through from their evil, sick Fifth Dimension, and the whole story was about sickness and illness.

But I didn't know at this time that I was slowly dying of toxic septicemia. And then I noticed King Mob actually gets to the point where he's dying, and three weeks after I write the story —I write the story where they all go through the whole bit, his death— I'm lying in hospital going through the entire parallel experience to his near death with septicemia, a punctured lung and pneumonia!

And so I thought, "Okay, good news. I survive this one." It was really... it was a worthwhile experience, a very interesting experience. I felt fantastic when I'd survived it. But I thought for Volume II of *The Invisibles*, I've got to give King Mob a good time and see what happens!

Rather than just try to get myself laid using the comic (laughs), I began to realize how I could do other things, and I would put things in that I wanted to happen in the world and watch them happen. You're basically making a little hologram, something that condenses a part of reality that you can then control —As above, so below, the Hermetic axiom— and hopefully by doing that, you'll control the large scale reality you're in.

I wanted to live in that world: I wanted to live in the world of super spies and super sex and international travel and yes, now I do. (Laughs). And real shamanic transvestites send me emails and tell me how to throw Molotov cocktails without burning your dress. And these people exist. They're all real. (Laughs).

RM: The element of "style" as a weapon in *The Invisibles* really impressed me.

GM: It's easy to write off Left-Wingers or anarchists or WTO protestors by saying they're shabby. God bless those people but it's easy to identify them as the enemy. If you were a cop, you'd know who to attack. So I kind of wanted to take it away from that and make it stylish and cool and use the weapons of the culture, which was fashion. It was all stuff I was interested in anyway. As a shallow person, you know, I liked that stuff. So I worked this into the deeper themes of magick and the occult and I think it had an effect. I think it's worked in a certain sense that it was cool to be a rebel. By now, they've absorbed it back into the culture and you know that's as clichéd as anything. But that image has now become the anarchist image of the bald headed guy and the leather coat and the tied trousers and the cool gun. I think it came directly out of *The Invisibles* and affected the entire cinematic culture.

RM: I'm assuming that like all teenagers, you had heroes and idols and people who you looked up to. People who you thought maybe knew more than you knew or that were special or who knew something that you didn't know, that you wanted to know. And now that you are on somebody else's pedestal, how does that feel and how do you react to that responsibility?

GM: I don't see it as any responsibility at all. These kids are *on their own* with that kind of thing, just as I was on my own when I read those books and was tempted into drugs and, you know, psychedelic experimentation and weird travel beyond time. I don't evangelize for these things. But it is a strange thing that if you do pursue that path, then this shit happens. I'm a skeptical person. Even though I come across as like a nut job, I'm very skeptical. I wanted to find what is real and what these experiences that I've had and other people have had, actually mean. What is this really connecting to and how do we get to the bottom of it? I hate bullshit and New Age candyfloss. So for me it was always, I'd read these books, crawling with instructions: *if you do this, certain things will happen*. That was the thing: *you go and do it and you'll see that it works*. Like Robert Anton Wilson saying that if you do *this* you'll contact beings from Sirius or any of these other people that I was interested in.

So being a skeptic I thought, "Yeah, bullshit, I'll try this" and when I tried it I found that it *actually worked*. Yes, you can make demons manifest. Yes, you can talk to beings from Sirius. What you're actually doing I still don't know; yet *it happens*. And you can follow these occult manuals available at any decent bookstore and you will get these results. So all that I hope is that all the people will ignore me and the pedestal and move on and do what I did rather than think "Yeah, this guy knows shit." I mean, I'd rather have them think, *"This guy is telling me lies. Let me test this method and see if it works."* And if you test these magical methods you'll probably find they work as I've found they work. But I don't want any responsibility for it, just read, the work is just *there*. It's like a piece of art. Interpret it how you choose. I hope people interpret it in wise and interesting ways, but beyond that it's up to them. And I'd like to see the end productions that come back from that inspiration.

RM: In the letter column in *The Invisibles* and on some of the Web sites that have been devoted to your work, there are often very elaborate explanations of things that were probably just dashed off, without a thought to it. How do you react to that and are you ever tempted to gently tweak a kid who writes to you with some grandiose idea about something that to you is just off the wrist?

GM: It is weird, because you find people who are analyzing what's on the tee-shirts that characters wear and all it was is that the artist happened to be listening to that particular band and they wrote it in. But people connect it into this huge thing and you know, suddenly, this is the most meaningful part of the conspiracy that somebody's wearing an "Air" tee-shirt! That's just the artist that wrote that in because he was listening to the Air record that day. But people say, "Oh Air is this and Air represents this and in the tarot Air represents this elemental quality." And they were extrapolating entire volumes of knowledge from this. *But the fact that they did it means, okay, it works. Let 'em do it.* I have my own master key to *The Invisibles* as to what it's about and what it means and how to unlock every little bit of it. And there are magical secrets in there; there are Tantric secrets in it.

RM: There are a lot of dog whistles in there. Obviously the Beatles references are a bit easier to decipher. I've spotted many a Noel Coward reference. There're Crowley references, of course. The *Voudon Gnostic Workbook* is mentioned a few times. That's pretty obscure!

GM: Yeah. This entire last volume, there's thousands of Arthurian references that nobody's even spotted yet, despite the fact there's a hand holding a gun coming out of a lake on the last cover. The last part of the story is about the Holy Grail and my interpretation of the Holy Grail being what happens when two people talk. It's that shape it makes in the middle, like in those optical illusion things. *What do you see, two profiles or a chalice?* To me that was the Holy Grail, *communication*.

But what I really wanted is for people to take it as, say, the same way you'd look at a painting or listen to a piece of music or interpret a tarot deck. Just play with it and see what you get from it. See what inspires; see what comes out of it. It should be dynamic. It shouldn't have an end, like *The Prisoner* or like *Twin Peaks*, which don't have an end. You can talk about them forever and they're the touchstones for your imagination.

RM: Earlier you were talking about the notion of writing things into existence, a very Burroughsian form of magick. When you were writing *The Invisibles* what were some of the things that started coming into your life whether you asked for them to or not?

GM: The entire general weirdness of *The Invisibles* invaded my life to the point where the two became indistinguishable, the comic and my life. It got to the point where I could put anything in, basically, *and it would happen*.

The intention was to make a super sigil. The magical idea of a sigil is to take a desire and abstract it into a figure or symbol. We're all familiar with magick symbols, weird looking *Witchblade* sort of alphabetical shapes. So the comic was deliberately intended to be a spell and I'd been reading a lot of stuff talking about writing as magick and writing as an actual act of writing across the fabric of the universe, almost. Scribbling on reality.

I was looking into this sigil technique and the basic sigil goes back to primitive man. If you wanted your desire to manifest, you could draw a bison on the wall and stick some spears in it and then you go out and hunt, and hopefully you'll kill the bison. The original sigil was primitive man's first attempt to control his environment by drawing on the walls, and that was, I'm sure, a major magical step for us to be able to do that, to create an image of something that existed in reality, and hopefully by manipulation of the image, to then manipulate reality.

That passed on through what we would call the alphabet. *There's a reason why spelling is called spelling*, and it's quite serious. The alphabet is a condensation of desire, but the magical way to do that was developed by Austin Osmon Spare early in the last century and taken up by the Chaos magicians and people like Genesis P-Orridge and Thee Temple ov Psychick Youth. They used the sigil method a lot.

The idea was you write down a sentence, you abstract whatever your desire is, what your intent is and you try to create this image. But the image I always thought is just static and it came to me, having written comics for a while, that we create these extended narratives which are basically just drawings and words put together, but they almost move. They seem to move because they fake time. And as I thought about the potential for comics to be used magically and because comics were my particular medium, it seemed that the best way for me to work my magick was to use my medium to make my magick work. I suddenly saw the comic continuum as a super sigil, in a dynamically extended process.

The Invisibles is a spell or an abstracted desire, which is actually spread out through what seems to be a story, which seem to be plot lines, which seem to have resolutions. In actual fact, *it's a sigil*. It's a huge, moving sigil, and it is not just drawn on a wall, it's drawn across six years. I think that it's a very powerful technique.

I want to do some more stuff with this and the future comic projects will probably deal with this a lot more. The fact I've managed to get my hands on corporate projects like *X-Men* means that I can take big corporate sigils and mess with them.

RM: Ah yes, getting next to corporate money and *reach* is a very good thing. Like I always say "If they give, you should grab!"

GM: The most powerful magick is being done by large corporations, governments and the military, but these techniques are available to anybody. If you want to study the best, go study McDonald's or The Gap or any of these corporations and see how they do it to extract money out of your pocket. These people are the inheritors of the Hermetic tradition, and...

RM: Without knowing it.

GM: Maybe some of them *do* know it. There're a lot of smart people who are involved in advertising and marketing and logo design. They're people like us, they're not dumb and they know that these things have certain psychological effects.

Since World War II there's been quite a vast dossier accumulated on using psychology to make people do things. Systems like Neuro-Linguistic Programming have been developed specifically for this purpose and they are in use by corporate bodies. We know that. You can go to NLP seminars and management seminars where you will be taught magick and personality modification techniques *that are profound*.

The corporations are using these things. And even the very idea of corporations, I think *they're* occult entities. You're dealing with what occultists would call *agregores.*

What is a corporation? The head of Disney has got nothing to do with Disney, really, except he's the head of Disney and he's decided to be *that* person, to become at best, the biggest piece of that huge, ghostly entity which haunts the world. And if you look at corporations that way, they are powerful occult entities. They are the new gods. They're the new loas and spirits of the world we're living in. I think it's time that we turned that back and time we all learned NLP and time we use those techniques from all the advertising gimmickry and wizardry that's been used to outfox us. We should turn it back on them. Watch for them, these techniques are in every advert and in every political speech and in everything you see every day.

RM: At what age did your interest in the occult commence? How did you get into it?

GM: I was probably pretty young. My mother reads tea leaves and the women in the family were always pretty witchy and we were kind of a bohemian family anyway, so stuff like that was accepted. I had all these comics with guys with super powers and Dr. Strange doing his thing, and I always wanted to do that kind of magick that comes out your hands, the real magick. (Laughs). I was all intellect and I was really mad because I didn't have these like, you know, powers of pre-cognition that my mother had when she looked in tea leaves. But my uncle, her brother Billy, was really into Crowley and into that stuff and he had a great occult library in his mad house with his kids and things.

He would give me books and at first it was a big scary thing and so you'd only read the books on mythology first because you could handle that. But then I got interested in magick and by the time I was 19, I just decided to practice it and see if these guys were telling the truth.

And, you know, all these years later, yeah, I can only say that *they're telling the truth*. All the manuals that were on Billy's shelf, *Magick in Theory and Practice* and whatever else. And then I got into Chaos Magick in the 80's, which is like punk magick. All those old books always said the first thing you have to do is clear your mind of all thought to be able to do magick. Nobody can clear their mind of all fucking thought, you know? (Laughs). The whole thing's nonsense. I felt like I'd never really do it, but the minute the Chaos Magick guys came along and said, "Make your own methods. Use your own gods. It can be Mickey Mouse."

RM: Yeah, forget about the eye of newt and the bubbling cauldron!

GM: Yeah, *forget everything*. Forget everything you think you've learned about magick! And I think that that's when the magick started to work, and since I discovered how to use the comics as magick, I've entered into a kind of state where *magick does me*. I don't do it anymore; I don't have to do rituals like I used to do. Things happen because I put 'em in the books.

GRANT MORRISON

RM: I know what you're saying. You can't sit down at a piano and start playing *Beethoven's Fifth*, but you can sit down and plunk out *Chopsticks* pretty easily. After you've learned what magick is all about, it's like a muscle that you can really use, and by that point, you've started certain processes along, which are then already in motion and it builds on itself. I see it as a process of self-discovery and like learning a martial art.

GM: It's the shit from gold ultimately. It's just the alchemical thing. Like I said, with my illness, if I hadn't been who I was I probably wouldn't have conceptualized it in the way I did, which was to assume, "Okay, I'm having a shamanic experience." I could just as easily have assumed I was having a really shitty physical experience and I was going to die. But I had this grandiose view of it because I'd been writing this stuff and because *it seemed like a good way to deal with an illness was to assume that it was trying to tell you something*. And if you assume that and it does seem to tell you something and you recover from it, well,

let's just say I feel as if I've got a kind of totemistic relationship with the *Staphlyococcus aureus bacillus*.

RM: Yesterday you were saying that the counterculture should be like Mad Cow disease and I thought that was great: "We should infect them like a virus and it will be years before they know that they've been infected."

GM: Well Mad Cow disease is an interesting disease (laughs); I've been reading a few books on it. And apart from the fact that it makes cows die in amusing and horrible ways, it destroys people's brains without their immune system recognizing that it's there. Your brain tissue will be eaten away and spongified before you even know it. None of your immune responses recognize this, so it doesn't get touched. Somehow it gets in and destroys everything without you knowing. So I saw it as a really good metaphor for what the so-called counterculture should be doing now, in the sense that the culture demands our ideas. So okay, they can have them, but you have to understand that these ideas will fuck with your head, and if there's…

RM: Which they don't understand!

GM: They don't understand. They don't understand that if you mass transmit these ideas you will mass fuck with heads and we're seeing the results of that I think, in the way that the culture is mutating. (Laughs).

RM: Yeah. It blows my mind that somebody decided to give *me* a television show. I'm not going to drop the ball on that. The idea that someone would allow me to hurl as much weirdness as I could into people's living rooms is utterly hilarious to me. If they only knew!

GM: Right, if they only knew. The nation is trained for weirdness and the more they get the more they want. And the more (laughs) outrageous it becomes. So that shows you how much of us they want and that's kind of like…

RM: A license to drive!

GM: I see it as a hamburger. We are the hamburger and they want this hamburger. They didn't realize that there's all these prions kicking about in the hamburger because they think it's just a tasty, nutritious meal from McDonald's. They're taking a bite and this thing's getting in and this thing is breeding fast and it's adapting and it's very rapid and it's very destructive to everything they hold dear. But it's in and it's out of control. It's out of their control. And these people don't believe in magick. They don't think such things exist, even though it's been practiced on them.

By Volume III of *The Invisibles*, the charge was over because I wasn't using villains anymore. It resolves and they just… they say, "Well, we're just part of a process. You *are* us. We've absorbed you now." The Invisibles and the enemy becomes one thing engaged in this dance. And ultimately it's the dialectic: they synthesize to create a new thing. *The Invisibles* ends by saying: *individuality is over.*

The freedom fighters that thought they were fighting for individuality —like Patrick McGoohan in *The Prisoner*, "I'm not a number!"— in the end realize that individuality was the trap that led to existential alienation, that led to boundaries and wars. It was useful, we had to become individuated, individuals. But *The Invisibles* ends with seeing the next stage beyond that is to take on multiple personalities deliberately. And I just think this world is working as it's meant to be, because even the worst thing is part of the process, because we're all in one continuum. The continuum is us. The space between you and me also defines who you and me are, but the space between us is there, and it's pregnant with possibility. It's phase space, to use a scientific term. And that's what the Invisibles are. They try and open up that possibility again. Forget the boundaries, drop all and advance into your enemy's space to the point where you understand why he's your enemy and he stops being your enemy because you're him now and he is you. Everyone just reverses through each other, is the way I saw it working.

Even the Gnostic Archons that appear in the book that appeared to be vast demonic Lovecraftian entities that have been clawing their way into our reality to dominate everyone, at the end they are revealed to be kind of pathetic figures. And I saw them ultimately as purely… they were there to catalyze events in the book. And they even realize that in the end, the great nightmarish Archon insect monsters from beyond. In the end they're revealed to be nothing less than a kind of infection that has been sent to Earth to inoculate our universe, in order for the universe to be born properly in the future. So the bad guys are the good guys. They're here to inoculate us. Evil is a thing we experience as an inoculation against evil and they just become purely part of this magnificent process that unfolds at the end of the book.

RM: How do you define evil in a more mundane sense?

GM: Evil to me is just stupidity, but I'm a snob. I'm an I.Q. snob. And I hate the stupid to the point where I'd like to devise a way of exterminating the stupid. These people have been running the world for so long and they've made a fucking mess of it. You know, just hand it over to the smart people and let us have a go of it. That's all I ask. So as far as evil, I don't think there's evil, I think that people just do stupid things. We re-label things, we label elements of our process with words like good and evil because we're inside this thing. But then seen from the outside, good and evil seem irrelevant.

RM: What's something that you would like to see coming up on the rise in the next five years?

GM: Number one, let's have some good music. (Laughs). I'd like to see some

GRANT MORRISON

good bands! Come on, kids, like do something, it's getting really rough.

RM: You want to exterminate the stupid. I want to exterminate all of these all-singing, all-dancing teen pop people. (Laughs).

GM: It's almost part of the same program I think. We'll get them all eventually. But one thing I'd like to see, one thing I tried to put in *The Invisibles* was the creation of a new youth movement. It ends with the girl who you see later on in 2012 has grown up and become an Invisible herself in the future but she's in the second to last issue where it ends up with a kind of passing the torch onto the next generation. And I just had her wearing secretary clothes but with a shaved head and *Fuck You* tattooed on her head because I thought that would be a really cool way to dress. Just dress like a secretary, carry a little handbag, but be the hardest core punk on earth.

And I was just trying to say: look, be this movement, please get beyond all this stuff that we've got now, you know, and start bands, start fanzines, start websites, *do something* and express this current because there's an incredible current flowing through right now. And nobody's put it to music yet and nobody's given it a name. That's what I'm interested in seeing: something *new*.

NORBERT H. KOX

Contemporary religious painter Norbert Kox is one of America's most important visionary artists. His self-described "apocalyptic visual parables" utilize powerful symbolic metaphors aiming to shake modern man from his spiritual malaise and clear away centuries' worth of mistranslations of the Bible.

"When I grew up I was taught that the Catholic religion was the only true religion, but when I started to study the Bible —and I believe that the Bible is the inspired word of God— I saw contradictions to the Catholic religion. I had to make a choice and I chose to go with the scriptures. What I do in my paintings oftentimes is reveal these findings where the scripture contradicts either Catholicism or modern day Christianity, and then I point out these contradictions in the paintings. That's what riles people up and causes them to get angry."

Not surprisingly, the Catholic church feels Kox's work is blasphemous and religious protesters picketed a 1999 exhibit. At first inspection there is little question why his art is so disturbing to religious people: demons peer out from darkness as Christ is tortured on the cross, Christ is represented as a cockroach sporting a "Superman" tee-shirt, as a Statue of Liberty tourist trap item or as a puppet manipulated by behind the scenes demonic figures. In one of Kox's most important works, *Chana Baal: Hierarchy of the Mother*, Pope Pious XII and Pope Paul VI (who never denounced Hitler) are depicted as Satan's shills, wielding their Papal power for evil, not good, as gold leaf snakes whisper atrocities in their ears and a sun demon (representing the Pagan elements of Christianity) smiles smugly above their heads. "I'm pointing out that not everyone who represents themselves as a servant of God is necessarily telling the truth," says Kox.

An extraordinary mixed media piece from 1999 called *Dis'Guised* takes the message even further with the Duchampian conceit of painting Rene Magritte's *"Ceci n'est pas une pipe"* from his *Treason of Images* in the mouth of Warner Sallman's iconic *Head of Christ,* arguing visually that "This is not a pipe, but this *not Christ*, either."

"Well, this is patterned after an image that was created by Warner Sallman in about 1940, I believe it was, and he was asked to create this image so that they could make small wallet-sized reproductions of it to hand out to the servicemen during World War II. That image was so widely distributed — and still is today— that this has come to be the traditional representation of Christ. When people look at it they think this is what Christ looked like. And it really has nothing to do with him, it's an artist's invention, and so therefore it becomes an idol."

Does Kox see Sallman's painting, arguably as recognizable as the Coca-Cola symbol or Mickey Mouse, as a "graven image"? Kox is unequivocating: "Yes it's a graven image. People look at this image and visualize Christ and think, 'I'm praying to Christ.' Some of the testimonials that they got from some of these servicemen were things like 'I look at this picture and I pray and this is my Jesus that I pray to and he's alive to me, living and alive and answers all my prayers' and so on, and it reminded me of the part in the Book of Revelations where it talks about the Beast and the creation of the image of the Beast or the icon of the Beast, and the Beast was allowed to give spirit to this icon so that it would be living. If Satan can give spirit then what is that spirit?"

"This particular painting —like all of my works— it points out certain things that are deceptions and falsehoods that have crept into modern day religions and it's my job to reveal truths and expose falsehood. Much of my imagery has to do with false teaching and false traditions, and at times this has been misunderstood and people think that I'm mocking Christ but it is certainly not a mockery of Christ because I'm a follower of the teachings of Christ. What this is showing is that it's a false image that was created by man and in the scripture all these prophecies warn of this counterfeit Christ. The Bible speaks of the Son of Perdition and it says that Satan masquerades as an Angel of Light and when you look that up in the original Greek it's a word that means 'to disguise,' so it says 'Satan is disguised as an Angel of Light and his ministers are disguised as ministers of justice.' (2 Corinthians, 11:14-15). And the scripture warns about this deception that's going to come through the Christian religion, because there's no other way that it could deceive the Christians, it has to come through the Christian religion and so that's why I believe that all the false imagery, false names and perverted doctrines are what has the Gospel of Christ so twisted and distorted that it doesn't even resemble what the original First Century Christians were following after."

Secret Babylon the Great: The Mega, 1996
61" x 31.5"

Kox was not always the devout, gentle, middle-aged Christian fellow that he is today: he was once a hell-raising biker who customized motorcycles and cars in a style similar to that of Von Dutch, Big Daddy Roth or Stanley Mouse. He was a heavy drinker and prone to violence. Kox friend, art professor David Damkoehler, quoted in *Apocalypse Culture II*, said this about him: "While [Norbert] was a biker, his actions were legendary. People who encountered the early Norb recount vivid, vulgar acts done with a flair and originality that compare to the most original performance art of the time."[33]

When I asked Norbert about this, he told me the following tale, trying to act like "Of course I'd never do such a thing these days" and telling the story that way, offering several disclaimers along the way, yet nearly breaking into an impish grin several times as the anecdote progressed: "Well, one of the things I did that people were talking about for a while was I went into this real nice restaurant, where everyone was dressed all fancy, like a country club or some place like that and I had my biker clothes and leathers on and I sat down in this place and I looked all around me. I looked at everyone there, one by one around the room, and of course they were all looking back at me to see what I was going to do and I took out this jar I had with me of real big night crawlers and I opened the jar, took one out and then I held it up, dropped it right into my mouth and ate it. I don't think those people will ever forget me!"

Probably not! But what was it that caused this *badass* biker to repent and find salvation? Kox tells the story himself in an excerpt from his unpublished book, *Six Nights Till Morning:*

It was the summer of 1974 at a motorcycle hill climb in Wisconsin Rapids; we would always go a day ahead of time and party hard until the hill climb.

[33] "Jesus, Lucifer, Santa/Satan: The Apocalyptic Parables of Norbert H. Kox," Adam Parfrey, from *Apocalypse Culture II*, Adam Parfrey, editor. Feral House, 2000.

I never experimented much with LSD. That night when the acid was being passed out, I was already stoned and overconfident. When I said I would take two hits, my friend wasn't able to dissuade me, knowing I had never done more than a half-hit before.

Before long, the acid was swimming in my mind, and everything around was either comical or beautiful. Everything that moved had a tail like a comet, and everything that shined had a million sparks. It was blowing my mind. I remember thinking, "Wow! This is fantastic." But the beauty was intermittently shattered by ugly visions and obscene words. The force was closing in on me and I started to feel its effect.

I became trapped in a circle of events, events which always brought me back to the same spot, but each time it would occur

The Big Banana and His Bunch, 1995
30" x 40.5"

I became a little more frightened. Events would happen exactly the same as before. It was not within my power to change one thing, not even the words I would speak. What I saw was an exact recurrence of previous events; the only thing different were my thoughts. I became more and more paranoid each time around.

Vicious dogs were in the air all around, snarling. Everyone was walking through fire, which wasn't unusual for our bunch except for the frequency and order it was happening in. My brother Magoo was wearing an underwater snorkeling mask. He broke the glass out while it was still on his face. He would laugh hideously, waving a broken-off car antenna, sparks flying in every direction. Fear gripped me deeper as I thought to myself, "I have to talk to someone. I am so scared, I've never been this frightened before." Then another guy I knew, Teen Angel, would jump out of the trunk of his car, and a new spark of hope would lighten my heart as I rushed towards him, then as quickly as he appeared, he was gone. I thought if only I could get some sleep, I might find rest. I knew I could not take much more. I would start to head for the tent, but only a few steps later I would stumble and begin to fall. Then I would find myself staring at the Coleman lantern while the moths would land in the fire and die. Every episode ended at the Coleman lantern, where it began, and then the horrible sights would begin yet again, and I knew I was in for another lap.

While at the lantern, I would feel a certain temporary relief. I would seem to recompose my

NORBERT H. KOX

DIS'GUISED, 1999
11" x 8.5", 4" frame

senses a little, somehow hoping that it was all over, but still knowing in my mind that the repeating chaos had just begun. Soon the fear would grip deep in my bowels. Was I alive, or dead? There was no way for me to know. I prayed that it was all my imagination and that the gang was just trying to freak me out. But to my dismay I would find myself staring once again at Magoo, seeing him through the shiny glass of the snorkeling mask, which would then again twist and break, glass falling down his heavy beard. It's one thing to watch the *Twilight Zone* TV show; it's another thing to live

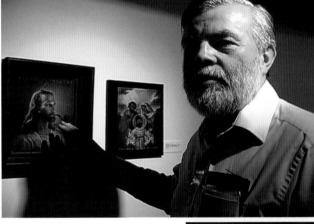

a creepy episode over and over again. I was crying. I was peeing my pants. I thought I would die of fear, but when death didn't come, I thought that I had already died and gone to Hell. I'd been through these Hell circles four, five, six times, and then they were still going. By now I had almost given up hope thinking that I'd ever see my family again. I was in another world. If I was not dead, I was a zombie locked in an insane asylum.

I wanted to repent. I wanted another chance. "Oh God," I said, "don't let me be like this forever." I do not know how long I prayed, or all that I said, but God did hear me.

The air began to feel different. The ice-cold chill had melted away in the summer breeze. The cases of beer which had been stacked high the last time around were now empty cans and torn cardboard. The perspiration evaporated from my forehead and I began to collect my thoughts. I could not believe it. It was too good to be true. Had Hell rejected me, or was Satan just building up for the big one?[34]

For ten years afterward, Kox lived as a hermit, sleeping in the back of a truck in the Wisconsin woods, spending his days and nights studying the Bible and creating his extraordinary body of work. Eventually, by the late 80's, he emerged back into society and began teaching art at a Wisconsin college, participating in several group and solo exhibits of his work. Today his paintings and sculptures have been seen worldwide and even though they are often denounced by religious leaders, with every new book, exhibit or TV show covering this devout outsider, his message is heard by —and resonates with— more and more people. As artists articulate the intuition of their culture, I wondered if Kox considered himself to be a prophet even in that mundane sense?

"I don't think it's too outrageous to say that I'm a prophet because if you really look at the dictionary definition of it, a prophet is somebody who bears the word of God or who tells the word of God and that's what I'm doing by yielding myself to the Holy Spirit as I work on these paintings and allowing God to work through me. In that sense I am a prophet bringing His word to the world. And it's not always what the world wants to hear, but the prophets of old were hated by the world also, so if I get a little ridicule out of it then I guess I knew ahead of time that it'd come."

[34] Unpublished manuscript, *Six Nights Till Morning* by Norbert Kox, quoted here in *Apocalypse Culture II*. Adam Parfrey, Feral House.

NORBERT H. KOX

Mother of Harlots: The Pie-Eyed Piper, 1996
35" x 30"

May's One: Image of Jealousy (Ezekiel 8: 3-16, & 22: 25-29), 1991
48" x 84.5"

The following is an extraordinary response to an email I sent Norbert when the scandal within the Catholic priesthood first erupted:

From Richard Metzger
To: Norbert H. Kox
Sent: March 18, 2002
Subject: "Who can take a sunrise, sprinkle it with…um… *dew*?"

Norb,

I gotta know: What do you make of Operation Candyman, the Department of Justice sting that nabbed dozens of people over the weekend, MANY of them Catholic priests, with kiddie porn?

And all of the lawsuits filed this week accusing these priests of molesting kids for *decades*? I think this is the beginning of a NASTY avalanche for the Catholic church.

Fuck 'em, it serves 'em right!

Maybe that's a poor choice of words here…

Best,

Richard

NORBERT H. KOX

From: Norbert H. Kox
To: Richard Metzger
Sent: March 18, 2002
Subject: Re: "Who can take a sunrise, sprinkle it with…um… *dew*?"

I have been so secluded lately that I had not heard about this sting. Glad they caught them. Now lets see what they do to them. I have been hearing for years about the Catholic priests with the little boys. Someone ought to figure out a suitable punishment for these praying mantises and put a stop to their perverted treachery against innocent children.

I do not understand how decent people can continue to be Catholics and even take communion from the hands of the same priests who are raping their children.

The Catholic church has since its historical beginning used the rank of priesthood to molest and sodomize men, women and children in the name of God. First they created a doctrine declaring themselves God and Christ on earth, so people would have to look to them for salvation. Then they used their unique position to deceive their victims into believing that whatever sexual favors are performed to satisfy the priest, are in reality pleasing God, since they are standing in God's place. This also meant that if they did not please the priest, they were actually displeasing God. How could they not do what the priest wanted, it would be disobedience to God. If they expected to be saved they certainly could not deny the priest his wishes.

This is a tactic used by the sadistic sexual criminals who call themselves priests. Over the past twenty years there have been many cases of priests being caught in their evil when someone had the courage to report them. Now so many are being caught that it can no longer be kept secret. It gives other victims the courage to come forward and tell their stories. It now looks like the majority of priests commit these evils. If there were any good priests left how could they stand by while children are being raped and sodomized, and how could they help the evil ones cover their tracks the way they do?

It is time for Catholics to realize that their hierarchy does not represent God. GOD IS NOT ON EARTH RAPING THE CHILDREN, BUT THE DEVIL IS.

If every Catholic in the world would walk out of the Catholic church at the same time and say, we are not going to be a part of this evil organization that uses its authority to commit evil, the perverted priests would have no one to molest but themselves.

You asked me what I thought about it. I hope they catch every last one of those scumbags.

What those nasty priests are doing physically to the little ones is what the false doctrines of the "church" are doing spiritually to its hypnotized populace.

Take care.

Talk to you soon.

Norb

a Baal-Hierarchy of The Mother, 1991-1995

" x 17"

NORBERT H. KOX

DUNCAN LAURIE

Duncan Laurie is an award-winning glass and metal artist. He produces the sort of large-scale interi-or design installations that you might see in the lobby of a New York advertising agency or a bank in Singapore. From his incredible glass and steel workspace–*cum*-laboratory located on a lush peninsu-la off the coast of Jamestown, Rhode Island, Laurie also experiments with some astonishing electronic devices and maintains a uniquely outfitted recording studio.

For years Duncan Laurie has been an enthusiast for topics related to *subtle energy*. He invited me to his laboratory to explore the "forbidden science" of radionics and demonstrate plant communication for the *Disinformation*® cameras. It was clear when we arrived that he was raring to go.

Kooky outsiders often populate the fringe science arena and what makes Laurie such a great pitchman for these radical ideas is his All-American persona. This is not a guy who is a crazed loner feverishly working on a perpetual motion machine in a squalid basement somewhere, but a well-spoken, well-bred, *reasonable*, East Coast old-money family man. Handsome, square-jawed, very much in the Gary Cooper/Harrison Ford mold. He has a keen sense of humor about these matters and he takes all of it with a grain of salt.

Duncan's participation and networking within The US Psychotronics Association led him to forge friendships with influential figures in the fringe science movement, such as Paul Laffoley and the late R.J. "Josh" Reynolds III, tobacco scion and the last to bear that name. Josh Reynolds who was, to hear Duncan describe it "for all intents and purposes, the patron saint, of the alternate science movement," for years helped fund various researchers and practitioners who would have found funding otherwise impossible to get. After illness curtailed Reynolds' ability to travel, Laurie and visionary artist and writer Aymon de Sales often did the scouting work for Reynolds, continuing to network within the movement and meet with like-minded individuals such as Andre Puharich, Elizabeth Rausher, Tom Beardon, Pete Kelly, Michael Bradford, Eric Dollard, John Keel and many others.

When we first got to his place, Duncan gave us a tour of the grounds. It's a wonderful spot on the landscape and has been in his family for generations. The peninsula where his lab sits is carved out of solid, granite rock laced with slivers of quartz. High-pressure water flows on either side of it, "charg-ing" the area as Duncan says.

A fantastic energy exists here and indeed it's one of the most beautiful places I've ever seen. It's wild and unspoiled, despite the popularity of the sailing mecca Newport just across the water. The lab, as I mentioned above, is made of glass and steel and it is as extraordinary as its setting. The bricks are all made of glass and during the day the lab is filled with dazzling light, an artist's dream space. At night, the structure glows from deep inside, illuminated by its inhabitant's activities and broadcasting good vibrations back to the highly charged landscape.

The structure of the lab conforms to the concepts of sacred geometry in architecture, not just in terms of ceiling height, length and width, but also the shapes of the windows and doors. As we make our way through the ground floor up to the lab, Duncan throws around terms like *The Golden Ratio* and *The Fibonacci Series* and I note that it feels like we're in a shrine. Duncan nods in agreement, as if that's the very point he's trying to make

The moment we reached the top floor of his sun-drenched, transparent workspace, Duncan Laurie's enthusiasm to impart to me some of the things he's learned didn't allow me to ask a question. He just launched right into it. A glance around the room revealed several electronic devices of unusual vintage and even more esoteric items such as the wired cattle skull ("It's a tuned cavity") hooked up to plants moonlighting as makeshift microphones. As he talked he flipped a switch and an unpredictable, slight-ly ethereal *feedback* noise started coming out of the speakers hanging in every corner. I soon realized I was listening to *the sound* of a plant!

DL: Back in the 70's, but even before, a lot of very interesting research concerning plant conscious-ness was beginning to come out. The best known involved the experiments of Cleve Backster, who was a professional at reading lie detectors and for some reason or another he wound up having a lie detector hooked up to a plant, which he found could then respond to certain signals that were going on in the room, similar to the way a person would. And if there was more than one plant in the vicinity, then another form of communication seemed to be taking place between them.

You had this plant symbiosis of signals. Backster conjectured some field phenomena was occurring between plants. He even went so far as to hook up shrimp on a timer and at a certain point while he was far away from the laboratory, the shrimp would fall into scalding water. They would die immediately and the plants on the electroencephalogram would go "Arrgrrraahh!" The signal would go crazy. They'd be screaming, essentially, feeling the demise of the shrimp. So this got a lot of attention and as a result there were government studies and there were studies in other countries. Everybody got into this for a while and then it all disappeared or went underground.

There are very vivid documentaries on this effect, such as *The Secret Life of Plants*, that show scientists tearing one plant apart while the other one is reacting audibly with what sounds to be great pain. This experiment was conducted over and over again in order to explore what was going on with these plants.

RM: What does that indicate? Does it mean that plants speak to each other in a telepathic, "faster than light" kind of communication, or through their root system? Or what? How do plants communicate with each other?

DL: A lot of the assumptions were made that the plants were communicating through the ether or through some sort of biological domain. Or was it, as is now generally believed, some type of a chemical, like a pheromone, that one plant would give off and another plant would receive? There's a lot speculation.

RM: How could an olfactory signal happen that fast?

DL: Well that's what prompted a lot of the research; people were astounded by the fact that these plants had this capability. A sensual reaction that was so instantaneous that it could be done at a distance without anyone present. It wasn't like, I sense it and the plant senses me, it was something the plants were sensing about each other. I don't know that a full explanation has ever been completely put forward; it's just an open question. Is there another domain that plants have access to that may have the potential for communication on some subtle level?

DUNCAN LAURIE

We're talking about subtle energy here; maybe this is one indication of it. My efforts have been to try and isolate a biological communication domain from other types of communication such as signals in the electrostatic fields. How do we know? There are so many things that are invisible. But if you were able to say precisely, "Here is a biological signal, it's not electromagnetic," then you would have proof that there was a medium of subtle energy. I think a lot of people believe that anyway, but we're actually looking for a way to demonstrate it. It's not a forgone conclusion. You have to isolate these things very precisely and that's not easy to do.

Here's a good metaphor for the way this works: the stethoscope hears the heartbeat in a very simple way. If you put the same signal into a CAT scan you enlarge that signal tremendously. You embellish it in a way that you can take a cross section of it and amplify it. You get much, much more information out of the signal by enhancing it electronically. I'm thinking that it's possible that by running these plant signals through audio processors —sophisticated ones— we're revealing more of what's in the signal. Not just adding something to a simple pitch shift. Because of the fact that there's a complex biology involved, we're opening that signal up. The more it opens up, the more it seems the plants want to do. The more range of expression you give them, the more they seem to work with that range and produce deeper effects, just like that [Laurie refers to a notable uptick of activity from the plant]. I'm talking about it and the next thing we know, the thing's boosting itself right up. There's this funny reciprocity between the plant and the operator and whatever else is going on in the room. You put on some music; all of a sudden they seem to be pegging themselves to the music. Like dancing to it. Is that a magnetic phenomenon? Or is that a biological pheromone? Who's to say it's not some gnome living in this plant that sees this as an opportunity for it to express itself? I can't say, but it's wild to see it happen.

These are the kinds of questions you ask yourself as you start to work with it. It brings you in touch with the nature of the organisms themselves. What is this environment? What kind of an environment do our plants create around us? When you listen to a bunch of them all together they sound like a circus. They're absolutely unpredictable in terms of where they're going to go and how they're going to jump out. And as such they almost have a completely non-egotistical connotation to them. They just are what they are. They have nothing to do with the human condition; you can't predict what they will do. The sounds are initially harsh to the ear, but as you get used to it, it becomes more and more and more interesting and spatial. It's like looking up at the night sky. You see it initially as a flat tableau, but the more you look, the more volume begins to creep into it.

RM: I notice that as I get nearer this one over here, the sound changes. It's like a Theremin.

Radionics Enthusiasts
L to R: Timmy Walters, Aymon de Sales, Josh Reynolds, Michael Bradford, Daffy Nathanson, Duncan Laurie

Jamestown, RI, Oct. 4, 1993

DL: This is a pitch shift with a slight delay added to it. It's very close to the purest signal. And as I move closer to it (he does so) it reacts (the tones get wilder). It's very sensitive. If I was thinking of this as an instrument and I could expand this field out into a room, a defined space, then a dancer could come in and out of this field, producing a tonal change.

The electrodes are acting like a Theremin. The amplifier's got a field structure around it that is very sensitive. We want a very specific signal in the plant, but what we have as a result is also a sensing device that will pick up movement and other things as well

RM: This kind of energy must get trod on by the forces of modern life. Cell phones, satellites, radio and microwaves…

DL: We have an idea of how consciousness evolved and expanded in prehistory: you have this design effort through cave art and architecture and everything else to make consciousness more vivid, to make knowledge of higher life forms more vivid, to potentially access invisible domains of knowledge in different ways and other things like that. Eventually we got to the point where there are so many people and there's so much information and there's so much technology and so many things intruding into our lives, subtle and not so subtle, that the problems change. Now we need something to de-condition us and *edit out* a lot of this noise and allow us to just focus on and enjoy the things that we want to enjoy.

This is where a lot of the experimental machinery in this room starts to come into play. What is in here is a combination of acoustic technology, radionic technology and psychotronic technology. The acoustic technology is all very straightforward. Amplification, digital signal processors, short wave radios, tone generators, other forms of input like microphones and just a variety of all the normal audio sources.

When we talk about *Psychotronic Technology*, this is the use of psychic phenomena in an electronic apparatus or through an electronic apparatus. Energy that is derived from the human body and/or the human mind and is projected into form via the ability of the medium to manifest this energy or to extract it from the individual and use it either locally or at a distance to affect something outside that individual, without him physically touching it. Psychic energy is pretty well established scientifically, now. There are statistical studies that have confirmed that this is real. It's been studied and militarized and every other thing that you can think of.

What happens when you combine this PSI energy with electronics of specific design is that you can augment the energy and you can direct it using the electronic device. We do this all the time, anyway. You can't watch a powerful movie or television show without feeling there is an energetic component to what you are seeing, that somehow this is viscerally affecting you. Advertising uses this in terms of subliminals, there's a long history of this. *We cook this energy into our food.*

DUNCAN LAURIE

What is important is that psychotronic technology has been opportunized by the wrong elements of society for a long time. There are very few people who view this type of technology in a constructive way as a potential application for environmental change, for personal growth or development, whatever you want to call it. Psychotronic technologies are devices that are underground; they are not for sale in your appliance stores or anywhere off the shelf that I'm aware of. They have to be specially ordered through the Internet or through organizations like the United States Psychotronics Association, which hosts many of these inventors every year. There's an underground network of inventors producing and refining these products.

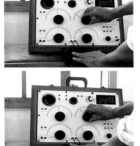

Radionic technology, on the other hand, grew out of medical instrument design at a time when medical science was more open to the idea of biological energy. It's inventor, Dr. Albert Abrams, MD, came from a wealthy San Francisco family, studied medicine at the University of Heidelberg in Germany and went on to teach pathology at Stanford where he became the Director of Medical Studies.

With radionics, you use an instrument, a link —and I'll get to that in a moment— and the applied intention of the operator to a condition requiring treatment. You have to apply your intention, which you direct into a device or into a design. This releases your ego from the responsibility of having to do this intellectually

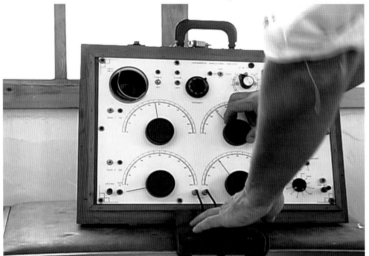

impossible task. The device has a responsibility for carrying this signal to wherever you want it to go and putting that signal to work on that situation. This is exactly what modern laboratory psychic research has found actually takes place under controlled conditions. But there is a discrepancy as to whether this is something almost physical that comes out of the individual and is projected, like a voice, or whether you have a field phenomenon which exists throughout nature which is switched on in the mind. It's possibly pattern recognition now, and that information travels to the source and it couples with another form of information in the receiver and then that information starts the ball rolling. This is where nobody knows for sure what is going on. We've got a lot of unknowns about how energy and information work. This is one of them. So we're looking at devices here that are *medically unsupportable*, *scientifically irrational* and potentially *illegal* depending on how you use them, and yet all over the world they're being used.

And if you look precisely at how indigenous societies used art to heal, you'll find precisely the same principles at work. A Navajo sand painting is a geometric manifestation of harmony being constructed while the healer is taking the disease out of the patient, and correcting it by virtue of assigning the harmonies of the sand painting to the individual. *It's pure radionics* and yet it's never perceived as anything more than just a metaphorical transaction. *This couldn't possibly heal anybody, it's too simple.* This isn't how healing takes place; you have to have a drug.

[35] The paranormal detection of underground water or mineral deposits (or lost persons and objects) using a divining rod or pendulum.

RM: Tell me what some of these devices do (gestures towards an array of instruments).

DL: Okay, a short history of radionics devices: this is called a *Pathoclast* and it's the closest thing that we have to the *Abrams Device* that was the first one. This is the *specimen well*. Into this you would put a representation of whatever it is you're working on. If it was a person, it could be a blood sample. It could be a photograph. It could be anything that indicated *what it was* that you wanted to work on, a link to it in some way. Basically you use this device in a dowsing[35] capacity to decide how you'd want to affect the thing that you put in that box.

RM: When you say that it could be a blood sample or a photograph, a blood sample is straight-forward, I get that… but *why a photograph*?

DL: A blood sample would contain DNA, but for some reason, a Polaroid, where you have both the positive and the negative of whatever it is that you're using, *for some reason it works*. I don't think any-body knows why a photograph would work, but in the case of this other machine, the *U.K.A.C.O. Device*, which is probably the most powerful radionics device every made —it was used entirely for agri-culture— the idea was to replace pesticides and fertilizers.

Aerial photographs of fields were placed on the device. They would actually cross out some of the crops —say there were bugs on the crops and they wanted to use pesticides— they placed a pesticide on the photograph in the shape of an "X", they put it in the device, they pushed the button (snaps fin-gers) and "Boom." They did this four or five times a day and they measurably reduced the predation on the fields, even selectively row by row. This is a matter of historical authenticity, as unbelievable as it sounds. This we know because this device was extensively tested by the Pennsylvania Farm Bureau Federation, in 1949, prior to all this stuff being outlawed. U.K.ACO was a company set up that went around on a "no cost basis," *no results, no cost*, and for a long time these humble looking devices were built and manufactured. The inventors were a group of Princeton graduates under a guy named Curtis P. Upton, the son of one of Thomas Edison's associates.

Initially the emphasis was on eliminating the parasites, but parasites attack weakened fields. The weakened biological structure of an organism is what the bug goes after. They don't go after a strong one, if there's a weak one there. So what they found was, instead of trying to kill the bugs —which they did— they could strengthen the crops to the point where the bugs would fly over and go to some-body else's farm where the plants hadn't been strengthened. It's complicated. This is where the dis-cussion gets very cryptic and also very surreal, but it's important to know.

RM: To say the least!

DL: Yeah, to say the least. It's also true that the Mafia has used these things. I talked to a couple of investigators who said they had consulted with the FBI in cases where devices of this kind, especial-ly that powerful one, were used in murders. This is all part of the underground spy literature of how these things have been militarized and turned into warfare technology.

RM: This reminds me of a famous story about William Burroughs. He hated the proprietor of a cigarette shop in Paris, this old woman. Just loathed her. He would take photographs of the street where her kiosk was and then doctor them, cut the kiosk out and move the photographs back together and tape them up. Soon after, her place burned to the ground.

DL: I've heard that story; it's exactly the same thing at work.

RM: These devices actually map Aleister Crowley's definition of magick on a one to one basis: *causing change in conformity with will*. They are truly *magical* devices.

DL: I think you could call them that, sure.

RM: It's occult technology.

DL: It's occult technology until they find out how it works and then it becomes mainstream technology.

RM: Science!

DL: Right. But for our purposes, sure they are. But they're also *an art medium* and this is what I wanted

to get at.

It's like the mouse on the computer: if you don't have that thing to direct the signal, you can't get anywhere. You can have millions of bits of information in the computer, but if you don't have the mouse, you can't get at it. So the radionics device is like a mouse for this energy. You can find a manual for the device. You can get books and you can find out how to use these devices; that's all part of the medical literature for it.

What's important is that if these things *metaphorically* have the capacity to affect energy forms of some kind, whether they heal, whether they augment growth in plants, they have other applications, too. They have artistic applications. They are no different than a sand painting. They are no different than a Tibetan weather ceremony where they bring in a weather front or any number of other applications that indigenous societies have used to move energy and have incorporated it into art and ritual.

What exists here, is a way of *looking at* a technology. Rather than focus on the ego potential of the operator to amass personal gain or power and then do various different things with it for a personal gain, this is sort of more oriented towards, "How can this technology be used in a creative context?" How do you want to use this to produce art? Can you move weather with it? Can you affect crops? Can you do something with this artistically that would be like a crop circle? Where a certain amount of the field you treat, a certain amount, you don't. It's a design.

Now if somebody did that using this technology, it would wake up millions of people to the potential of what this kind of energy is. The Native American people did this a lot, but we view it through that lens. We view it through a cultural lens based on the technical level that they had at that time, when they were working with bows and arrows and hide and everything else. We think it's got to be on that level, it can't be more sophisticated, until you look at the fact that information is being used here in a subtle way, coupled with earth energy. So now you go out and you look at all these petroglyphs that are inscribed in the most inhospitable places of the Southwestern landscape. Generations of people have gone to these places and have put their symbol on it.

Imagine that that symbol is a personal intention that this individual, as an operator, is directing on a highly activated spot on the landscape, energetically, to broadcast his intention to affect a condition that he wants to improve. Say he has some tribal suffering. There's a lack of water. They go to these places and they hammer one into the wall, they put this prayer into it and all of a sudden you have an energetic change, you have a rainstorm coming in. I saw this hap-

pen out in the Hopi Pueblos *with dance*. Every year the snake dance would be performed in an area where they have six to eight inches of rainfall a year. Within 20 minutes, it was raining. You can't tell me that's just coincidence.

Somehow they were using *directed intention*, through design, through art, coupling it with physical energy and subtle energy of some kind and making things happen. Why aren't we doing that? We're supposed to be *so advanced*, you know? How come our artists are sitting around making these self-reflective, metaphorical pieces that are just basic commodities?

It's not just *an object*; it's a method that you could use *artistically* to *change reality*.

Further reading:

Blueprint for Immortality: The Electric Pattern of Life, Dr. Harold Saxton Burr, Neville Spearman Ltd, 1972

The Secret Life of Plants, Peter Tompkins and Christopher Byrd, various editions

Report on Radionics, Edward W. Russell, C.W. Daniel Co. Ltd, Essex

The Cosmic Pulse of Life, Trevor James Constible, Borderlands

Principles & Practices of Radiesthesia, Abbé Mermet, T. Nelson & Sons, NYC

Future Science, John White and Stanley Krippner, Anchor Press/Doubleday

The following books are available at Borderlands Research Foundation, www.borderlands.com

Abram's Method of Diagnosis and Treatment, Sir James Barr.

Radionics: New Age Science, editors, Borderlands

ERA: Electronic Reactions of Abrams, Dr. Albert Abrams,

My Search for Radionic Truths, Murray Denning.

PAUL LAFFOLEY

Thanaton III
1989
Oil, acrylic, ink, lettering on canvas
73" x 73"

SUBJECT: A Visitation by a Flying Saucer and Alien

SYMBOL EVOCATION: The tortoise as the Earth-Mother, the Support of the World

COMMENTS: The painting depicts an extraterrestrial's exhortation to me, explaining how to:

1. Link life to death in a continuous experience.

2. Utilize the resulting thanatonic energy to travel faster than the speed of light, turn matter into consciousness and back again, alter evolution at will and exist simultaneously at every moment of time.

3. Move the entire universe into the Fifth Dimensional realm, and say when in history it is possible for this to happen.

I have also received other information I cannot understand.

> Since this information was given to me directly but not for me per se, it must be communicated to others, many of whom are better prepared than I to receive it. Accordingly I was also shown how to make the painting into a psychotronic, or mind-matter interactive device which is activated by approaching the painting, stretching out your arms, touching the upright hands and staring into the eye. By doing this, *new* information will come to you through the active use of the divine proportion, which is the proportion of life connecting to death.

PAUL LAFFOLEY

In the earlier interview with artist Paul Laffoley, we explored the three main areas of Paul's work: the issue of "symbolic evocation," his plans for a time machine and *Das Urpflanze Haus*, Laffoley's unique spin on "Green architecture." In this second interview with Laffoley we focus on just one painting, Laffoley's 1989 masterpiece, *Thanaton III*, a painting he claims is *alive*.

RM: Paul, this painting, *Thanaton III,* which you completed in 1989, is probably your most famous work. Why do you think that this piece has become so representative of your paintings?

PL: It contains most of the imagery that I've used and probably will continue to use: the Great Pyramid, things to do with the near death experience, UFOs, images of the aliens, my theories of history and, of course, that it is participatory.

RM: When you say it's participatory, what do you mean by that?

PL: The nature of this painting is almost entirely participatory. This is something that has a life of its own and will respond to the person who is using it. You can

use the imagery, almost machine-like, but not quite. It's like a psychotronic generator or radionics device whatever you want to call that kind of stuff, maybe "mind matter interaction." (Smiles) By touching it, by looking at it, by projecting your own energy onto it, it will respond to you.

RM: In most of your work you present schematics and plans for unbuilt devices or for living architecture like your *Das Urpflanze Haus*, but *Thanaton III* is different because, in this case it's not a plan to build something, it is *the thing itself?*

PL: It's a way of achieving communication and I'm communicating with a higher dimensional realm. And its two dimensionality is the key. My personal theory is that the subconscious and the collective unconscious is totally two dimensional and therefore the flat format of modernism can fit perfectly onto it and you can have a one to one, point by point correspondence. It is kind of like taking money out of a bank machine, when you're looking at a screen and you're called upon to touch the screen. You do know that you can't go through the screen but you do also know that there's something behind the screen that's organizing the experience that you have, and the result is the payoff of money. This operates in basically the same way only in this case the payoff is not money but a type of knowledge. A type of transformative knowledge, a knowledge which will literally bring you for an instant into the Fifth Dimensional realm.

When people use a bank screen, they know that it's something they can only partially participate in. They can't alter the program of the screen just as you cannot alter the program of authentic symbols. They come into play when someone comes upon the situation and are forced to address their own subconscious. It uses what I consider objective symbolism: symbolism that is not, let's say, reactive to your personal subconscious. It comes from the collective unconscious, whatever Jung meant by that. It's coming from almost a Platonic realm.

RM: Are you saying that there's a kind of an energetic feedback loop that's going on between the viewer and that which is viewed?

PL: Right. Carl Jung talked about a collective unconscious meaning that there are symbols that work for everyone, regardless of their condition in life. They can be educated, uneducated, from different classes, social groups... but these symbols will *literally operate on them*.

RM: In the same way that a stop sign or a red light tends to be used in cultures all over the world and everybody seems to know what that means?

PL: Only that's a convention. You could use any other symbol to mean stop. A green light could mean stop. These symbols don't operate that way; they are literally *objective* and have a single informational payoff.

The painting uses symbols that have been tested by time for producing transcendence and as a result of that, it's got to be information that is objective to the person. It gives you the appearance of something that's working with you, but it actually has its own agenda and you either go along with it or you may just turn away...

If I'm correct in what I'm saying, these are symbols that are coming from a higher dimensional realm and therefore I cannot know what they are except via my experiences of them and of other people's throughout history. This is an example of work in the visionary genre, which is an eternal genre. There is no point in history when art like this or with that intention has ever not existed.

RM: (Reading) "Utilize the resulting thanatonic energy to travel faster than the speed of light, turn mass into consciousness and back again, alter evolution at will and exist simultaneously at every moment of time." "Thanatonic energy"? What does this mean? It's *death* energy?

PL: That's right. Thanatonic energy is an energy that's efficacious without motion. I've always felt that the near death experience has within it a condition of knowledge. What it's providing is a way in which you can connect to the actual collective unconscious and what's being processed in it. As a result of that you're actually getting absolute knowledge.

RM: You say that the painting is a way to "connect life to death in a continuous experience." Is the person who's looking into the eye and touching the canvas of *Thanaton III* in touch with a near death experience?

PL: Well I think it's beyond a near death, meaning that you actually are in contact *with death*. The structure of it in terms of its proportions deals with the *divine proportion,* which is the proportion of death. In our body the proportions that we have when we mature conform completely to those proportions .382... to .618... and you begin to die.

RM: A child doesn't have this proportion but when you reach adulthood, you have achieved these proportions?

PL: That's right. And therefore it is usually adults who are going to receive the information. A child can receive some part of it, but it will be very blurry as opposed to an adult who is ready is ready to receive it and what they'll receive is, well, it's like being moved into a world where life and death are completely continuous, meaning that if you were to live physically forever you would not be able to ignore the thanatonic energy, meaning the energy of death. You would be processing information that would appear to be totally inappropriate to a person who had a life that they knew would end with death and so would not be concerned with it until they actually died. This would be a way in which the death energy would be with them all the time and would be in a complete balance. In our life, which will be cut off, the balance is that as you grow older the death energy begins to take over, as opposed to the life energy. And so with this, both those energies would be operating simultaneously in every instant.

RM: In lieu of an instruction manual how does one approach the painting to download this information?

PL: Just do this. Have your heart chakra here at the bindu [center point], place your hands on the pads

PAUL LAFFOLEY

and then stare directly into the eye. The eye will start to activate because you are sending energy to it and it's sending it back to you. I can see that it's already begun to pulsate and there is a light blue ring that's starting to circulate around the black pupil so the painting is officially "on." Watch in this area, watch the ring of light it'll start to circulate either to the right or to the left. When it's rotating to the left, it's giving off energy *to you*, when it's rotating to the right, it's taking energy *from you...*

RM: Is that a good thing?

PL: It was taking your thoughts and utilizing them... So it was taking consciousness from you through your eyes into it.

RM: It seemed to be rotating in a clockwise direction.

PL: What it was doing with you is that it was discovering if it wanted to give you anything. It was monitoring your mind. I've already been monitored by it, and so I keep getting information. Now you will discover whether or not that happens with you.

RM: Why do you have to touch the painting in order to receive this information, why can't you just look at it?

PL: In the hand you have these chakras on what is called the Plane of Mars, and each one of the mounds on your palms and fingertips contains brain cells. It's an extension of your brain and it's sending out energy. Your eyes are actually a much more direct connection to the brain and the eyes send out energy. They are not passive receivers, neither are our fingers passive receivers. An unsighted person can learn a lot simply through their fingers. If you were to keep your eyes closed for a day as an experiment you would find out the extent to which the hands and fingers do a lot of the work. The eyes are sending out a lot of energy, but the fingers are actually receiving information. What you are being sent might be described as similar to Morse Code. I'm saying that the hand/eye coordination is what's going on, but they perform two different functions: when you look at a computer and you're using fingers on the keyboard, you are checking with your eye as to what's happening with your fingers so that they have to be in sync with each other. So as information starts to come through you can then send information *back*. This is actually the mechanics of the feedback process.

RM: Why are the smaller, three fingered alien hand pads superimposed over the human hand pads?

PL: To give you the sensation that there is somebody on the other side of this that's connecting.

RM: That they're putting their hands up to you like a patty-cake...

PL: Right. When somebody holds your hands up and you touch them, that's a real communication with somebody. You normally don't do that with people, you shake hands or what have you, but having hand on hand is more of a communication between two entities.

RM: So the viewer of the painting should imagine that there's somebody behind this on the other side doing the same thing and that this is actually its eye *looking* out at you

PL: Well, yes, but the alien might be a gaseous form of energy...

RM: Are you saying this may be just a theatrical disguise that the alien wears, and that the alien might really look like a gas?

PL: Think of this as a stage set, you know where it all opens up and it's like a play and then you can fold the whole thing up when the experience is over.

RM: What is the information that someone interacting with this painting should expect to get?

An alien communicates with Paul Laffoley. Boston, Dec. 31, 1988.

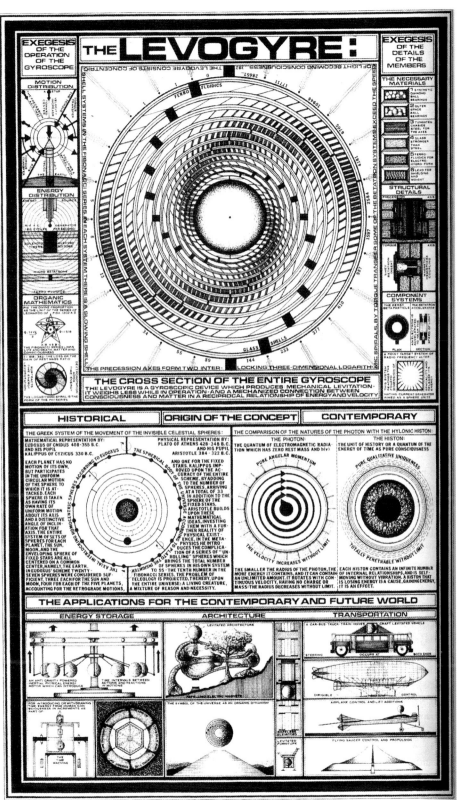

The Levogyre, 1975
17" x 27"

PAUL LAFFOLEY

PL: It's an organization of your experience. Our entire existence is information. Our cells process information. Our brain cells are doing that. We're getting information from our senses and we're sending it out. Here is a way in which you are the closest to pure information that you'll ever be on this side of the Fifth Dimension.

RM: Going back to your book, in the commentary it says "the painting depicts an extraterrestrial's exhortation to me explaining how to link life to death in a continuous experience. Utilize the resulting thanatonic energy to travel faster than the speed of light, turn mass into consciousness and back again, alter evolution at will and exist simultaneously at every moment of time and third, move the entire universe into the Fifth Dimensional realm and say when in history it is possible for this to happen." *Say when in history it is possible for this to happen*: is this for you, the artist Paul Laffoley, to say to the human race?

PL: Perhaps, but I also think that it's the judgment of the correctly formed conventicle. I think that it's a collective piece of information from all the people who will see the painting. That it forms a conventicle —a group of people who have special information— from the painting that converges in time and space. It cannot be a single individual because it requires so many skills, so many different kinds of readings of reality that have to fit together like hands clasping.

RM: Is the painting a kind of an oracle?

PL: For the collective, yes. For the individual it's simply a transformative device.

RM: *Simply a transformative device*, meaning what?

PL: Well it prevails upon you to change, but to change to form a conventicle, to be part of it. You won't actually understand all of it or you won't get the whole picture until all of the various people or entities involved in it have come together in a single place.

RM: Well that's very interesting! This painting has been exhibited a few times, but for most of its life since 1989 it's been in storage in your studio...

PL: It's had a limited provenance, as it were.

RM: Okay, now should its provenance by increased by more shows and more viewings? Is it true to say that the more people who see this, the more that a sort of a zeitgeist or a worldview around this painting and around this symbolism will form in the culture?

PL: By its own internal logic, I'd have to say yes.

RM: Would it be desirable for copies of this painting to be exhibited in town squares all over the world so that the public in many different countries could interact with it?

PL: That's right, only I wouldn't call them copies, a cloning analogy sounds a little better. As long as the image is completely presented, it is the same thing. This painting is sized for the average human being. You could have it smaller or larger depending upon the height of a general population in an area.

RM: What would actually happen after this painting has been exhibited all over the world and tens of thousands of people have had a chance to interact with it?

PL: It will begin to select those members of the conventicle that will actually be able to produce it, the change from the Fourth to the Fifth Dimensional realm. So it's not just that if everybody sees this that they will want to be involved in the construction of the conventicle. It's giving information to people that have capacities that can be used, because a conventicle really means a small group of people or a small group of entities that have a special knowledge.

RM: I think I'm starting to understand a little bit more. In one of our past conversations, you said that the painting represents a clarion call, correct me if I'm wrong, for a group to self select itself —this conventicle that you're speaking of— who will say "Okay right, it's a good idea to move out of the Fourth Dimensional realm that we as, er, "meat devices" live in and move into and exist in the Fifth Dimensional realm, and then to begin to work towards that goal...," yes?

PL: Right.

RM: And the idea is to move us all there?

PL: It's really about penetrating a surface. That's what's meant by portalling. To go from the Fourth to the Fifth Dimensional realm, you can penetrate by a Mobius strip, you can penetrate by going through a surface, but you don't want to rupture either yourself or the surface in the process. It's like in that Buster Keaton movie when somebody comes out of the movie or they go into the movie, right onto the screen. You are not destroyed in the process and that's like passing through a dimensional portal.

It's literally a new a new form of science, a new content of science and I think this is an inevitable goal. In many ways this is almost a rehash of Gnosticism and the elements of early Christianity that people have lost track of. When it's understood properly it will lose a lot of its, say, traditional or historical pull. When the cobwebs come off, it'll be shown to be vital again, that it never really lost its vitality. It should be seen as a new way of understanding how the universe is objectively observed.

RM: A facile definition of Gnosticism is a direct connection to the divine, do you consider yourself a Gnostic?

PL: I have leanings in that direction, but I think that if you if you follow the Gnostic mythology carefully, then there are a lot of things that are totally inappropriate to my life. I think people are looking for meaning in the universe and the meaning is in the tension between fate and free will. And of course, "A Direct Connection to the Divine" is part of the definition of mystical experience.

RM: (Reading) "...an alien's exhortation to me." When you say an alien, you're talking about one particular alien, correct?

PL: In most mythologies when they talk about guardian angels for people or a town or tribal gods in that way, what they're really talking about is the fact that there are assignments of entities for different parts of the universe. You know "Clarence now has a job, he's got to press the button for a while." He was just sitting there for billions and billions of years and now he's going be part of the picture.

RM: So is the alien on the canvas a representation of the being who came to you and said "Paul Laffoley, Earthling artist, you've got to do this thing that will show the human race how to move from a Fourth into a Fifth Dimensional space"?

PL: No, that's just a generic image that we have of aliens.

RM: So this is kind of a Hollywood alien just for simplicity's sake.

PL: Yeah, okay. (Laughs).

RM: Back to the book: "I have also received other information that I do not understand." So you're saying some of what the alien told you was jabberwocky.

PL: Well, *to me* but obviously not to him or her or it or whatever it was. I've been trying to take that information and use it like looking at a coded book and you don't know the code. Trying to figure it out, so maybe at some point in my life I will understand some of that information but not now.

RM: In the hierarchy of the epistemic ladder that you talk about where does *Thanaton III* fit in? Is it a sign? Is it a symbol?

PL: The *sign* is information that's completely by convention, like we were talking about before. In my system of epistemic engineering, I have a number of steps, in a kind of epistemic ladder and the first step is a *sign*, that's information by convention. The second is an *index*. This is like forensics, like animal tracks in the snow. You know that something's there but you you're only made aware of it by indirection. The next one is an *icon*, which is an attempt to actually depict what it is you're after either with sound or touch or some individual way.

And then the next one up is an *archetype*. This is very close to Jung's idea that you can have information that is moving towards the completely objective. In other words you're after something that's objective and not something that's simply a projection of yourself, like a hallucination. Finally, a *symbol* is literally absolute knowledge. It has taken Plato's system to the extreme.

Thanaton III is in between the symbol and the archetype, where you are going into an authentic trance. But you must progress towards that through the image that I presented, because that's been given to me as information [from the alien]. This is where the revelation part, for me, works; it was told that I must do it in this form, it doesn't work unless you are able to go through these states and go deeper into it.

RM: Is it accurate to say that *Thanaton III* is a kind of meditation device?

Cover: *Architectonic Thought-forms,* 1999.

PL: Well it's not just an auto-scope because that's what a meditation device is. You could use anything to focus on. That is not what this is. This can be used in its most trivial form as that, but it has greater potential.

RM: Is that to achieve an authentic revelation?

PL: I think we want to get rid of all the veils, we want to uncover everything so that in the end there's no such thing as revelation left. We actually have the answers.

RM: What happens if and when mankind does have all the answers?

PL: That's when I believe that the physical universe will be transformed from the Fourth into the Fifth Dimensional realm. It boils down to understanding dimensionality in a way that's not necessarily mathematical, not necessarily religious, not necessarily philosophical, but has subsumed all three.

GENESIS P-ORRIDGE

As the never-ending dialectic of pop culture marches on, neutering and commodifying "rebellion" and "outrage" for mass market consumption, some rebels manage to retain their artistic credibility by constantly reinventing themselves and finding new and improved ways of confounding the status quo. One such figure is artist, musician, writer and "cultural engineer" Genesis P-Orridge. For three decades now, as a performance artist, as a prime mover behind both "Industrial Culture" and the early Rave scene, and as the anti-Pope of his own magico-religious order, Thee Temple ov Psychick Youth, P-Orridge has infuriated the powers that be with his deliberately provocative and innovative body of work and ideas.

After a near-death experience left him determined to follow his notion of becoming a Beatnik writer, the young P-Orridge's instinct for finding other "genetic terrorists" like himself led him to the psychotherapeutic boot camp of the Exploding Galaxy/Transmedia commune (which also included filmmaker Derek Jarman). Members were required to sleep in a different location every night, to take meals at different times during the day, and to act out assigned roles and attitudes, often in costume and with unerring earnestness, going so far as to have atypical sexual encounters (in character!) or risk getting badly beaten up if a situation warranted it.

The commune's anarchistic spirit and insistence on life as art and art as life inspired the performance art events of COUM (pronounced "coom") Transmissions. Staged primarily by P-Orridge and part time pin-up model Cosey Fanni Tutti (born Christine Carol Newby, 1951), COUM's outrageous "happenings" were parallel to the work of Viennese Actionist Otto Muehl and Hermann Nitsch's *Orgies Mysteries Theater*. COUM's *shamanic improvisations* involving enemas, blood, roses, wire, feathers, sexual intercourse, milk, urine, licking up vomit, crucifixion, maggots and self-mutilation were often not conceptualized until the very moment of the performances, if at all. Indeed, the *point* often escaped the performers themselves. For P-Orridge and Tutti it was about freeing themselves (and the spectators) of their own taboos by performing benign exorcisms of a sick society's malignancies.

COUM's ephemeral oeuvre was celebrated in an ironic "retrospective" at London's prestigious Institute of Contemporary Art in October of 1976. The show, called *Prostitution* —a wry, multi-leveled commentary on the artist's role in society— consisted of beautifully framed photographs of Cosey cut straight out of the pornographic magazines that she'd posed for; P-Orridge's post-Fluxus[36] sculpture which utilized her used tampons; and photo documentation and props from past COUM actions. Most importantly, the opening night party featured the official debut of the *musique concrete* freakout of Throbbing Gristle.

Great Britain's self-appointed moral guardians, predictably, went apoplectic at COUM's decidedly avant-garde provocation. *Prostitution* became a symbol for everything that was wrong with the country and, compounding the furor, the exhibit had been staged at the taxpayers' expense. P-Orridge and Tutti appeared live on primetime television after a week of media overkill with over 100 magazines, newspaper headlines, even cartoons (mostly) denouncing the duo. Tory Member of Parliament Nicholas Fairburn declared the show "A sickening outrage. Obscene. Evil. Public money is being wasted here to destroy the morality of our society. These people are wreckers of civilization!"

All of this, it should be pointed out, was a few weeks before the Sex Pistols swore their way into history at talk show host Bill Grundy's expense and long before Andres Serrano's *Piss Christ* or Karen Finley's yam-stuffed asshole caused similar firestorms in Reagan-era America. *Prostitution* was one of the most highly publicized art scandals of the 20th Century and with it "the music of 1984" had arrived a bit early. Throbbing Gristle's "mission of dead souls" had begun.

For Throbbing Gristle, P-Orridge and Tutti were joined by Chris Carter (synthesizers, rhythms) and Peter Christopherson (prepared tapes, electronic percussion). Carter had constructed light shows for bands like Yes and Hawkwind. Christopherson designed album covers as a partner at the legendary 70's design firm, Hipgnosis. P-Orridge played bass, electric violin and fronted the group. Tutti played the guitar. The TG sound ran the gamut from soft (albeit doomy) improvised proto-ambient instrumentals (*In the Shadow of the Sun*), to punishing rhythms and electronic squall played at top volume layered with P-Orridge's psychotic screaming (*Subhuman*) to Carter's beloved ABBA influenced synthpop (*United*). "It was John Cage meets Stockhausen meets the Velvet Underground" P-Orridge says.

The group deliberately encouraged myth and confusion by titling its debut album *Second Annual*

I AM

APRIL 22 1986 No. 402

SYCHIC TV TERRORISE VIRGIN

[36] International interdisciplinary arts movement that began in the 1960's. John Cage, Yoko Ono, LaMonte Young, Aye-O, Ben Vautier, Joseph Beuys, Nam June Paik, Terry Riley and founder George Macunias were all considered Fluxus "members."

[37] David Henderson, *Sounds*, cited in *Wreckers of Civilization*, Simon Ford, 1999, Black Dog Publishing.

[38] This intro is largely the same as the one I prepared for *Painful but Fabulous* (Soft Skull). I think I got it right the first time and saw no need to reword it for this chapter.

[39] *Cease to Resist*, L.A.I.C.A., Los Angeles, California, November 23rd 1976.

Report and its flirtation with quasi-fascist symbolism such as the now familiar red and black TG "electric bolt" logo, reminiscent of the National Front symbol *and* the anarchist flag, further muddied the waters. Lyrically TG continued COUM's policy of not toning down the members' interest in the darker areas of the human psyche. The red light district of London's seedy Soho, deadly viruses, burn victims, mass murderers like Myra Hindley, Ian Brady and the Manson Family were all grist(le) for the lyrical mill. TG's disturbing obsessions liberated the concept of what could serve as thematic fodder for pop music for all time, yet it was difficult to tell if the group was endorsing their subject matter or just saying *"Here it is."* The group's dangerous ambiguity was meticulously calculated to force the audience *to think;* not so much conceptual art, rather it was "deceptual art" as P-Orridge friend, painter Brion Gysin, described their work.

It's been said that "the legend of Throbbing Gristle was easily as important as the outbreak of punk,"[37] but other than a small handful of substantial articles (RE/Search, Rapid Eye, Tape Delay), by and large, COUM and TG's histories are hazy and apocryphal. Now with the publication of several books like Simon Ford's authoritative COUM and TG history *Wreckers of Civilization* and the *Painful but Fabulous* art career monograph, Genesis P-Orridge —one of the last living links to the Beat Generation, it's worth pointing out— is finally getting his due. Not surprisingly it comes at a time when the "sickest man in Britain" —forced into exile by moralist hysteria like Oscar Wilde before him— is at a safe distance, far from England's green and pleasant land and living in New York City.[38]

COUM lithograph, 1976.

RM: What was a COUM performance like?

GP-O: At the very beginning they were more like street theater and *Theater of the Absurd*, very improvised, based around different mythical characters that we invented. Later on we started to explore taboos: sexual taboos, behavioral taboos, even deeper, and got into what would now be called *transgressive art,* although at that time there was no category for that.

As it got more intense and intimate, it became reduced to, in the end, just two characters: a male and a female character. Cosey and I would alternate and I always saw that as being androgynous —not two people— that they were one creature, separated, trying to find unity with its deeper self. It developed over the years. Of course, as it developed it created more problems with the media and the status quo.

RM: It would seem that there were two kinds of COUM performances; there was a light version, if you will, and then a darker, more shamanic version, if you could describe both...

GP-O: In Milan, during 1976, we performed for the British Council and we did something called *Towards Thee Crystal Bowl*. We basically built a geometrical structure out of black scaffolding in a huge galleria, a big shopping arcade, but beautiful, baroque, 50ft high galleria in the center of Milan and at the bottom of the scaffolding structure was a square and a circle, a white square and a white circle. The white square was about three feet deep filled with polystyrene granules —it was originally meant to be filled with milk but the local car factories went on strike saying that it was a capitalist waste of food if we used milk— so we had to use plastic instead. I was all in black with makeup and long hair and she was in a see-through silver body stocking and basically I started at the bottom and she was at the top and we reversed roles, as slowly as we possibly could and it took us about 45 minutes, which was very physical. We had chains and clips everywhere and we would have to move as slowly as we could, and when I say *slow* I mean that the hand would move like this (gestures very slowly), but while it was moving like this, ready to try and grab another place to hold onto, this arm was having to maintain balance and keep the rest of the body supported in space from a chain until that got somewhere else to take some of the strain off the other arm. It was incredibly rigorous physically, but we tried to make it look fluid and like a ballet. Eventually Cosey completely disappeared into the white granules, while I was hidden on the top with a camera and I took photographs from above. It looked like a canvas with bits of her body as she disappeared and then that was the end of the performance.

On the other hand, at somewhere like the Los Angeles Institute of Contemporary Art,[39] by that point we'd gotten very much into the limits of our own bodies, and the limits of our own imaginations, so we would tend to ask ourselves what would we be surprised or even shocked to do? What would we do in private that we would be very uncomfortable doing in public? Why should it matter, if we are driven to do something, then a public should not matter, a public space should not matter, the drive and the need should be what governs behavior. So we became much more sexually oriented. The performances came to include bodily fluids, vomit, nails —trying to swallow big nails— all kinds of things like that, twigs hanging on strings. Flowers, tampons, roses, ice cubes, and we would have the combination between real physical pain and fake physical pain. One of the things that I always found interest-

ing was that most audiences would be fixated on what was false and artificial, and absolutely unaware of what was real. Cosey would be pretending to cut herself from her stomach to her vagina and theatrical blood would run out, down her body. That would be completely fake. I would be somewhere else being a lot less physically dramatic, but I would *actually* be swallowing a ten-inch nail and my feet would be on ice cubes and nails that were sticking into my feet more and more as time went on, but people didn't notice that because it was subtle.

So I was very interested in the way that perception describes something. People would say, "*I saw this*." But they *didn't* see *that*, they saw something else much more physically demanding and missed it. That's where I became interested in editing and inherited perception. People are very easily manipulated into believing something that didn't happen and being *convinced* that they saw it and I still am fascinated with that. I think it's at the root of a lot of our culture. People will be adamant about what they saw in a video. We've had problems with that ourselves and yet something that has real human importance can be dismissed. It's

GENESIS P-ORRIDGE

Cease to Resist, L.A.I.C.A., Los Angeles, California, November 23rd 1976.

GENESIS P-ORRIDGE

149

seen in popular culture when people are very concerned about what Madonna does but probably haven't asked each other how are the people in Africa for over a decade. So their attention is directed away from physical reality to consensus reality and I think there are reasons for that and I'm still interested in why that happens.

The tampon sculptures

RM: When the *Prostitution* show was held in London's Institute of Contemporary Art in 1976, this was pretty far out stuff that you were doing —in any institution, let alone one that is owned by the Queen— so I'm wondering, do you think that the Queen actually knew about the tampon sculptures and the pornographic photos that were hanging and what was going on, just down the street from Buckingham Palace that night?

GP-O: Well, there's no question that the Queen or her direct representatives knew, because before the exhibition opened word had got out that some of the content would be at least controversial, and three law lords were sent down who said that they were sent as representatives of Buckingham Palace. Law lords in England are a strange, bureaucratic group. They are answerable to the Queen but are also a little bit like the Supreme Court, somewhere in there. They're important, but don't have civil power as such, it's more of a behind the scenes kind of power.

And they came down and said, basically, "*This show must close, it must never open.*" Being somewhat cheekier at that time than I am now, I told them that that it was not going to happen, that if they wanted to close the show, they were very mistaken if they thought I would be intimidated and if necessary we would occupy the art gallery and turn it into a "free art zone," paint the building in camouflage, put up sand bags and have a standoff just like guerrillas who'd taken over an embassy or something, which at that time had happened a couple of times, so they understood the imagery very well.

RM: So what did the public see when they entered the Prostitution exhibit?

GP-O: It was a great big rectangular Georgian room. On the left were all the black and white and color photographs of COUM actions to that date. Except for a few they were all taken by random passersby, which we thought were interesting. People that came up afterwards and said "I took photos would you like some?" And on the opposite wall to those, framed beautifully in silver frames, very much like the *Systems Art* and conceptual art at the time, were pages from what in Britain are called *glamour magazines*, featuring Cosey Fanni Tutti doing nude modeling.

In each one there was the same person but different made up names with made up stories by the copywriters, so all of those were other people's views of her and none of those were really true. On the third wall were the press cuttings, from the first day of the show and each day we'd put up more and of course as the show got more notorious there were more and more and more press cuttings so it started with one or two little ones and it went bigger and bigger and bigger and bigger and bigger until the wall was full. And that was the mass media's fictional version of what was going on. The press cuttings were getting more and more hysterical and ridiculous, so there were three walls that were all other people's views of us, none of which we felt were in any way accurate.

And the rest of the exhibition was for all intents and purposes, a satire on the idea of the museum. And a lot of this was basically spontaneous. We were asked to do a retrospective, I said "Yes of course," and then improvised with what we had. In the basement of the ICA I found these museum display cases with glass tops that would normally have archeological finds in them or rare books. I just said "Can we use these?" And they said "Sure." So we dragged them upstairs and then the question was "What should we put in them?" So it was basically "What have we got that's like art relics?"

So we took things we'd worn in performance art actions and props and things from the house —just anything that appealed to us— and put them all in, neatly labeled as if they were archeological finds. Some of the sculptures and installations that we'd used in the more theatrical performances we also rebuilt. So there was an orange and blue room

October 19th – 26th 1976

SEXUAL TRANSGRESSIONS NO. 5

PROSTITUTION

COUM Transmissions:- Founded 1969. Members (active) Oct 76 - P. Christopherson, Cosey Fanni Tutti, Genesis P-Orridge. Studio in London. Had a kind of manifesto in July/August Studio International 1976. Performed their works in Palais des Beaux Arts, Brussels; Musee d'Art Moderne, Paris; Galleria Borgogna, Milan; A.I.R. Gallery, London; and took part in Arte Inglese Oggi, Milan survey of British Art in 1976. November/December 1976 they perform in Los Angeles Institute of Contemporary Art; Deson Gallery, Chicago; N.A.M.E. Gallery, Chicago and in Canada. This exhibition was prompted as a comment on survival in Britain, and themselves.

2 years have passed since the above photo of Cosey in a magazine inspired this exhibition. Cosey has appeared in 40 magazines now as a deliberate policy. All of these framed form the core of this exhibition. Different ways of seeing and using Cosey with her consent, produced by people unaware of her reasons, as a woman and an artist, for participating. In that sense, pure views. In line with this all the photo documentation shown was taken, unbidden by COUM by people who decided on their own to photograph our actions. How other people saw and recorded us as information. Then there are xeroxes of our press cuttings, media write ups. COUM as raw material. All of them, who are they about and for? The only things here made by COUM are our objects. Things used in actions, intimate (previously private) assemblages made just for us. Everything in the show is for sale at a price, even the people.   For us the party on the opening night is the key to our stance, the most important performance. We shall also do a few actions as counterpoint later in the week.

PERFORMANCES: Wed 20th 1pm - Fri 22nd 7pm
                 Sat 23rd 1pm - Sun 24th 7pm

INSTITUTE OF CONTEMPORARY ARTS LIMITED
NASH HOUSE THE MALL LONDON S.W.I.   BOX OFFICE Telephone 01-930-6393

with a pyramid above it and everything in the room around the table was half orange and half blue. This never got mentioned in any newspaper. There was a steel rectangle made of a mile of silver chain that you could walk through but it looked solid when it caught the light. This too never got mentioned in any of the newspapers. There were walking sticks. There were diaries, clay sculptures, just all kinds of silly domestic things, too. Never got mentioned.

But in one of those display cases there was a walking stick that had a spiral of used tampons on it, which had been used in the Paris Biennale, a very prestigious art event. And that of course did get mentioned. And there were also some Fluxus sort of sculptures that I made at the last minute because there was a space left on the wall. One of them was an art deco clock, with one month's used tampons in it and underneath was the title *It's That Time of the Month,* which I thought was schoolboy, but funny, you know, silly stuff. There was another one that was like a tiny baby doll but the body of the doll was a used tampon and it was in a little bed like you would find in a doll's house with a little picture and it was done like a living room in a doll's house and it was called *Living Womb.* And there was a Venus di Milo whose arms had tampons dangling from them, and that was called *Tampex Romana.* I just thought they were throwaway jokes.

GENESIS P-ORRIDGE

'These people are the wreckers of civilisation

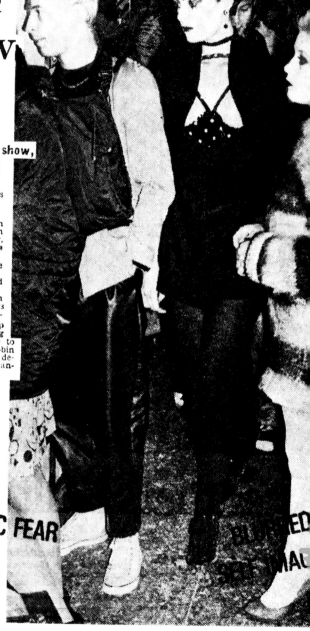

TORY MP Nicholas Fairbairn fought his way through Hell's Angels and young men with multi-coloured hair, lipstick and nail varnish last night —

AND SAW

sex-show

A STRIPPER, accompanied by a rock group called "Throbbing Gristle." far, far worse than anything I have ever seen. I was appalled.

"They must be very sick people indeed."

A WEIRD porn-and-pop show,

Its filth is exceeded only by its banality.

their pornography can only destroy the values of our society.

Nicholas Fairbairn . . . outraged.

And the MP's critical appraisal was : 'It's a sickening outrage. Sadistic. Obscene. Evil.' money is being wasted here to destroy the morality of our society. These people are the wreckers of civilisation. They want to advance decadence.

'I came here to look, and I am horrified,' said the MP.

THROBBING GRISTLE

ARE attemptiong "to destroy the difference between good and bad, and right and wrong

"I'm sickened "This show is an excuse for exhibitionism by every crank, queer, squint and ass in the business."

Mr. Fairbairn said he saw:

SADISM with sticks and flails.

WEIRD music from what exhibition organisers called the Death Factory, by a rock group called "Throbbing Gristle." allowing people to promote every swill-bin attitude they can to degrade language, meaning and thought"

Stripper

The show includes a stripper accompanied by masochistic performances by a rock group called Throbbing Gristle; They are devoid of any sense of proportion and respect for the decencies of life.

MASOCHISTIC performances by a rock group. may be a scabrous symbol of one facet of Britain today ; but not yet, thank heavens, of the whole. And the underlying impulse is not one of survival but of destruction and the death-wish—

controversial pop-and-porn show

T.G.

A rock group called Death Rock will be taking part at the opening. They will be singing songs about mass murder and about the child murderer Ian Brady. "They offer no

CEASE TO EXIST

CTION

GENETIC FEAR

Visitors . . . what today's connoisseur is wearin

152

But these were the items that led to questions in Parliament, of us being accused of being *wreckers of civilization,* of subverting the entire British way of life, that we should be executed, vilified, put in jail, that this was evidence that finally Great Britain had been destroyed and there was no moral fiber left: just insane. Completely insane. And of course all of this also went up on the walls, all these commentaries, and it just became more and more obvious that people see what they wish to see and are upset by something that they wished to be upset by. And interestingly too, there was quite a lot of outrage that the magazines which you could buy outside on a newsstand about 50 yards away, somehow became outrageous pornography by being put in a frame, but were acceptable when they were on the street available to anybody.

So a huge dialogue developed between what was art, what wasn't art and one of the most exciting moments for me was to see the *Evening Standard* newspaper, which is normally quite Right Wing, do an editorial discussing *Dada* and the history of absurd art in order to put a context on what was happening at the ICA, and I was very proud of that. I doubt that it's happened before or since. And there were questions, as I say, in Parliament. There was a TV special, primetime, live from the ICA. It was a very bizarre time and this was all prior to the Sex Pistols and what was to come. So in a way it's probably true to say that the ICA began the storm that accelerated with the Sex Pistols.

A lot of the photographs of the audience arriving at the ICA included people like Siouxsie and the Banshees, and the very early punk rock stars to be. It was an incredible moment and it was very frightening to have the entire establishment of your own nation turn on you, ferociously, for basically just being what I thought was witty. It was remarkable.

RM: But surely you knew that the *Prostitution* exhibit was going to be controversial, you were intending to provoke the establishment, weren't you?

GP-O: I was curious to see what would happen. I did make a list. I bought all the daily papers and I made a list of all the news editors and I sent all of them invitations, but it was very much a shot in the dark; I didn't know what the response would be or if they would even care, but I was curious to see what would happen. One of the weirdest memories I have of it is all though that time I was still working for St. James Press doing a big art history book,[40] so I was going to an office every day and then going to the ICA afterwards. On the second day of the exhibition I was on the subway going home and I was holding onto the strap and I looked down the carriage and more than half the people in the carriage were reading the evening papers, as they do in London, and on the front of each one was *"Sex Show Man's Amazing Free Tour"* and *"Pornography Show Outrages an MP"* with photos of *ME*, and I was thinking, "Oh no, they're going to realize it's me" and beat me up, and go crazy... (shakes head)

Nobody realized it was me and I noticed very quickly that it's all fiction, and in a way nobody *wanted* to know I was real. They wanted me to be a cartoon character that they could either sympathize with or despise, but the journalists did not want to actually interview me, nor did the public really care if I was a real person or a fictional character. They wanted to build their own myth and believe it for their own reasons and that was a very significant moment for me. And has been ever since. That was when I knew nobody cares who you are, they only care about what reinforces their own prejudice and their own preconception of what they don't want to have happen to disturb their safe view of life. And that's very empowering, because then you realize *you don't exist*. You are fictional and you have no restrictions as a fictional character, in terms of what you might want to address.

RM: What were some of the names that you and Cosey were called in the popular press?

COUM action, date unknown.

[40] *Contemporary Artists,* co-written with Colin Naylor, 1977, St James Press. *Contemporary Artists* is an overlooked gem amongst P-Orridge's prodigious output. This 1,077 page book is perhaps the single most exhaustive modern arts survey of the 1970's and has become hotly sought after by collectors.

GENESIS P-ORRIDGE

GP-O: Well, *Sex Show Man* was one of them. *Sex Troupe. Porno artist. Tampon Man…*

RM: That's a good one.

GP-O: (Laughs) Yes, *Tampon Man,* which is sometimes still what people know me as in England. They think "Oh you're that guy with the tampons, right?" And that's the downside of something like this: you are forever the *Tampon Man*.

But it was a very intense evening. We had transvestite security guards, who were all over 6'6", and we had kegs of beer instead of wine for the opening, we had a striptease dancer and an obscene comedian. Throbbing Gristle played and then LSD, which was one of the first times that the media had seen a punk band, *ever*. So it was a big catalyst and it was the moment when all these disparate underground movements that I believed were inevitable, all appeared visibly at the same time, in the same place, and that's another reason that it short circuited the media so much: it wasn't like there was just COUM, it was punks, transvestites, an anti-art stance, satire, sex —all the ingredients they would have loved to have known about in advance— but they just got hit with it out of the blue. And you could see they were shocked. I mean they were just completely flabbergasted, and the main thrust of all of it was a real sarcastic commentary on the floundering of their way of life. In a way they were completely right to see us all as enemies of the status quo. It was a very particular moment socially where British history was about to change and the neo-Victorian witch hunt was thrashing in its death throes and partly through that show I became an ongoing scapegoat for that neo-Victorian thrashing.

RM: What was it that the Tory MP Nicholas Fairburn said about Throbbing Gristle?

GP-O: I can't remember exactly but it was something along the lines of "All the most vile worms and decadent amoral creatures from the gutter were represented here tonight. These people are the wreckers of civilization."

RM: It's a difficult job, but someone's got to do it.

GP-O: Do you know what? This MP later got arrested for indecent exposure and his secretary committed suicide outside his office because they'd had a love affair that went wrong. He was not exactly Mr. Moral!

RM: So how did Throbbing Gristle develop out of COUM?

GP-O: Well we got to point with the art world where we just realized that we could have a career, we were starting to do the Musee d'Arte Moderna, events in Brussels, Paris and big British Council shows in Milan, and there comes a moment where you can see that if you start to do nice, big, blow up photographs, beautifully presented and you wear better clothes and become a little bit more aloof, and more of a dilettante by nature, and you can have a very nice life and teach at an art college and eventually have things in museum collections and one day have a monograph written about you, and just do variations on the formula that you've developed. In other words, carry on being the *Tampon Man*.

Though that's not really why I do anything. I do things to find out what happens, I'm not in the least interested in art, I'm not in the least interested in music. Performing is interesting because it's a deadline more than anything else. The only true interest I have is words, in and of themselves. So I can abandon anything when I can foresee its future. I'm not there to make money, I'm not there to get praise, I'm there to prove something can be done, to prove a change can occur, or to pinpoint a soft spot in our culture in order to have a healthy psychic hygiene occur, but I'm not there to keep repeating it. So we decided between ourselves that it was time to attack another monolith. We'd attacked the art world, we'd succeeded and in a way the ICA just compounded the success of the commentary. We thought *"What are we least trained and able to do?* Be a rock band! None of us play music. Is that a corrupt and formalized cultural medium? Yes. Let's attack that. Let's see if we can apply our nihilistic, sarcastic, artistically and intellectually strategized ideas to that and let's see if we can do music." So that's how we began: *what have we lying around?* We had an old guitar that was broken and we fixed it. I insisted there should be no drums because that was the thing in rock and roll that most tied everything down to a style, so no drums. Chris Carter could make synthesizers and gadgets. Peter Christopherson was fascinated with tape recorders and William Burroughs' tape experiments. So we just took the skills we had and our formula always has been and still is, *whoever is there find out their skills or their obsessions, these dictate what the project is.* You don't decide what you need, you let the project be the sum total of the people involved and that's a good technique.

Then all you have to do is *wait, be patient, think and listen* and that's what we did, for a whole year. Every weekend we would meet, build equipment and play Friday, Saturday and Sunday, and just be together for three days. And at the end of a year of doing three days a week of explorations with sound and taping everything and listening back finding out which bits you enjoyed hearing, we assembled what became a style. And when we were ready that's when we did the ICA. And of course, we were going off at such a tangent to everyone else. Punk was basically Chuck Berry with naughty words, and the premise of *learn three chords, form a band.* And I thought why learn *any* chords if you're going to try and do something new? You throw out every rule, so that's what we did.

TG logo

I was given the job of doing vocals because I was the one who talked all the time, and Cosey decided she wanted to play lead guitar because she didn't really like lead guitars. She would just make completely atonal sounds with the guitar and she used lots and lots of effects.

Sleazy [Christopherson] built his own special, um, what would be like a *sampler* now but using cassette decks. He had six Walkmans and he converted them, so with a small keyboard he could play either side of the stereo on each cassette tape, which meant he had 12 sources of sound that could be 45 minutes long. When he played he could have anything on those tapes and he would play, as long as he held down a key, the sound, whatever it was, would come through. He could also make it sequence as well, which to this day I think is a very radical instrument.

(Below) TG Self-portrait. From left, Peter "Sleazy" Christopherson, GP-O, Chris Carter and Cosey Fanni Tutti.

RM: Wasn't a lot of the equipment built for the band specifically?

GP-O: Chris was always the main electronic wizard. When we'd met him he'd already built a huge piano sized modular synthesizer, a big huge analog synthesizer, and he and Sleazy would look through lots of electronic magazines for new gadgets to build or new things that people were thinking of building and he would often make them himself. He built the "Gristlisers" that gave us our special pulsing sound. And as time went by he built more synths until Roland began building things and then he would tend to buy Roland equipment. The whole PA, we built ourselves. We had huge 4 x 4's of Goodman speakers and then above those we had bass bins and then Piezo horns across the top, so it was a huge wall of speakers and it was just all bass, all middle and all treble so we could separate the sounds out completely. The bass bins were so big I could climb inside one. They were huge.

Industrial Records logo

And we used to experiment on ourselves in the Death Factory, what we called our studio space, turning everything up as loud as we possibly could and leaving it on. We'd have it all wired into itself, and it would play itself, and sometimes we'd take that and use that as the backing for something else. One time, Chris and I stood there for maybe an hour and he got tunnel vision, his eyesight changed, our clothes were moving just from the vibration of the sound flapping, and the lights on chains, the big fluorescent lights were swinging and I could see zigzag patterns in the air. It was incredible, so we would experiment on ourselves, on the physical aspects of the sound as well.

RM: You have called the Death Factory, an *alchemical musical laboratory*. Can you explain what you meant by that? What was going on magically that created the TG sound?

GP-O: Before we called the music *Industrial Music*, we were thinking of calling it metabolic music. My personal interests —and each person in the band had a different subjective view of what was happening— my personal interest was very much to rebuild a magical approach to sound. I still to this day believe all sounds in and of themselves are linked with archetypes and metabolic functions and psychic functions and they don't have to be in a cultural pattern that's obvious. In fact, *sometimes chaos is preferable because the unlikely can occur.* One of my first ever inspirations to begin making any music was the book *Zanoni* by Edward Bulwer-Lytton,[41] in which there's an alchemical violinist who talks about the legend that there are a certain combination of notes that you can play on a violin that are not normal musical notation —you can only find them by a combination of faith and random chance— and when you strike those notes together, if you do, you leave this world and you enter another dimension. You transcend being reincarnated, being in a human body and you *leave*. It's a key, it's a key to a divine being and I think that's what music was originally. In ancient times we had a different consciousness. It wasn't the kind of consciousness that we have now. When people made sounds they could see other beings still. We only forgot to do that when we developed Western language and perspective in architecture. Our consciousness changed as we developed the idea of perspective and fixed language.

So what music originally did has been forgotten and that was something that I wanted to try and rediscover for myself, and to this day I believe it's possible. That's why I would always have a violin on stage in TG, although I rarely played it, in case I felt that I might be able to hit those notes. It was there symbolically, every single gig, and that was my totem to say, "I may leave this world and you may come with me," because if you're in the room, locked in, with this event and your body and your neurology are also to some degree controlled by the sounds, at that point who knows what could happen? And we've had people who hallucinated, we've had people who had visions, we've had girls say they had spontaneous orgasms, we've had people become violent for no apparent

[41] Sir Edward Bulwer-Lytton (1803-1873) was a Victorian novelist. Now best known for having written the following sentence: "It was a dark and stormy night; the rain fell in torrents--except at occasional intervals, when it was checked by a violent gust of wind which swept up the streets (for it is in London that our scene lies), rattling along the housetops, and fiercely agitating the scanty flame of the lamps that struggled against the darkness." From *Paul Clifford*, (1830).

reason and not understand why. Music is very powerful, and it doesn't have to be a recognizable form. The power in and of itself of any sound is enough. Tibetans know this. Tibetans use *singing bowls* not to sound pretty and sell in shops. The original singing bowls are very specific frequencies, which release specific chemicals in the brain and body in order to alter the state of consciousness. So we took that idea, *high frequencies alter consciousness,* that's why we got Piezo horns, before they were common, and put them right across the top, but we didn't have a formula or a specific destination. We were happy just to see what happened; that's why it was a laboratory.

RM: What happened at the end of TG and why was the mission terminated?

GP-O: Same reason as we stopped COUM Transmissions... basically we'd gotten to the point where we had become a rock band without drums. And we had become an institution that was viable. We were making money. And we were bored, and we were beginning to be formalized because we were bored. We weren't pushing ourselves towards another peak or another chaotic discovery, we were falling back on what we knew would work. And although we didn't really sit around and say that to each other we'd been so close and so intimate so long that all of us knew, and could feel it. And when we got to America it was obvious that we didn't even feel like communicating with each other anymore. And there are different versions of how that was announced; my version is that we were on a radio station and when they said "Well what's next for Throbbing Gristle?" I spoke up and said "We're splitting up after San Francisco, because that's where the Beatles and the Sex Pistols split up and it seems like the best place: the graveyard of the seminal English rock band."

_Psychic Television

In 1982 Genesis P-Orridge formed Psychic TV, a rock group with a built-in cult. For a few stamps, Thee Temple ov Psychick Youth would send you a magical toolkit for creating your own designer reality.

RM: What was the initial concept behind Psychic TV and Thee Temple ov Psychick Youth?

GP-O: That's a whole book really (laughs). I guess I just decided that if I was going to do more music, instead of hiding the ideas that I had about music and life subliminally camouflaged in another project, it would be interesting to see what happened if you were completely blatant about your line of inquiry and your agenda. And at that point I had got to a place in my private life where I was more and more interested and affected by what one could loosely call *psychoactive ritual*.

Attempting to access altered states and other dimensions and to leave the physical body and push the physical body to a point where you were somewhere else, to learn about other worlds, if you like. And from those researches certain basic

techniques seemed relevant to everyone to demystify that. So we wanted to demystify people's conceptions of what magic, what music, what popular culture could really be about. To make it intelligent and anthropological and to also, rather than have something like a fan club, say to people: "The reason we do what we do is because we live this way and we believe this way of living is more beneficial to evolution of the self than the way we inherited from society and we are prepared to share, with anyone who's enthusiastic, some of what we feel is going on and give you that information, so perhaps some of it will in turn help you to maximize your potential and let go of traumas and neurosis and emotional anchors that hold you back from being the maximum possible human you could be." And that was really what it was for, it was to say: *there is a lost tribe*. There are people who feel more kinship with each other than they do with their blood family or their supposed peer group. That there are, all over the world, individuals who are just like us, who are both mystified and amazed by life. And who don't believe the inherited and the dogmatic and the suppressive ideas of the particular society that they were born into and they have a right to be special and they have a right to be magical and they have a right to be spiritual and they have a right to liberate their mind and their psyche and in a sense, *their soul*, in order to find their destiny. And that's why we're here, it's to recognize the illusion of life and through that let go of the material world and become something far more incredible that can give energy back to those who are still confused. That was what it was for.

RM: How did people who were interested in joining Thee Temple ov Psychick Youth, who were interested in becoming initiated, contact you?

GP-O: The band, Psychic TV, was the public face of TOPY and we used to put an address, a PO box, on the records initially and anyone who was interested could write in. And then to a degree, we took the structure of a magical order or a Masonic order and one of the things that we wanted was for people to be serious about wanting to change. Because the basic bottom line is, as we said over and over again, *we believe in change*. We believe people should change, that change should be constant. Nothing should remain fixed. You should be in the present moving to the future. And that takes a commitment, you don't want to waste time talking to people who just want to have a signed photograph. So we built a structure that required people to *initiate themselves*, by sending them, first, leaflets and in the leaflet there were two manifestos about our version of reality and if you were interested in that manifesto you could write again and purchase *Thee Grey Book*. *Thee Grey Book* was 23 pages long and it had some more manifestos and then an example of a ritual that people would do in private, which involved having an orgasm, which is where the conflict with the establishment began again.

And in that ritual people would write down something that they truly desired and wanted. It could be very simple, it could be to pay the rent, it could be —and often was— to have a girlfriend or a boyfriend. That was very common. For some people it was more abstract. And sometimes it was written down in such a way we didn't even know what it said, and of course it didn't really matter what it said, what mattered more than anything else was that people *analyzed themselves* and actually started a mental process of choosing a desire and a willed place to get to in their life. They learned how to strip away all the artifice and all the more cosmetic needs of life and isolate one thing they really wanted and that in itself was the real idea of the whole thing: to help people learn, one by one, what their agenda in life really was and then by focusing on that and doing something really specific, but pleasurable, they would train their consciousness... their inner consciousness, the unconscious if you like, to move them in terms of decisions they would make from then on towards always deciding in favor of getting to that place, and that is a *fantastic* thing to learn. Because you find that you manifest things that you want because you actually *move towards them*. Most of us don't really move towards what we want, because most of us don't really have a clear idea of what we want.

RM: That's as clear a definition of magick as I've ever heard. What was the form that these spells took?

GP-O: Well most people at the beginning would send them in on paper and they would put themselves in a quiet room with candles, maybe some music, and then they would meditate, concentrate, focus on what it was that they really felt they wanted and then they would make some kind of graphic image and then they would also add, sometimes not always, pubic hair, sexual fluid, and some blood, as a consecration, and then that would be put in an envelope and sent to the TOPY headquarters. And those would be filed under a person's name, they had a code name, everyone had a code name so nobody knew who anybody was.

And after 11 they received a gift, with a free book that they didn't expect which basically contradicted the first book and was much more abstract about ways of thinking. That was called *Thee Black Book*. And if they did 23, which was the number they were told they had to do, one a month on the 23rd of the month, for 23 months, having had several free gifts and several items at certain points when they didn't expect, people would assume something really special would happen on the 23rd time. In fact we never wrote again. That was it. If someone got to 23, we just threw everything away.

RM: So either they felt gypped or they laughed and they got the joke.

GP-O: Well either they got the idea that they were learning how to deal with themselves or they didn't. That was the basic structure. And funnily enough most people who reached 23 and got no more response are still in touch with me and all of them are very successful at

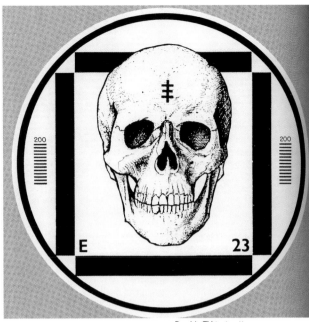

Psychic TV test pattern

what they're doing. I have to say it's incredible, so I think it worked, I think there's nothing better than training one's mind, body and soul to want the same thing.

RM: When I was 17 I was living in London and I saw pretty much all of the original Psychic TV gigs, as you know. I enquired about Thee Temple and I

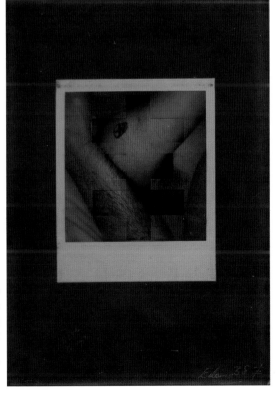

TOPY initiation sigil

sent in a sigil and as I recall the sentence of desire was that I wanted to fuck the Scarlet Woman, not *a* but *the*... and the woman who I had in mind, of course, I *nailed* about six months later. So it works, kids...

GP-O: Well that's a rather crude way of explaining it (laughs) but I can believe that. There was a high success rate and I don't think that it's such a big deal. I think it's an old, tried and tested technique. Sexual magick is something that's done in all cultures, Tibetan culture, Aztec culture, in fact probably in Catholic culture. I would argue that celibacy in the Catholic church is sex magick. Because the combined energy of all those celibate people praying is the same sexual energy *in reverse*, a negative charge going to one place which is the Vatican. And likewise with Tibetan monks, celibacy is used as a magick battery. Of course the Tibetans are interesting because they use Tantric magick as well and they have sexual practices, too.

RM: Well, if the Pope is the repository of this celibate sexual energy, then you as the *Anti-Pope* of TOPY in some ways must have benefited directly or indirectly from these activities. I don't know if that was necessarily your idea or the goal behind it, but the same logic stands to reason, that you would benefit from the energies of the people who were doing this.

GENESIS P-ORRIDGE

GP-O: It's possible that the combined ongoing sexual energy of the network went back to the center, but it wasn't exactly a pyramid. There was a central office with people working for free, but the overall feeling was much more of an extended family or tribe with real loyalty and kinship and trust. It was remarkable the way that people took care of each other and did all the things that you're supposed to get from your own relatives. I could turn up in America and there was somewhere to stay in every town. I could travel the world and be taken care of and that's fantastic, *but so could everyone else!*

At one point in Brighton, where we were based in the end, we had three houses, two of which were just for people who were coming through and once a year we had a world TOPY conference and there might be 70 people in Brighton and at that time we would take care of everybody else, so it was a reciprocal empowering.

RM: Did you ever look at the situation of being the architect of Thee Temple ov Psychick Youth and say to yourself, *"This is really weird"*?

GP-O: No, not really. I remember being at Arbor Low, which is a stone circle up in Derbyshire that we used to go to once a year and have a big camp out. The farmer would let us all go and stay there. And seeing basically an entire encampment of people from all over the world with tents and structures, a bonfire, children —there was a children's tent because there were quite a few children— and just thinking, not so much it was weird in the sense of *odd*, but it was incredible that it had *gotten that far*, and that we were being given such free reign to gather somewhere that was private. And how interesting it was that

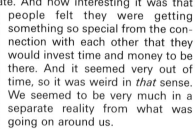

people felt they were getting something so special from the connection with each other that they would invest time and money to be there. And it seemed very out of time, so it was weird in *that* sense. We seemed to be very much in a separate reality from what was going on around us.

RM: Why did you end TOPY?

GP-O: Because it became a pyramid structure, and there was an underlying pressure for me to be patriarchal. It became very much that I was supposed to give encyclicals out and keep coming up with ideas and it was just becoming cumbersome, and it was becoming

a safe place for people not to think anymore, there were so many levels at that point... It became quite huge. There were almost 10,000 people actively involved and people were saying it should be registered as a religion and calling *Thee Grey Book*, "The Holy Book" and it seemed to the people who were actually running the office that it had gotten out of control. There were people becoming involved because they just wanted to have a tattoo and just wanted to be able to say that they were involved in TOPY but they had no inkling or idea of the origins and they didn't really want to know, they just wanted to belong to a gang, and that wasn't the idea. It was meant to be an anti-cult. Part of the interest for me too was: *can we set this up, what will happen?* Well the answer was *"Yes,* you can set this up." To a degree it's beneficial and then after that if you really believe in individuals, you have to let them go. A friend of mine said he thinks the most fantastic thing about TOPY was that I walked away.

He said no one ever does that, *that no one sets up a cult and then leaves*, and no one does it and doesn't make money. I used all my own money so it wasn't like people were sending in subscriptions or something. We were paying from our own money, Psychic TV, to print everything so in that sense it was very unusual.

RM: Well it's very difficult to imagine L. Ron Hubbard walking away from Scientology, but how did it feel to break with that? It must have been very freeing to walk away from the whole thing.

GP-O: For me it was very, very liberating, but I got so much of a backlash of anger and even hate mail. I got hate mail for years from people who claimed to be members of TOPY. One of the things that I know immediately if somebody says they were a *member* of TOPY, is they're not telling the truth. Because we never called people *members*, they were *individuals* and they were connected only as long as you chose to connect yourself, as long as you found something useful for you in what we were doing. If you found you were no longer interested, then you disconnected yourself and that was it.

My feeling was, too, *I've got a life!* I had no intention of being a bureaucrat, no intention of being anyone's dad, except for my children. And so I was actually surprised, I never expected a backlash like that. I thought it was obvious that it had to stop, or it would become that which it was criticizing, it would become a dogma, a religion, and the idea was to demystify some of the useful parts of various religions or techniques and give them away and that was it. When it was given away, it was truly given away.

RM: You are generally thought of as being one of the cultural engineers behind Rave and what used to be called *Acid House*. How did you go about effecting the rise of Rave?

GP-O: Well the cultural engineering I do of anything is really simple: I just talk it up a storm and print a lot of propaganda and distribute it wherever I can until I just get a hold of everybody and just bend their ear with the idea until it takes root. It's very simple, and it works, anyone can do it pretty much. You do it with *Disinformation*®. You just direct people's attention to a topic and you just obsess over it, immerse yourself in it and become a fanatic for a while. Fanaticism and obsession are incredibly compelling states of being to other people because most people aren't obsessive or fanatical or driven about *anything*. So anyone driven is a magnet to at least a certain proportion of people, usually those who are already driven to some degree themselves and recognize something there, so it's a resonance effect. With the Rave thing it was a very simple process, we were traveling around, already trying to develop a psychedelic dance music, as we called it in the beginning. It seemed to me, having worked with The Master Musicians of Jajouka, that one thing missing at that time in the popular culture was a really psychedelic multimedia experience *that was also danceable* so that ritual states of trance could be achieved. And that was partly coming from the fact that we had our own tribe and we were we were trying to discover ways in our own gigs as Psychic TV, how to take the entire process further as a tribe, and we would tend to play four or five hours —that was our average then— but it wasn't always quite rhythmic enough to induce a constant group trance, so that was why we were looking at that idea. One thing I knew with Jajouka was that the speed of the rhythm is really important, but we hadn't quite assembled the elements to make something that worked and that was also modern. In Chicago, whilst doing a free-form radio broadcast for a college radio station using lots of turntables, cassette decks, microphones, just everything and just improvising with rhythm loops and then free-form collage sounds, somebody called Derek Carter came to the gig and said "I heard what you were doing on the radio, man, and it's fantastic. You've just got to come to this shop, you're going to love the stuff people are doing in Chicago." So he took me to this tiny little record shop in the black area of the city and Derek May was behind the counter mixing things live and Derek Carter was DJing and they played me a couple of records they had that I didn't think were very interesting —they were pretty much gay Garage House— and I said in my typical way, "What's the most extremely awkward record you've got in the shop that you find really hard to listen to?" And they had these four white label records and I bought those.

I didn't have a chance to listen to them until I got back to England and when I played them (snaps fingers) *it was like that.* I knew that this was the key, *that* rhythm that they were doing in Chicago was the key and you could float anything on top and it would work. So you could build hallucinogenic abstract tonal landscapes, you could put any kind of sound and cut up through and it'd sit on this rhythm. It was very exciting, so I made a cassette, got in the car, drove around and got Dave Ball from *Soft Cell* and said, "Listen Dave, this is what's going to happen. This is what's coming next, listen to it and think what we can do with these rhythms, imagine it with this on top," and that's really how it

GENESIS P-ORRIDGE

began. And I played it to Richard Norris and I played it to Tim Simenon, who was our baby-sitter at the time, who became *Bomb the Bass*. Dave Ball and Richard Norris became *The Grid* and as an experiment we started to include DJing in our gigs and started to make these loops of sound and incorporated it. So we were really the first people —not DJing what became Acid House and Rave— we were the first people doing the full on live event before that was happening, but it was one of those classic things that I always say, *it was inevitable.*

We started talking it up a storm, we met other people like Danny Rampling and we went to *Shoom* and thought "Wow, it's happening" and everybody knew each other. It was one of those beautiful moments when everybody got excited by everybody else and it was just *BOOM*. Within months it was huge and we were one element of this process of inevitability.

RM: **Tell me what happened when you were in Nepal.**

GP-O: At the end of 1990 we sent out a post-card to the network and it just said, "Changed priorities ahead." And by that time one of the main activities that we were engaged in, in Britain, was picketing the dolphinarium in Brighton, in order to get the two dolphins freed and rehabilitated into the wild, which we succeeded in doing.

And at that time as well, I've always been interested in Tibetan Buddhism and Tibet so we started to go to Samye Ling, the Tibetan Buddhist monastery in Scotland. One day I was talking to the retreat master, Lama Yeshe and I said, "What do you think I should do? I'm kind of tired of being in a rock band and glad that I've ended this TOPY thing," and he said, "Well why don't you go to Nepal? We have a monastery in Kathmandu and they would really appreciate your help." Okay! Sometimes it's good to be impulsive. So we went to Kathmandu in Nepal, helping the Tibetan monks with soup kitchens, contrary to my image as a wrecker of civilization and a terrible satanic force in Great Britain. There we were getting up every morning at 5:30am, we'd grab a quick breakfast at the Vajra Hotel[42] and then to take a taxi ride across Kathmandu to Boudenath Stupa. There we would help the monks cooking rice and dhal and lugging great big vats of food and fresh water to where we would feed all the beggars and refugees and children that turned up. Sometimes 300, sometimes even 800 and we would feed them twice a day. My daughters Caresse and Genesse were there and they always helped, smiled, and never complained. They knew what they were there for and why. Wonderful children. Mainly for our part we contributed our record royalties, as well as just paying for ourselves to be there. So it was a shock having been there for a while and really getting into the mood of good works and compassion to receive a fax that said, "*Phone home, there's a real problem.*"

So I walked all the way into Kathmandu to where the international phone was —there was one place you could phone from at that time— and I phoned up and I was informed that our house in Brighton had been raided by 23 police and detectives and that they'd taken away two tons of my belongings in a big van. And I said *"What"*? And I just couldn't believe it at first, and they said, "Well, yeah it's very serious. You should think carefully about what you want to do next." And it transpired that some fundamentalist Christians had written a book and the idea of the book was a last ditch attempt to convince the world that Satanism and satanic abuse and ritual killings and killing goats and eating babies and all those terrible specters of evil were real, because in Britain at that point it was pretty much already discredited. So this was a final attempt to convince the world it was true, and *I was the one they picked as the scapegoat.*

They stated that in the basement of my house there were terrible, terrible satanic rituals taking place where people were being chained and kept prisoner and then they were drugged and raped and forced to have babies and then they were made to eat their babies and the house was full of dead bodies and on and on and on in this hysterical mish mash of comic book fear. *Scotland Yard claimed they'd been observing the house for a year before raiding it. And yet none of them had noticed there was no basement.* The house was basically an open house, the front door was hardly ever locked, and people came and went constantly. We had children's parties; we had parents' meetings with the school. Like *where* was this taking place? You know there wasn't anywhere… we had nowhere secret, we lived the most public lives possible. We could hardly get to the toilet without somebody asking us something. You know, the office was there. The place was full of people the whole time. So there was just a witch-hunt, just an insane, fabricated, ludicrous witch-hunt. Of course the police very quickly realized that they'd been led up the garden path, but they are obliged to go if someone tells them a story like that. So then on Saturday there was a piece in the *Guardian* newspaper saying *"At Last: Proof Satanic Rituals*

Really Happen". And then all the tabloid Sunday papers printed pictures of me, *"Leader of satanic cult"*, you know, *"The most evil man in Britain"*.

First I'm *a wrecker of civilization* now I'm *the most evil man in Britain*? Meanwhile I'm in Nepal cooking rice for lepers, you know, and this is something that probably none of those fundamentalist Christians have ever bothered to do, actually go and take care of people, with their own money? *I was doing missionary work basically*. And then on the next Tuesday there was a one-hour documentary film on Channel 4 called *Dispatches*, which I still haven't seen. I have a copy but I just can't face looking at it because I know I'll get so irritated. And it was this huge outcry and lots of stuff in the newspapers and then one small little piece saying, "You know this never actually happened and we know very well it's not true." The *Daily Mirror* were the only ones that actually bothered to do an investigation, and to their credit they found the people behind this documentary film.

[42] The Vajra Hotel was the scene of Grant Morrison's "alien abduction experience" discussed at length in the Morrison chapter.

It was shown on Channel 4 without being cleared. No one checked to see if anything in it was true. They used as their "proof," ironically, some old videos that Derek Jarman and Psychic TV had made, which had been commissioned by Channel 4 in the first place. *The idea of these videos was to show how people think they're seeing things that aren't there*, how when things are edited people assume they hear words that are not said and we were commissioned to make the videos to prove this was possible. Isn't that ironic?

They took that, *knowing that they had commissioned it*, and pretended that bits of it were real and then intercut it with things that were nothing to do with it, and they changed the voice-over. This was their evidence, this arts program TV show that they paid for in 1982. So, of course, the newspaper said, "This is actually something that was made just for Channel 4, it's not real." Derek Jarman was there, so they interviewed him, he said, "Of course, it's not real." Then they found the two witnesses, the two women who claimed they were held in the basement.

Genesis with Tibetan holy men

They had no idea. *They didn't even know what Thee Temple ov Psychick Youth was. They had never heard of it*. They made up some name like "The Satanic Grimoire of something, something" and it turned out that —illegally— the fundamentalist Christians had found them in a mental hospital by going through their records. These were very disturbed, very unhappy women who had been taken to a Christian safe house and held against their will, shown who knows what kind of videos and then when they were completely and utterly freaked out, they were told what to say so that it could be edited to appear as if it was about us.

And it was a Right Wing, Christian lawyer in Liverpool who accessed the illegal files. But they never printed an apology, they never gave me back my archive, and in that archive are many hours of Brion Gysin being interviewed, talking about his notebooks, showing things, paintings, drawings, explaining all kinds of incredible things. He's dead now. That's gone. There was a movie that

GENESIS P-ORRIDGE

Derek Jarman made when we brought William Burroughs to London. Derek filmed William all the time, went around with me and filmed everything. There was only one print of that movie and it's gone. There are Throbbing Gristle concerts that there were only one master of, gone. Just incredible stuff. All the photo albums of the children growing up, gone. A stuffed dolphin toy, gone. The girl's *Carebears* videos, gone...

I mean it's just incredible and it's still missing. That department of Scotland Yard was disbanded not long after, two of the detectives died within a year and now it's just impossible to find anyone who says they know anything about where everything is. Of course we were never charged with anything, because we hadn't done anything. So there I am, I'm in Nepal, I've lost a house. I lost that house because I couldn't go back and I couldn't carry on paying the mortgage if I had no income. I had about $5,000 left, cash, and I went to His Holiness Dzongsar

Khyentse Rinpoche who was a very, very high holy Tibetan Lama and through an interpreter I had an audience with him and I said, "I'm a refugee now, too." And he laughed, and he said, "Yeah, it's not so bad is it?" (laughs) or words to that effect. I asked, "What shall I do next?" He said, "Why don't you go to America? You'll find your destiny there." I said okay, and then I happened to know that he needed money for a small, simple, primitive hydro-electric system for his monastery up the side of Mount Everest. They were worried about cutting down the trees to heat the monastery in the winter and boil water, but they have lots of really fast running mountain streams, so if they could put in a big pipe with a turbine in it they could make enough electricity for some electric light bulbs and some heat, and they needed $5,000.

So I gave him all the cash that I had and said "This is to build the electric generator for your monastery" and he said, "Thank you very much." And then I went back to the hotel where we were staying, which was run by Tibetans and I said, "I have no money," and they said, "It doesn't matter, we'll put you in the best suite and you can stay for as long as you want and we'll take care of you." So they did. They took care of us until we could find out a way to get to America, which was we rang people up. Wax Trax Records sent us tickets and we were thinking, well, *where will we go?*

And this is where it gets really interesting, from my perspective, and it's one of the reasons that I am more and more convinced of two things: first, the universe is kind, innately kind, and the second is that if you believe in focused and effective will and if you believe in yourself, being true and telling the truth, then *events protect you in ways you would never expect*. So after I'd seen the Rinpoche, I went back to the hotel and who knows why I remembered this, I still don't know, but as we were leaving the house months before, the post had just arrived and rather than leave it on the carpet, I grabbed it and stuck it in my carry-on bag for the plane.

And I had carried it from Thailand to Japan to Nepal, back to Thailand to the jungles of Burma, back to Nepal and never thought about it and somehow I ended up looking in the bag and there was an envelope from Michael Horowitz[43] in Petaluma, California and I'd never opened it. So I opened this envelope, pulled out

[43] Michael Horowitz is the owner of Flashback Books, a rare book dealership specializing in Psychedelia. He is also the curator of the Timothy Leary archive. He and Cindy Palmer are the co-editors of *Sisters of the Extreme: Women Writing on the Drug Experience* and the parents of actress Winona Ryder.

a post-card and on it, it said basically "Hi, how are you? Loved the show in London" and then it said, "If you ever need a refuge just call this number, love, Michael."

And I just thought, "Well I guess I need a refuge!" (laughs) So I traipsed all the way back into Kathmandu to the international telephone and I phoned the number and Michael picked up the phone and I said "Michael we can't go home, we're stuck in Nepal" and I explained what happened. And he just said, "Can you get to America? We'll meet you at the airport. Come to San Francisco and you can live in our house as long as you have to, no problem." So that's what happened. We arrived in San Francisco and there were Mike and Cindy with a pick-up truck and they threw all of our stuff in the back. We had a couple of big bags full of Tibetan clothing and children's clothes that we had made to sell, and we ended up living with Michael and Cindy, which is just the most incredible kindness, I just couldn't believe it. I mean, I'd met him twice, had dinner with him at his house once, and there, you know, I was sitting there in his living room.

One thing that Michael has done for years is he takes care of the Timothy Leary archive and has done since the early 70's. So Timothy would sometimes call up the house. On this one particular day, Timothy Leary called and Michael said, "Oh you'll never guess who's living here: Genesis is here with his family," and Timothy said "Put him on the phone, put him on the phone," and he was really enthusiastic, and said, "I know what it's like, I had to go on the run. I know what it's like when your own government doesn't want you, but don't worry about it, *it's a compliment*. Don't take it badly, just think that you must have done something *right*, you must have said something *true* and they didn't like it." And he just said any time you want to come to Los Angeles just come down, you know "my house is your house." So that was how I ended up meeting Timothy Leary, so it did turn into a fantastic adventure.

And I can look back now and just see it really was the death throes of that neo-Victorian, conservative, Thatcherite Britain, and someone had to be the target. Someone unlikely. They couldn't attack Communists anymore, it was inappropriate to attack homosexuals, they had to have something, some boogeyman, some nasty demonic fear that they could try and play on to frighten some people into voting for a conservative life again, but it failed. It was just a knee-jerk flailing and it did me a world of good. It got me out of Britain and I think it made me a much healthier person. I feel quite honored to be one of the few forced into exile by the British way of life. There's Oscar Wilde, there's Quentin Crisp, not many, both people who I admire, so I'm in good company and good company is one of the great blessings of life.

RM: Obviously your situation paralleled Leary's incarceration and his running from the law. It also parallels what happened to Aleister Crowley when he was vilified by the *John Bull* newspaper and the British tabloids in the 1920's.

GP-O: But Crowley made the mistake of going back and fighting and one thing one has to learn from history is *strategies*. It was obvious to me that going back was definitely the wrong policy at that time. Too much had been invested in turning me into a scapegoat for it to be let go lightly and the British way of dealing with a problem is to vilify something and then humiliate the person, like Oscar Wilde too, who tried to fight, and destroy them, there and then, or else just let time pass and forget about it and not make a public scene.

So I knew that the strategy was to let go, although that was difficult, particularly when you have children. And Timothy's take on everything was that he was very sure that they weren't really interested in me, *they wanted my archive*. And he said that this was true of himself, as well, that if someone builds an archive of an alternative perception of life, no matter what that is, no matter how radical or odd or quirky or how intellectual, that when someone builds a body of work or an investigation that's *very specific* and *very thorough*, it becomes, inevitably, of interest to those behind the scenes. Those who are involved in *Control*. And those are the people, the faceless ones, that you cannot go head on with because you don't know where the conflict really is. You don't know what's really happening or who's behind it so you're fighting a cloud and I think he was probably right because the archive was what was secreted away and lost.

And I've built a new one, now, what can I say? There's always more information, but it's a waste. There are museums and archives that would really like access to that material and one reason I stored it was so I could give it away later, to universities, museums, researchers or whoever and now it's just gone.

GENESIS P-ORRIDGE

It's in sacks somewhere and that's a shame. If one of them knows where the archive is, it would be very nice if you would inform one of my representatives and help it get returned, because it was taken illegally. I never did *anything*. In the end I wasn't even *accused* of doing anything. It was all just an illusion. But my archive was taken. And for the sake of an alternative popular culture of which I've been a part I think it should be given back, so I can make those films available to people who are interested.

And so all those notebooks are also available for anyone in the future who wants to do more writing about someone who was involved. And more than anything else I'd like the children's photo albums back, because to this day they feel like the first years of their lives were stolen and don't exist. They could never go back and see their friends, they didn't go back to school, didn't meet their friends after their holiday, they have no pictures, have no telegrams saying congratulations, nothing. And there's no reason for that. There's no reason for taking that from them, so I would like that back for them.

RM: **What was it like when you returned to Great Britain for the Psychic TV reunion concert at the Royal Festival Hall?**[44]

GP-O: It was incredible and it was strange. *The Guardian* newspaper did three full pages basically rehabilitating my image: *"Weren't we silly thinking he was a bad boy? He's really just an English eccentric…"* —you know— *"…who's paid his dues and now we welcome him back with open arms."* That was the media's attitude, the same newspapers that had been vilifying me eight years ago.

The Royal Festival Hall holds nearly 3,000 people and it was nice that we were allowed to have my family and friends and the people who had supported me all the way through all those weird times sit in the royal box where the Queen and her family sit when they're there.

And this was a building specifically built for the royal family and the upper class of Britain to listen to classical music and entertain themselves. And it was given over *to me*, to curate an evening, with my friends from my tribe and all the people that I wanted to have there. Quentin Crisp was the master of ceremonies; he was huge on the video screens, introducing everything, to make that connection with exile for a way of life. And when I first walked on the stage, everyone went crazy, cheering and yelling and you felt like people, for whatever reason, right or wrong, saw me as a symbol of having succeeded to disagree with authority, *on behalf of them*, which was part of the whole idea. If I am a figurehead, it's not to be in control, it's not to be at the top of a hill, it's to take on the responsibility of saying *that which should not be said* or that which is normally not polite, on behalf of all the other people *who were thinking it*. Just like satire is there for, and I think there was a real emotional reaction that I was *alive*, even, and that was almost the best part, the fact that we pulled it off, and after all those attacks on my ideas and my lifestyle and my attitudes and philosophies that the government paid to bring me and my friends from all over the world back to play and to entertain in the most prestigious place!

RM: **When you look back over your long career, what are the consistent themes you see?**

GP-O: Well, basically my entire life has been dedicated to trying to understand the mystery of being alive, trying to understand what being alive implies and what can be done with that mystery. What is the absolute maximum possible desire and dream that one can have, that you can execute whilst in this body, and to aim for that. And so my real interest from the very beginning has been the nature of being, the nature of reality, and how to manipulate, comprehend and work with those ideas themselves and with music and art, performance, talking, writing, constructing, imagining —those are just tools that I can use to draw in resources, other ideas, collaborations— but the main thrust is always spiritual, is always the nature of reality, and the mystery of life, that's what it's for and as I get older I think I'm getting more and more precise in isolating what those particular areas are that might just work as keys to adjust the stupidity of humans.

I'm always just flabbergasted at the number of ways people hurt themselves and hurt others. It's mind-boggling. So one has to be separate from society and one has to be separate from the status quo, one has to choose visibly and audibly to be other than what is considered the average human, because the average human is trapped inside a problem and until you're outside the trap you can't necessarily see a solution. So that's what it's about, it's not entertainment, it's not purely education; though it's more education than entertainment, it's something more incredible. The search to succeed in calling down the impossible and proving that it can actually work in a really good way.

When I left school I went to a friend's house and his mother, who was an ardent Catholic with 13 children, said to me "So Neil, what are you going to do now that you've left school?" And I said, "I'm going on holiday for the rest of my life."

And she looked at me with horror and threw me out of the house and said to [44] Held on May 1, 1999 the whole family "Don't you ever let that person back in this house and don't ever speak to him again." And all I meant was if work is something that you do begrudgingly, then it would be great to have a life where everything you did was something that you chose to do, and that was creative: that would be a holiday. And I still feel that I'm blessed. I've had the most fantastic life, and I've got to do, so far, everything I'd imagined and more, and I've still got time. So I'm lucky, very lucky, but it's attitude. You have to truly believe that everything can change.

GENESIS P-ORRIDGE

STILL ESSENTIAL

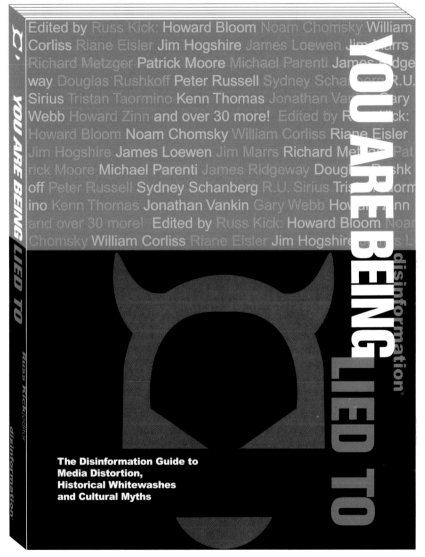

Edited by Russ Kick: Howard Bloom Noam Chomsky William Corliss Riane Eisler Jim Hogshire James Loewen Jim Marrs Richard Metzger Patrick Moore Michael Parenti James Ridgeway Douglas Rushkoff Peter Russell Sydney Schanberg R.U. Sirius Tristan Taormino Kenn Thomas Jonathan Vankin Gary Webb Howard Zinn and over 30 more! Edited by Russ Kick: Howard Bloom Noam Chomsky William Corliss Riane Eisler Jim Hogshire James Loewen Jim Marrs Richard Metzger Patrick Moore Michael Parenti James Ridgeway Douglas Rushkoff Peter Russell Sydney Schanberg R.U. Sirius Tristan Taormino Kenn Thomas Jonathan Vankin Gary Webb Howard Zinn and over 30 more! Edited by Russ Kick: Howard Bloom Noam Chomsky William Corliss Riane Eisler Jim Hogshire James L

YOU ARE BEING LIED TO

The Disinformation Guide to
Media Distortion,
Historical Whitewashes
and Cultural Myths

Russ Kick (editor)

disinformation

YOU ARE BEING LIED TO   THE DISINFORMATION GUIDE TO MEDIA
DISTORTION, HISTORICAL WHITEWASHES AND CULTURAL MYTHS

Edited by Russ Kick • Published by The Disinformation Company
Oversized softcover • 400 pp • $24.95 • ISBN 0-9664100-7-6

ALSO FROM
DISINFORMATION

Quality Paperback Bookclub Main Selection

EVERYTHING
YOU KNOW IS
WRONG

THE DISINFORMATION GUIDE TO SECRETS AND LIES

NAOMI KLEIN • HOWARD BLOOM • HOWARD ZINN • PAUL KRASSNER
WILLIAM BLUM • ARIANNA HUFFINGTON • NOREENA HERTZ
THOMAS SZASZ • GREG PALAST • JAMES RIDGEWAY • WENDY
McELROY • KALLE LASN • RICHARD METZGER • TRISTAN TAORMINO
JONATHAN VANKIN • PETER BREGGIN, M.D. • LUCY KOMISAR
MIKE MALES • JOHN TAYLOR GATTO • EDITED BY RUSS KICK

EVERYTHING YOU KNOW IS WRONG
THE DISINFORMATION GUIDE TO SECRETS AND LIES

Edited by Russ Kick • Published by The Disinformation Company
Oversized softcover • 352 pp • $24.95 • ISBN 0-9713942-0-2

disinformation®